Plato on the Rhetoric of Philosophers and Sophists

In this book, Marina McCoy explores Plato's treatment of the rhetoric of philosophers and sophists through a thematic treatment of six different Platonic dialogues, including *Apology, Protagoras, Gorgias, Republic, Sophist,* and *Phaedrus.* She argues that Plato presents the philosophers and the sophists as difficult to distinguish insofar as both use rhetoric as part of their arguments. Plato does not present philosophy as rhetoric-free but rather shows that rhetoric is an integral part of the practice of philosophy. However, the philosopher and the sophist are distinguished by the philosopher's love of the forms as the ultimate objects of desire. It is this love of the forms that informs the philosopher's rhetoric, which he uses to lead his partner to better understand his deepest desires. McCoy's work is of interest to philosophers, classicists, and communications specialists alike in its careful yet comprehensive treatment of philosophy, sophistry, and rhetoric as portrayed through the drama of the dialogues.

Marina McCoy is assistant professor of philosophy at Boston College. A former National Endowment for the Humanities Fellow, she has published articles in several journals, including *Ancient Philosophy* and *Philosophy and Rhetoric.*

Plato on the Rhetoric of Philosophers and Sophists

MARINA McCOY

Boston College

CAMBRIDGE UNIVERSITY PRESS

CAMBRIDGE UNIVERSITY PRESS
Cambridge, New York, Melbourne, Madrid, Cape Town, Singapore, São Paulo, Delhi

Cambridge University Press
32 Avenue of the Americas, New York, NY 10013-2473, USA

www.cambridge.org
Information on this title: www.cambridge.org/9780521878630

First published 2008

Printed in the United States of America

A catalog record for this publication is available from the British Library.

Library of Congress Cataloging in Publication Data

McCoy, Marina, 1968–
Plato on the rhetoric of philosophers and sophists / Marina McCoy.
　　p.　cm.
Includes bibliographical references and index.
ISBN 978-0-521-87863-0 (hardback)
1. Plato. 2. Rhetoric. 3. Philosophers. 4. Sophists. 5. Gorgias. I. Title.
B395.M296　2007 184 – DC22　　　2007007242

ISBN　978-0-521-87863-0 hardback

Contents

Acknowledgments

So many people have contributed to this book's development that it would be impossible to name them all. Still, I will make an effort and ask for pardon from anyone that I inadvertently overlook. I am indebted to all of my teachers from Boston University but especially to Charles Griswold and David Roochnik. I am always inspired not only by the quality of their writing but also their passion for philosophy. I have learned a great deal from them through conversations both in word and in print. Most of all, I am thankful for their philosophical friendship, and I dedicate this book to them.

My colleagues at Boston College have been most supportive and helpful. I thank the College of Arts and Sciences for a Research Incentive Grant that made writing this book possible and John Carfora for his assistance in developing the project for the grant. The support and friendship of colleagues such as Eileen Sweeney, Patrick Byrne, Mary Troxell, Kerry Cronin, Brian Braman, and Paul McNellis, SJ, was invaluable. My graduate research assistants over the past years, Matt Robinson, Phillip Braunstein, and especially Jeff Witt, worked tirelessly, and I thank them for their aid. Also important have been graduate students in my seminars who helped me to think through these issues with their many insightful comments and questions. In particular, I thank Joshua Shmikler for helpful conversations and comments on the *Sophist.*

I am grateful to many friends, colleagues, and scholars whose thoughts in various ways contributed to the development of this book. Again, I thank David Roochnik and Charles Griswold but also Colin Anderson, John Cleary, Gregory Fried, Jill Gordon, Gary Gurtler, SJ, Katya Haskins, Enrique Hülsz, Michael Kelly, Thornton Lockwood, Arthur Madigan, SJ,

Joe McCoy, Matthew Ostrow, Nick Pappas, Nick Smith, and Ronald Tacelli, SJ, for helpful comments on chapters or related talks or articles. Two anonymous referees also gave wonderful comments that greatly improved the book. Special thanks are due to my editor at Cambridge University Press, Beatrice Rehl, for all her work and amazing efficiency in working with the book. Thanks also to Mary Cadette, my project manager, and her staff. Any errors that remain are my own.

I thank my whole family but especially my parents and my husband, John, and children, Katherine and James, for their understanding, support, and love while I was writing the book. They inspire me both as a scholar but more importantly as a human being, and I am always grateful for their loving presence.

Portions of this book formerly appeared in print and are reprinted in part herein with permission of *Ancient Philosophy* and *Polis*: "Protagoras on Human Nature, Wisdom, and the Good: The Great Speech and the Hedonism of Plato's *Protagoras*," *Ancient Philosophy* 18 (1998): 21–39; and "Sophistry and Philosophy in Plato's *Republic*," *Polis* 22 (2) (2005): 265–286.

1

Introduction

I.

This book explores how Plato separates the philosopher from the sophist through the dramatic opposition of Socrates to rhetoricians and sophists. In one way, its thesis is simple. Plato distinguishes Socrates from the sophists by differences in character and moral intention. In the broadest terms, Plato might agree with Aristotle's claim in the *Rhetoric* that what defines a sophist is "not his faculty, but his moral purpose" (1355b 17–18). In another way, the problem is difficult, for the philosopher and the sophist share many characteristics in how they speak and act; these similarities are not superficial but go to the very heart of what Plato presents as philosophy, sophistry, and rhetoric. The tendency of contemporary scholarship has been to emphasize the distinctiveness of Socratic or Platonic philosophy in terms of a technical method separable from rhetoric.[1]

---

[1] Commentators who have emphasized a technical method in Socrates' or Plato's thought in distinction from sophistry include Gregory Vlastos, *Socratic Studies* (Cambridge: Cambridge University Press, 1994); Terence Irwin, *Plato's Gorgias*, translated with notes (Oxford: Clarendon Press, 1979); Jacques Bailly, "What You Say, What You Believe, and What You Mean," *Ancient Philosophy* 19 (1999): 65–76; Richard Robinson, *Plato's Earlier Dialectic* (Oxford: Clarendon Press, 1953); and W. K. C. Guthrie, *A History of Greek Philosophy, Volume IV: Plato the Man and His Dialogues, Earlier Period* (Cambridge: Cambridge University Press, 1986). Guthrie emphasizes the difference between eristic and dialectic in Socrates' thought but admits that Socrates often uses eristics to best his opponents. See Guthrie, *History*, 275–283. See also Frank D. Walters, "Gorgias as a Philosopher of Being: Epistemic Foundationalism in Sophistic Thought," *Philosophy and Rhetoric* 27 (2) 145. G. B. Kerferd, *The Sophistic Movement* (Cambridge: Cambridge University Press, 1981), argues that what distinguishes Plato's conception of philosophy from the sophists is the use of dialectic and its relation to forms, although Kerferd sees antilogic as the first stage of

One reason for this assumption is that Socrates seems to point toward the possibility of such a method in the *Gorgias* in his contrast between the political art and merely imitative rhetoric (*Gorgias* 464b–466a). However, when one turns to other dialogues, the relationship among philosophy, rhetoric, and sophistry becomes murkier. The *Phaedrus* seems to show philosophy and rhetoric as compatible, while Book One of the *Republic* presents a sophist with an intellectual position about justice alongside Socrates, with arguments that can seem sophistical. Plato's *Sophist* defines the sophist but, at one point in the dialogue, the Stranger equates "noble sophistry" with a practice that sounds much like Socrates' questioning activity (*Sophist* 230b–c). Plato's *Apology* opens with Socrates' claim that he is not a clever speaker, but he then goes on to rely upon numerous forensic and rhetorical techniques. Even in the *Gorgias*, Plato's voice must be distinguished from Socrates' voice as Plato uses the *Gorgias* in order to raise as many questions about philosophy and its value as he does about sophistry and rhetoric. The relation of philosophy to rhetoric and sophistry is complex.

Additionally, the contrast between philosophy and sophistry is a theme that permeates many Platonic dialogues. If one considers the number of dialogues in which Socrates finds himself conversing with a sophist, a professional rhetorician, or one of their followers (e.g., *Euthydemus, Gorgias, Protagoras, Hippias Major, Hippias Minor, Republic*); in which Socrates discusses sophists or a particular sophist (e.g., *Apology, Theaetetus*); or in which the definition of the sophist is abstractly compared with other related enterprises (e.g., *Sophist, Statesman*), the list is long. If one notes that the term *rhetor* was commonly used to refer to any speaker in the Athenian Assembly – adding political works to the debate – then few dialogues would seem *not* to contribute to a discussion of the issue.[2] Still, there is no unified account in the dialogues of a specific set of characteristics that define either the sophist or the rhetorician. The *Sophist* itself claims that the philosopher and the sophist are difficult to distinguish (*Sophist* 216c), and the variety of definitions given – as well as the dramatic contrast between the Eleatic Stranger's method of philosophizing and that of Socrates, now silent at his feet – illustrates its difficulty as well.[3] The

---

dialectic. As Kerferd, *Sophistic Movement*, 4–14, shows, many interpreters have treated the sophists as either subjectivists or as not being intellectuals at all, but such an interpretation is not borne out by a careful examination of the historical sophists.

[2] See Harvey Yunis, *Taming Democracy: Models of Political Rhetoric in Classical Athens* (Ithaca and London Cornell University Press, 1996), 10.

[3] Socrates says of philosophers: "And in the opinion of some they are worth nothing and of some everything, and at times they take on the apparitions of statesmen, and at times

lack of a clear definition of philosophy in the dialogues makes a clean and easy separation of philosopher from sophist all the more difficult. Plato seems less concerned with offering definitions of the philosopher and sophist than with opposing through dramatic conflict the *person* of the philosopher, Socrates, to a number of different sophists and rhetoricians.

In this book, I examine the distinction between the philosopher and the sophist in six of Plato's dialogues, with particular attention to the differences between philosophical and sophistical rhetoric. My argument focuses on three interrelated theses. First, I argue that Plato's treatment of Socrates in conversation with sophists and rhetoricians indicates that he thought that the distinction between philosopher and sophist was difficult to make. There is no single method or mode of discourse that separates the philosopher from the sophist. One cannot simply say that the philosopher is logical while the sophist is illogical, that the philosopher uses pure reason with no attention to rhetoric while the sophist persuades apart from reason, or that the philosopher has a successful method of speaking while the sophist lacks one. Nor are the sophists consistently presented as disinterested in knowledge or as morally corrupt. The meanings of the terms *philosopher* and *sophist* are disputed at the time that Plato is writing; for Plato, the claim that Socrates is a philosopher rather than a sophist is a normative rather than merely a descriptive claim. At times, Plato's dialogues even express some ambivalence as to whether the distinction can be made as clearly as the character Socrates himself wishes to make it. Careful attention to the multiple layers of Plato's dialogues reveals a Socrates who sometimes looks more like his opponents than he would like to admit and vice versa.

Second, I argue that philosophy, as Plato understands it, includes important rhetorical dimensions. While at times Plato associates the sophist with the rhetorician, he also presents Socrates' philosophical practice as rhetorical.[4] While the term *rhetorikê* was a relatively new term at the time Plato wrote, and its meaning shifts from dialogue to dialogue, when I use the term *rhetoric* here, I mean its broad, contemporary sense of "the means used to persuade through words." My definition of *rhetoric* here is deliberately general, for Socrates does not limit his use of rhetoric to one or two devices; his rhetoric is guided by the particular needs of the soul of

---

of sophists, and there are times when they might give some the impression that they are altogether crazy" (*Sophist* 216c). Again later, the Stranger claims that it is no easy work to distinguish the sophist, statesman, and philosopher (217b).

[4] See Yunis, *Taming Democracy*, who argues that Plato is "a rhetorical theorist of the first order," 16.

the person with whom he is speaking. Socrates is interested in persuading his audience and not always or exclusively through affecting the intellects of his interlocutors. For example, Socrates often attempts to affect others' senses of shame, anger, confusion, happiness, pleasure, and displeasure. In the *Republic*, Socrates seems as interested in making Thrasymachus feel flustered and ashamed as in disproving his claims about the nature of justice.[5] This is because the goal of Socrates' argument is to affect a person as well as to prove a thesis. Socrates also uses techniques common to sophists and rhetoricians such as *eikos* (probability argument), *êthopoiia* (portrayal of character), antithesis, cross-examination, and parallelism. In addition, he is ready to use myths, poetic interpretations, images, and other devices in order to affect his audience.

To an extent, Socrates' philosophical practice is continuous with the rhetoric of others whom Socrates would not consider philosophical. For this reason, a single definition of philosophical rhetoric that distinguishes it from sophistical rhetoric is not possible. The rhetoric that a philosopher must use is determined not only by the content of his subject matter but also by the audience to whom he speaks. While later philosophers such as Aristotle, Cicero, and Augustine took pains to distinguish and to separate the rhetorical elements of speech from dialectic or philosophical discovery, we find no such clean separation in the Platonic dialogues. Instead, we find a close connection between philosophical practice and rhetoric. At times, Socrates' questions seem to be designed to refute or to defend the content of some specific thesis but, more often than not, we find that something else is also going on: for example, Socrates examines the soul of the person whom he is questioning or hopes to affect the *thumos* of his interlocutor rather than his intellect alone. I argue here that Socrates' rhetorical practice, and his very concept of philosophy, relies more upon *phronêsis* and *kairos* than upon a technical approach to philosophical method. Plato, too, exhibits this sort of rhetorical attentiveness to the particulars. As author of the dialogues, Plato separates Socrates from the sophists by dramatically juxtaposing them in different circumstances. Plato uses elements of forensic speech, tragedy, comedy, sophistical set pieces, and other Greek genres in his

---

5 See Jill Gordon, *Turning Towards Philosophy* (University Park, PA: Pennsylvania State University Press, 1999), 25. Gordon argues persuasively that dialectic is not only about logical consistency but also about affecting the emotional responses of the audience. While her focus is on how the literary elements of Plato's dialogues turn the audience toward philosophy, my emphasis here is on how Socrates and Plato use rhetorical strategies that are in continuity with a longer tradition of rhetoric.

dialogues in a way that affects our own perception as readers of Socrates and his opponents.[6] One cannot offer a comprehensive definition of "Socratic rhetoric" or "Platonic rhetoric" because what constitutes good philosophical and rhetorical practice changes, depending on the topic and audience. Philosophy and rhetoric are closely interrelated. The content of thought and its discovery and formal expression in speech are intertwined.

Third, I argue that Plato differentiates the philosopher from the sophist primarily through the virtues of the philosopher's soul. One consistent thread in Plato's differentiation of Socrates from the sophists is how Socrates embodies moral virtues. The difference between the philosopher and the rhetorician is not to be found in a distinctive technique or method, in the absence or presence of rhetoric, or in some sort of foundational knowledge. Instead, Plato's ultimate defense of philosophy is to be found in the philosopher's person – that is, in his character and the orientation of his soul to the forms. Dialogues such as the *Gorgias*, *Republic*, and *Phaedrus* contain extensive descriptions of the virtues of the philosopher, but these accounts have too often been ignored as secondary to questions of method. However, for Plato, these virtues are closely connected to the proper expression of ideas in speech. For example, the *Gorgias* focuses on not only knowledge but also goodwill (*eunoia*) and frankness (*parrhesia*) as central to the evaluation of what constitutes good *logos*. The *Phaedrus* distinguishes between different types of souls, each oriented toward different goods, some of which are higher than others; good rhetoric is connected to loving the forms and one's partner in conversation. The middle books of the *Republic* focus overwhelmingly on the soul of the philosopher and the characteristics that both separate and make him apparently close to the sophist. Above all, Socrates' questioning is guided by his love of and his desire to care for the souls of those to whom he speaks.

A central defining characteristic of the philosopher is his desire for the forms. However, this theoretical commitment to the forms should not be understood primarily as a matter of having the correct metaphysics or as a positive epistemological state. That is, it would be a mistake simply to say that the philosopher knows the forms while the sophist does not. Instead, these dialogues emphasize the philosopher's desire for the forms as his primary connection to them; his quest for better knowledge

---

[6] See Andrea Nightingale, *Genres in Dialogue: Plato and the Construct of Philosophy* (Cambridge: Cambridge University Press, 1996).

of them stems from his love. This love of the forms has consequences for the philosopher's character. Plato closely connects moral virtues such as wisdom, courage, openness to criticism, and self-knowledge to the love of a transcendent good outside of oneself. Moreover, the philosopher's love of the forms affects how he speaks to others – ultimately, in order to guide others to love and to seek the forms as well. In this sense, the philosopher's theoretical stance ought to be understood in terms of the more primary meaning of the Greek term *theoria* as a kind of a vision of the world and oneself in relation to that world. His theoretical commitments are part of his character and identity as a person. However paradoxical it may seem, the philosopher is characterized by a love of the forms that precedes his knowledge of them. In other words, the philosopher is someone who is "turned toward" the forms as the object of his love; his stance is a moral rather than simply an intellectual position. Such a position helps to explain the inseparability of rhetoric and philosophy, moral virtue and intellectual virtue. Plato suggests that the understanding of our own desires grounds our theoretical outlook on the world and, in turn, our rhetoric is guided by our moral-theoretical vision.

While Plato evaluates rhetorical practice on the basis of these virtues of character, character is difficult to discern from the outside. To put it simply, who we are determines how we speak, but it is difficult to discern the character and motive of a speaker from his words alone. For example, Socrates might be genuinely concerned with improving his interlocutor but seem to others only to be interested in winning the argument. It is especially difficult to show intellectuals who already reject the philosopher's commitments that the philosopher's intentions are really the best. For these reasons, Socrates at times appears to be sophistical and the sophists at times appear to be philosophical.

Plato's dialogues do not sweep aside these complexities but rather present with care the problems inherent in distinguishing philosophical from sophistical practice. Plato is not only aware of the potential confusion of the philosopher and the sophist: at times he also even heightens the difficulty, instead of resolving it, in order to further explore the nature of philosophy. Plato's dialogues do not always present a clear and decisive victory for philosophy over rhetoric or sophistry from the point of view of the sophists themselves. More often than not, figures such as Protagoras, Gorgias, and Polus walk away from conversation with Socrates not at all persuaded that the life he advocates is better than their own. The sophists and rhetoricians with whom Socrates argues do not even seem to understand what Socrates' real aims are: Callicles in the *Gorgias* calls Socrates a "demagogue" (*dêmêgoros*) (*Gorg.* 482c); Polus says that Socrates takes delight into leading others into inconsistency (*Gorg.* 461c); and Thrasymachus says that Socrates refutes others out of a love of honor (*Rep.* 336c). Protagoras more generously suggests that someday Socrates will become famous for his wisdom (*Prot.* 361e), but his implication is that Socrates is above all striving for a good reputation. If Socrates' opponents in the dialogues all too often have a hazy sense of what he is doing in his discussions with them, Plato as author does not immediately and decisively clear up the problem for us. Instead, the dialogues force us to consider the value of philosophy in contrast to sophistry in a more nuanced way. In this sense, Plato as dramatist acts as a philosopher as well, using rhetoric to draw his own readers into questioning the value of philosophy, so to encourage the development of virtue in his readers.

II.

Before beginning an inquiry into how Plato understands philosophy, rhetoric, and sophistry, it is worth considering how his contemporaries approached the problem. Some commentators have argued that Plato was so concerned to separate the sort of rhetoric associated with sophistry from that associated with philosophy that he invented a vocabulary in order to assist him in this enterprise. Although modern readers often associate the term *sophist* with something along the lines of a clever argumentative individual with no concern for the truth, the reality is that the meaning of the term *sophist* (*sophistes*) was rather fluid in the fifth and fourth centuries. As Kerferd has argued,[7] the term *sophist* was originally applied to poets, musicians, rhapsodes, Pre-Socratic philosophers, and traveling teachers of "excellence" (*aretê*). Aristophanes' *Clouds* groups Socrates together with the sophists, while Plato's *Apology* attempts to separate him from them. Socrates himself, without a hint of irony, calls Diotima the ultimate sophist (*hoi teleoi sophistai*) in the *Symposium* (*Symp.* 208c).[8] The term *sophist* was used to describe, more narrowly, teachers of excellence who took fees for their services as they traveled; and, more widely, intellectuals who put a priority on the value of speeches for living

---

[7] See Kerferd, *Sophistic Movement*, chapter 4.

[8] Similarly, Socrates in the *Phaedrus* suggests that the term *sophist* would be too high praise when he claims that those who speak with knowledge ought to be called philosophers (278d); this implies that *sophist* need not be a wholly derogatory term.

well; or, most broadly of all, a "wise person." The shift from the broader and more positive sense of the term to a more negative and limited one seems to have taken place gradually over the course of the fifth century.

Schiappa has argued that Plato most likely coined the term *rhetorikê*, a term found in the *Gorgias* and *Phaedrus* (although, surprisingly, not in the *Protagoras* or *Sophist*), while the fragments of the historical sophists contain only more general terms such as *rhetor*, or *logos* and *legein*. He suggests that Plato may also have invented the terms *eristikê*, *dialektikê*, and *antilogikê* as part of this endeavor to distinguish philosophy from sophistry.[9] While Schiappa is right that Plato played a formative role in developing the terms *philosophia* and *rhetorikê*, he was not alone in his attempts to use such language to defend a particular rhetorical practice vis-à-vis other rhetorical practices in Athens at the time. Not only Plato but also Isocrates and Alcidamas lay claim to the title of philosophy and criticize sophistry. All three compare and contrast philosophy to rhetoric and sophistry. Alcidamas even uses the term *rhetorikê* in his essay, "On Those Who Write Written Speeches," a speech roughly contemporaneous with Plato's writing.[10] However, what each author intends by the term *philosophia* is quite different and, in some cases, perhaps not even identifiable as philosophy from the standpoint of a modern reader.[11] Alcidamas writes an extensive defense of the greater value of the spoken word over written speeches, associating philosophy with those who devote themselves to becoming good speakers and sophistry with those who pursue writing. For Alcidamas, both *rhetorikê* and *philosophia* are terms that apply to a life devoted to learning to become a better speaker; written speeches only distract or impede a person from pursuing this life of excellence. In contrast, Isocrates disagrees openly with both Alcidamas and Plato about the best rhetorical activities. Isocrates is not only a leading competitor of Plato's in offering a distinct kind of moral and political education. He is also a competitor for the very title of philosopher and repeatedly makes

---

[9] See Edward Schiappa, "Did Plato Coin *Rhetorikê?*" *The American Journal of Philology* 111 (4) (winter 1990): 457–470.

[10] J. V. Muir dates the composition of Alcidamas' "On Those Who Write Written Speeches" as approximately 390 BCE, about the same year as Isocrates' "Against the Sophist." But Muir admits its purely speculative nature. See Muir, *Alcidamas: The Works and Fragments* (London: Bristol Classic Press, 2001), xv. My own view is that dating Plato's dialogues is notoriously difficult and perhaps impossible in light of his continual revision of them. Still, commentators have often dated the *Phaedrus* at around the same time. See, e.g., Debra Nails, "Plato's Middle Cluster," *Phoenix* 48 (1)] (spring 1994): 62–67; and Spiro Panagiotou, "Lysias and the Date of Plato's *Phaedrus*," *Mnemosyne* 28 (1975): 388–398.

[11] See Nightingale, *Genres*, chapter 1.

normative claims about the true nature of philosophy, which he associates with his own rhetorical practice. For Isocrates, the practice of *philosophia* is something more akin to being a steward of culture, being well educated in cultural traditions and then using those traditions in writing and in speech to contribute back to the *polis*.[12] For Isocrates, *philosophia* is concerned not with abstract ideas but rather with speeches oriented toward making others act in concrete and specific political situations. Philosophy ought to concern itself with "noble" projects, while sophistry is overly concerned with abstract arguments over useless matters. Good rhetoric presents a clear course of action to follow and preferably addresses those with the power to effect change. One finds no role for the transcendent in Isocrates' conception of philosophy.[13] Plato's attention to the forms as objects of knowledge and his concern with general and abstract truths, not always connected to historically located political concerns, separate Isocrates and Plato.[14] But if Plato does not always treat *rhetorikê* as a political practice, he is the exception to the rule: for most Greeks, a *rhetor* would have called to mind a speaker in the Athenian Assembly, and the practice of oratory automatically would have been taken to mean public discourse.[15] When Socrates suggests to Phaedrus that the domain of *rhetorikê* includes both public and private discourse, Phaedrus is puzzled, for this is the first time he has ever heard of such a thing (*Phaedrus* 261a–b). For the ancient Athenians, rhetoric is understood primarily as a civic art.[16]

Nonetheless, Plato and Isocrates share more in common with each other than with their predecessors. Like Plato, Isocrates was a follower of Socrates, although Isocrates also studied with Gorgias. As is true in Plato's case, Isocrates is known primarily as the author of written works rather than as a speaker; yet, both write works in close imitation or adaptation

---

[12] See, e.g., Isocrates' descriptions of philosophy in *Panegyricus* 47 or *Against the Sophists*. For elaborations on Isocrates' understanding of philosophy, see Takis Poulakos, *Speaking for the Polis* (Columbia: University of South Carolina Press, 1997); and Ekaterina Haskins, *Logos and Power in Isocrates and Aristotle* (Columbia: University of South Carolina Press, 2004).

[13] See, e.g., David Timmerman, "Isocrates' Competing Conceptualization of Philosophy," *Philosophy and Rhetoric* 31 (2) (1998): 145–159; and Haskins, *Logos and Power*.

[14] However, Isocrates sees the difference as a reason to make Plato and Socrates as useless as the sophists. At the beginning of Isocrates' *Encomium to Helen*, he disparages both those who say that courage, wisdom, and justice are all the same thing and those who like to make contradictions about unimportant matters for their own sake.

[15] See Yunis, *Taming Democracy*, chapter 1.

[16] See George Kennedy, *A New History of Classical Rhetoric* (Princeton, NJ: Princeton University Press, 1994), 3.

of dramatic or oratorical forms. Isocrates goes out of his way to deny that
he is a "*rhetor*" (*To Philip* 1; *To the Rulers of the Mytilenaens* 7.5). He also
distinguishes himself from the sophists, whom he sees as concerned with
useless and abstract matters such as "deposits" or "humble bees and salt"
(*Panegyricus* 188–189; *Encomium to Helen* 12). Isocrates wants his philosophical education to help others to become better citizens or leaders;
Plato in the *Republic* sets out a similar role for philosophers of the best
city.[17]

Moreover, there is a moral core to both Isocrates' and Plato's visions
of education, even if their understandings of how we discover justice are
different. Isocrates argues that speeches ought to help us to become more
just, and he does not view justice as completely relative to opinion. While
we must rely upon opinion (*doxa*) rather than knowledge (*epistêmê*) –
since *epistêmê* is beyond human beings to acquire in political matters –
Isocrates also links speech to practical wisdom (*Antidosis* 255; *Nicocles* 7).[18]
Wisdom is not the mere ability to persuade a crowd but must include
intelligence and good judgment as well. A good speaker must possess
experience as well as have a natural talent for speech and good training;
he must understand the past well enough to aid him in good deliberation.[19] While typically Plato has been seen as holding knowledge far above
opinion, Socrates' reliance on his interlocutors' opinions as the starting
point of inquiry (e.g., in the *Gorgias*, *Protagoras*, and *Charmides*) and his
reluctance to make knowledge claims (e.g., denying that he is a teacher)
suggest the importance of opinion in good argument in Plato's thinking as well.[20] Isocrates sees philosophy as linked to everyday affairs, but
the dramatic form of Plato's dialogues also consistently connects philosophical argument to dramatic and political events contemporary with
the characters – for example, the setting of the *Gorgias* is Gorgias' visit
to Athens to persuade the Assembly to send troops to protect his *polis*.
Isocrates' and Plato's rhetorical practices overlap in important ways, but
they are competing with one another for the title of philosopher rather
than rhetor or sophist.

---

[17] E.g., Isocrates makes some of the same suggestions that Socrates makes about good
   education in the *Republic*, as when Isocrates claims that astronomy and mathematics
   have protreptic value for philosophy; see Isocrates' *Antidosis* 266 and Plato's *Republic*
   522c–531c.
[18] See Poulakos, *Speaking*, chapter 5.
[19] See Poulakos, *Speaking*, 87.
[20] See Alexander Nehamas, "What Did Socrates Teach and to Whom Did He Teach It?,"
   Review of Metaphysics 46 (December 1992): 279–306.

In short, the terms *philosophia, rhetorikê,* and *sophistês* do not have clear-cut uses even within the context of the Greek intellectual tradition of the fifth and fourth centuries (however, by the time Aristotle offers his own definitions, this seems to have changed). Some commentators have concluded from the lack of a clear distinction in vocabulary that the concepts of rhetoric and of philosophy have no real place to play in Greek thought prior to Plato.[21] However, even if the term *philosophia* was not always used, many thinkers were preoccupied with discerning the nature of *logos*, and widely differing practices in the use of *logos* often are accompanied by reflections upon what it means to use *logoi* well before Plato's time. Parmenides, for example, closely connects *logos* to truth (*aletheia*) while writing in poetic and mythic form, whereas Gorgias imitates the Eleatic style but then explicitly disconnects *logos* from perception and from being itself in his *On Non-Being*. Many Greek authors were concerned with the effect of *logos* upon those who speak as well as those who listen (consider, e.g., the reliance upon the recitations of Homeric poetry as a source of moral excellence).[22] As Yunis has argued, Thucydides is as much a dramatist making points about the problems of demagoguery and democracy in Athens as he is an historian of events.[23] The Greek mindset at the time of Plato is one of passionate interest in the nature, power, and danger of *logos*: terms such as *philosophia, rhetorikê, sophist,* and *rhetor* become part of the weaponry in the battle.[24]

Plato, of course, wants to defend philosophy and criticize non-philosophical rhetoricians and sophists. One might expect in such a situation that Plato would feel compelled not only to use a new vocabulary

[21] See Thomas Cole, *The Origins of Rhetoric in Ancient Greece* (Baltimore and London: Johns Hopkins University Press, 1991). Carol Poster has argued that the central opposition in early Greek thought is not between the sophist and the philosopher but rather between those who have schools of being and of becoming. See Poster, "Being and Becoming: Rhetorical Ontology in Early Greek Thought," *Philosophy and Rhetoric* 29 (1996): 1–14. On a related note, Nightingale has argued that the poet–philosopher distinction has no clear place in Greek thought prior to Plato. See Nightingale, *Genres*, 62–63.

[22] See, e.g., Gregory Nagy's presentation of the importance of Homeric poetry and the Greek hero in Nagy, *The Best of the Achaeans* (Baltimore and London: The Johns Hopkins University Press, 1979). See also Richard J. Klonoski, "The Preservation of Homeric Tradition: Heroic Re-performance in the *Republic* and the *Odyssey*," *Clio* 22.3 (1999): 251–271.

[23] See Yunis, *Taming*, chapters 3 and 4.

[24] Alexander Nehamas also argues for the claim that one cannot argue independently in Plato's time for what constitutes philosophy. See Nehamas, "Eristic, Antilogic, Sophistic, Dialectic: Plato's Demarcation of Philosophy from Sophistry," *History of Philosophy Quarterly* 7 (1)] (January 1990): 3–16.

but also to set clear boundaries for what counts as good philosophy and what must be excluded as mere sophistry or rhetoric. Some have suggested that this is precisely the purpose of Plato's use of terms such as *rhetorikê*. As Schiappa writes, it is likely that "Plato felt the sophists' art of *logos* was in danger of being ubiquitous and hence in need of definitional constraint."[25] However, part of the purpose of this work is to show that Plato does not define either the terms *rhetoric* or *philosophy* in a precise way that is sustained throughout the dialogues (although at times, *rhetoric* is defined for the purposes of a particular philosophical conversation in order to make specific claims). Instead, Plato carves out a notion of philosophy that is sometimes placed in opposition to rhetoric (as in the *Gorgias*) and sometimes harmonized with rhetoric (as in the *Phaedrus*). His notion of philosophy is not primarily defined through words but instead through the actions and the dramatic portrayal of the character of Socrates in relation to non-philosophers. That is, rather than simply stating how philosophy is different from sophistry, Socrates often uses sophistry (and sometimes "rhetoric") as a kind of foil for philosophy in order to explore the value of philosophy.

Separating philosophy from sophistry is also made difficult by the fact that the sophists themselves did not adhere to a unified method, subject matter, or school of thought but rather disagreed with one another about many issues.[26] Some ancient authors associated the sophists with natural scientists, as did Aristophanes in his *Clouds*. Some commentators have sought to unify the sophists through their apparently universal claim to teach rhetoric or at least persuasive political discourse (see *Protagoras* 318e; *Gorgias* 452d; *Euthydemus* 272a; *Meno* 95c; and *Theaetetus* 178e),[27] and Plato often strongly associates rhetoric with sophistry. For example, while the *Gorgias* distinguishes the two briefly (465c), Socrates

---

[25] See Schiappa, "Did Plato Coin *Rhetorikê?*," 467.

[26] See Kerferd, *Sophistic Movement*. Plato's *Protagoras* also dramatically displays the conflicts between the sophists when, for example, other sophists make fun of Prodicus, or Protagoras disparagingly suggests that other sophists offer their students the same old traditional education, while he offers something new (*Prot.* 318e).

[27] See E. L. Harrison, "Was Gorgias a Sophist?," *Phoenix* 18 (1964): 183–192, for evidence of the sophists' concern with rhetoric. Michael Gagarin, *Antiphon the Sophist* (Austin: University of Texas Press, 2002), 23, claims that not all the sophists were interested in rhetoric, though all were fascinated with *logos*. Since here my claim is that what "counts" as rhetoric is in development in Plato, and that other thinkers were concerned with similar issues even when they did not use the term *rhetoric*, it is enough to say that the sophists were universally interested in how words relate to truth, reality, and persuasion.

later claims that they are very nearly the same (520a). However, the terms *sophistry* and *rhetoric* are not presented identically in the dialogues. At times, Socrates seems highly critical of the activity of rhetoric, as when in the *Gorgias* he first calls it a mere imitator of justice (*Gorg.* 465c) but later claims that good rhetoric is to be used in support of what is just (*Gorg.* 527c). The *Phaedrus* sets out a picture of good rhetoric even while criticizing those who are in love with speeches for the wrong reasons. Moreover, no specific definition of rhetoric in the dialogues remains standing as an acceptably refined definition of the rhetorician's practice. While the *Gorgias* famously defines rhetoric as a "producer of persuasion," this definition is almost immediately shown to be problematic when Socrates widens the notion of persuasion: the teachers of crafts are also persuaders (*Gorg.* 454a). If there is any difference in Plato's use of the terms *sophist* and *rhetorician*, it is that *sophist* frequently has a pejorative connotation, while *rhetorician* may be positive or negative depending upon the context.

The sophist's close association with the rhapsode further complicates the notion of the identity of the sophist. As Blondell has argued, by Plato's time, the term *rhapsode* refers to those who recited others' poetry and then offered reflections on the meaning of the poems, often at public festivals for awards and honors. Figures such as Gorgias and Protagoras used poetry as a useful tool in moral education.[28] But despite Socrates' famous criticisms of poetry, he sometimes also uses it himself. For example, he frequently alludes to Homer in the *Republic* and, in the *Charmides*, quotes him as a key part of his strategy in refuting Charmides' second definition of *sôphrosunê* (*Char.* 161a). In the *Protagoras*, he interprets Simonides' poem for philosophical purposes. Moreover, Socrates' mythical descriptions of the forms, of human life before birth and after death, and of the nature of recollection rely heavily on the Greek poetic tradition. Neither Socrates nor the sophists are easily separated from the poets. Plato, too, relies upon poetry in the construction of his dialogues.[29]

Divisions among commentators on Plato echo the murkiness of the historical situation. Among commentators, there is virtually no agreement about what forms of speech or methods define philosophy as distinct from sophistry. Some commentators have located the essence of philosophy in

---

[28] See Ruby Blondell, *The Play of Character in Plato's Dialogues* (Cambridge: Cambridge University Press, 2002), 97–100.

[29] See Blondell, *Play of Character*. See also Gordon, *Turning*, especially chapter 3, on how Plato as author is both a poet and a dramatist.

dialectic. Robinson, for example, views dialectic as a method by which one searches for the essence of a thing and finds certainty about its nature.[30] Walters sees philosophical dialectic as seeking knowledge with closure, while the antilogic of the sophists finds truth in contradictory claims. As Walters describes the sophists' antilogic, it is "a continuous and recursive process. Though it yields knowledge, the knowledge gained is yet a new *logos* for the continuation of the antilogical process."[31] But other commentators locate the true nature of philosophical discourse in *just* this sort of antilogical process: the refutative process of Socratic questioning characterizes the philosopher but *not* the sophist or non-philosopher who is overly confident about his conclusions.[32] Plato's dialogue form includes opposing arguments and, in this way, displays some similarity to the antilogical oppositions of Protagoras and Antiphon. Moreover, the sophists do not restrict themselves to the practice of antilogic since they engage in epideictic speeches and, at times, even prefer them (as in the case of Protagoras in the *Protagoras*). And while Socrates says that he prefers short question and answer to long speeches (*Prot.* 329a–b), he nonetheless also engages in long speeches, sometimes with apologies or qualifications (*Gorg.* 465e; *Prot.* 347c–348a) and sometimes not (as in the *Myth of Er* in the *Republic* or the *Palinode* in the *Phaedrus*). As I hope will become clear in the following chapters, Plato's Socrates does not even have a single "method" that could be understood on the model of a *technê* or science; rather, his choices as to how to use speech are more reflective of a concern with finding the right kind of speech at the right time and

---

[30] See Richard Robinson, *Plato's Earlier Dialectic*. For Robinson, dialectic is difficult to unify as a concept because it sometimes seems to refer to a method of discussion and sometimes to collection and division. As Robinson puts it, "The fact is that the word 'dialectic' had a strong tendency in Plato to mean 'the ideal method, *whatever that may be*.'" See Robinson, *Plato's Earlier Dialectic*, 70. For a good overview of different senses of dialectic, see the appendix to David Roochnik, *Beautiful City: The Dialectical Character of Plato's Republic* (Ithaca]: Cornell University Press, 2003), 333–351.

[31] See Walters, "Gorgias as a Philosopher," 145; and Kerferd, *Sophistic Movement.*

[32] Although these authors disagree in important ways as to the nature of Socratic questioning, and even whether it is a "method" with discernable rules, authors who emphasize the place of refutative questioning include David Evans, "Dialogue and Dialectic: Philosophical Truth in Plato," *Diotima* 31 (2003): 21–26; Francisco Gonzalez, "The Socratic Elenchus as Constructive Protreptic," in Gary Scott (ed.), *Does Socrates Have a Method? Rethinking the Elenchus in Plato's Dialogues and Beyond* (University Park: Pennsylvania State University Press, 2002), 161–182; Jeffrey S. Turner, "'Atopia' and Plato's *Gorgias*," *International Studies in Philosophy* 25 (1)(1993): 69–77; and James S. Murray, "Disputation, Deception, and Dialectic: Plato on the True Rhetoric (*Phaedrus* 261–266)," *Philosophy and Rhetoric* 21 (1988): 279–289. Nehamas, "Eristic," 9, also notes the similarity between Socratic questioning and antilogic.

right place. That is, his approach relies more upon *phronêsis* and *kairos* than *technê*.

The past few decades of Plato scholarship have increasingly shown the central importance of literary and poetic devices in Plato's own work as author of the dialogues – that is, the importance of Platonic rhetoric.[33] As many have argued, Plato's dialogues themselves are poetic constructions that use images, characters, literary allusions, and other non-argumentative forms of presentation. These forms of presentation are not merely ornamental or of pedagogical interest; instead, commentators have increasingly recognized the philosophical content of the literary and dramatic elements in the dialogues. Plato presents not the historical person, Socrates, but rather a character named Socrates, no doubt close in spirit to his own teacher but not necessarily identical to that historical person. Throughout this work, when I use the term *Socrates*, I mean only the character of the dialogues – that is, Plato's Socrates. Similarly, when I discuss the sophists, I have in mind only the sophists of the dialogues. I suspend judgment on the questions of the accuracy of Plato's portrayals of Socrates and the sophists or the relationship between the dramatic characters and their historical counterparts. My project here is to present Plato's vision of philosophy and sophistry. At times, Plato seems to speak through the voice of Socrates but, at other times, Plato's voice is distinct, as when Plato alludes to historical events that have not yet occurred in the drama of the dialogue (e.g., allusions to Socrates' own trial in the *Gorgias*) or voices criticism of Socrates (e.g., in the *Republic* when Socrates finishes arguing against Thrasymachus and Glaucon remarks that Socrates has only seemed to prove the case against Thrasymachus; cf. *Rep.* 357a).[34]

Plato also draws heavily upon the genres of tragedy, comedy, and the Greek dramatic and poetic tradition (usually adopting elements of more

[33] To offer a few prominent and recent examples: Blondell, *Play of Character*; Bernard Freydberg, *The Play of the Platonic Dialogues* (New York: Peter Lang, 1997); Francisco Gonzalez, *Dialectic and Dialogue: Plato's Practice of Philosophical Inquiry* (Evanston, IL: Northwestern University Press, 1998); Gordon, *Turning Towards Philosophy*; Charles Griswold (ed.), *Platonic Writings, Platonic Readings* (New York: Routledge, 1988); Ann Michelini, *Plato as Author: The Rhetoric of Philosophy* (Boston: Brill, 2003); Gerald Press (ed.), *Plato's Dialogues: New Studies and Interpretations* (Lanham, MD: Rowman and Littlefield, 1993); and John Sallis, *Being and Logos: Reading the Platonic Dialogues* (Bloomington: Indiana University Press, 1996).

[34] For a clear explanation of various forms of Platonic irony, see Charles L. Griswold, "Irony in the Platonic Dialogues," *Philosophy and Literature* 26 (1) (April 2002): 84–106. See also Yunis on the problem of the absent author in Plato, in Yunis, *Taming*, 189–212.

than one genre within the same dialogue.)[35] His dialogues are dramatic in the sense that they often include an element of conflict, either between characters themselves or between ideas closely connected to the characters who espouse them. In addition, it is plausible that the dialogues themselves may have been performed or read aloud, either by a single individual presenting the entire dialogue or by multiple individuals.[36]

Rather than give detailed rules for how to incorporate the drama and rhetoric of Plato the author, I allow my examination of Plato's (and also Socrates') rhetoric to speak for itself in the chapters that follow. The proof as to whether the drama of the dialogue really helps us make better sense of Plato's philosophy is best found in the practice of explaining dramatic and poetic devices in relation to the spoken words of the dialogue rather than in an abstract defense. However, a few brief comments about interpretation are in order. First, while Socrates often has one audience (i.e., his interlocutors or other characters present), Plato's audience of readers is always distinct from Socrates' audience. The rhetoric of Plato is not reducible to the rhetoric of Socrates. I give attention in the following chapters both to Socrates' questioning *and* to Plato's "voice" in the dialogues. Second, I wish to emphasize that when I do speak of "Plato" or Plato's intentions, I mean by that what a given dialogue taken as a whole communicates to us. Little is known of the historical person, Plato, and speculation as to his personal beliefs on the basis of the dialogues is problematic. My use of the term *Plato* reflects this orientation toward Plato as philosophical author.

If the dramatic and poetic elements of Plato's dialogues are closely intertwined with the arguments given in the dialogues (and not merely decoratively designed to make them more alluring or easier to understand), then one cannot distinguish between philosophy and rhetoric by claiming that the philosopher offers rational arguments free of rhetoric while the rhetorician merely tries to persuade. That is, the sort of distinction that one finds in Aristotle's *Rhetoric* between dialectic and rhetoric – in which dialectic is the realm in which discovery takes place, while rhetoric persuades an audience what the dialectician has already discovered – is not identical to Plato's own separation of philosophy and rhetoric.[37]

---

[35] See Nightingale, *Genres.*

[36] Diogenes Laertius reports on at least two occasions where Plato may have read aloud his dialogues. See *Lives* III.35–37. See Blondell, *Play*, chapter 1, for a summary of many of the relevant issues; and Gordon, *Turning*, 1999, 68.

[37] Even in Aristotle, such a distinction is probably too facile, as Aristotle himself discusses issues such as the appropriateness of images for conveying the right features of particular

The task of separating the sophist from the philosopher becomes all the more interesting since Plato does not reject the use of rhetoric or see it as entirely separable from philosophy but rather views philosophy and good rhetoric as mutually interdependent.

In place of definitions and abstract arguments, we find in the dialogues a dramatic defense of the person of the philosopher set in contrast to the sophist. Plato explores the nature of the philosopher and defends his practice through his dramatic conflicts with the *person* of the sophist or rhetorician. The conflict of the dramas even reflects the sophistical tradition of opposing two arguments to one another (as in the *Dissoi Logoi*, or as the historical *Protagoras* claimed to do); not one *logos*, but two or more are given about most issues explored philosophically in the dialogues. Both those whom we today would commonly consider philosophers (e.g., Parmenides, Zeno, Socrates) and those considered sophists (e.g., Protagoras, Gorgias) were interested in the power of paradox and the very fact that one can give contradictory accounts. Early oratory arose in the context of the courtroom, in which "justice" was determined through adjudicating two oppositional arguments.[38] Plato uses a similar technique of placing arguments in opposition in order to explore philosophy.

Some of the sophists in the dialogues are uninterested in rational accounts of why the philosophical life is better: from their point of view, any reasoned argument in defense of philosophical rationality is circular and not worthy of attention when other priorities are more pressing. As I hope to show in the following chapters, the non-philosophers in these dialogues have such fundamentally different assumptions about the nature of language and reasoning that arguments alone are ineffective at persuading them of the philosophical standpoint. These non-philosophers have a fundamentally different theoretical stance or vision of the world than the philosopher. Plato is well aware of this problem and actively points it out to his own audience in the course of the dialogues. Plato's ultimate response to the sophists is not to offer a universal, rational account of why being a philosopher is better than not being one: Plato knows that no rational account succeeds in persuading the non-philosopher of the commitments of philosophy. However, Plato defends philosophy by comparing the souls and practices of the philosopher and the non-philosopher. That is, Plato's central means of

problems and how rhetorical argumentation has a heuristic value. Still, Aristotle emphasizes the priority of dialectic over rhetoric in Book One of his *Rhetoric*.

[38] Gagarin, *Antiphon*, 24.

defending philosophy against these non-philosophers is not to give a definition of philosophy but instead to make a series of claims about *who the philosopher is* (his character) and *what he does* (his practice).[39]

This helps in part to explain why Plato used the dramatic form to offer a defense of philosophy; as Aristotle later claims in his *Poetics*, the most important point of drama is its plot and the connection between the plot and characters.[40] We find this same emphasis on character and action at points in the dialogue when reason seems to fail. Socrates' arguments are not always persuasive to all individuals, even when logically valid. Sometimes they are even fallacious.[41] But Socrates' character and his love of the good make him the hero of Plato's dialogues; they ground his philosophy. In an important sense, Plato's defense of philosophy goes hand in hand with his defense of his teacher, Socrates.

For Plato, this defense of philosophy does not begin with a naïve and uncritical view of reason. As I hope will become clear in the following chapters, one of the key features of philosophy is that it is self-critical about its own foundations and continually revisits the very nature of *logos*, as well as the relationships between beliefs (*doxa*) and reality. Essential to philosophical practice is the ability to question the foundations of its practice. Philosophy does not presuppose a method but instead maintains a kind of openness as to what sorts of *logoi* are helpful for discovering the truth, as well as an openness to the very question of what *logoi* are and how they relate to truth. We see this in Socrates' own diverse uses of rhetoric as part of the process of philosophical discovery. This is not to say that certain beliefs about *logoi* or about practices are not better than others; quite to the contrary, the philosopher in Plato's portrayal cares above all about finding the truth. Plato is careful to emphasize the transcendent nature of this truth and its transformative power in myths such as those about the forms in the *Phaedrus* and the *Republic*. However, Socrates frequently confesses ignorance of the forms, as in the *Republic* when he suggests that he has only opinion but not knowledge of them (*Republic* 506c–d). Socrates does not present the philosopher as someone who first knows the forms and then loves them but rather as someone

---

[39] George Grote was among the first to emphasize the distinction between philosophy and sophistry as being a moral one: see Grote, *Plato and the Other Companions of Sokrates* (Bristol, England: Thoemmes Press, 1992), Volume II, 198–203.

[40] See Aristotle, *Poetics* II.6.

[41] See Roslyn Weiss, "When Winning Is Everything: Socratic Elenchus and Euthydemian Eristic," in Thomas Robinson and Luc Brisson (eds.), *Plato: Euthydemus, Lysis, Charmides* (Sankt Augustin: Academia Verlag, 2000), 68–75.

who loves and desires them, and so seeks to know them, and succeeds to varying degrees. The *Republic, Phaedrus,* and *Symposium* all place love rather than knowledge of the forms at the heart of philosophy.

It is the philosopher's very desire for the truth that requires him to keep revisiting foundational questions in light of new experiences, in particular in the face of challenges to it from non-philosophers. Put somewhat differently, the naming of a certain practice as *philosophia* is always already a normative claim about it – that is, a form of praise. But part of what is praiseworthy about the philosopher is his simultaneous commitment to the truth and his openness to questioning his own status in relation to that truth. For Plato, this self-criticism requires a continuing discussion of the nature of philosophical *logos* in light of challenges to it.

The problem, then, of discerning the nature of rhetoric and sophistry is simultaneously a normative and descriptive project for Plato. That is, to take on the title of philosopher for oneself is already to have a certain conception in mind as to what constitutes a better rather than a worse understanding of language and its relation to reasoning and reality. *Rhetorician, philosopher, sophist,* and *poet* are not merely terms that describe a set practice like *doctor* or *painter*. Instead, these terms are still in development, words being fought over in the battle about what *logos* can or should do. Plato's dialogues reveal his sensitivity to these difficulties about the proper use of *logos*. On the one hand, Plato acknowledges that the only way in which to approach the truth is through conversation with others; all human discourse about the truth is closely tied to the character and concrete needs of the persons engaged in the search. On the other hand, philosophy includes a commitment to moral virtues and to the idea of a truth outside of oneself by which our own individual ideas must be judged. Plato defends a theoretical stance or vision of the world in which the philosopher is oriented outward toward the forms, not inwardly toward only himself. Dialogues such as the *Phaedrus* affirm the presence of the forms as forces that literally move the soul through our human desires, even as our recovery of the truth is partial and limited. At the same time, philosophical discovery is always a process of becoming and not being: any expressions of truth will always be in part poetic, historical, and limited rather than presented in a transparent, ahistorical, and complete *logos*. Philosophy exists precisely in this tension between the universal and the particular, between the world of the forms and that of human discourse and desire. For this reason, the philosophy within Plato's dialogues is always rhetorical, as the philosopher orients himself both to loving the forms and to loving the souls of those with whom he is engaged in discourse.

III.

The task of examining Plato's approach to the philosopher–sophist contrast presents a difficulty for the commentator: to include only one dialogue on sophistry narrows the scope too much, but to extend it to the entire Platonic corpus is unmanageable. Therefore, for the purposes of this book, I approach the question of the philosopher–sophist distinction by focusing on one theme in each of six Platonic dialogues: *Apology*, *Protagoras, Gorgias, Republic, Sophist,* and *Phaedrus*. I choose the *Protagoras, Gorgias,* and *Republic* since they feature Socrates in conversation with a sophist or rhetorician and the *Phaedrus* since it directly focuses on the nature of good rhetoric. The *Sophist* takes on the project of defining the sophist, while the *Apology* features Socrates defending himself against the charge of being one. In each of these dialogues, both the content of the characters' speeches and their interaction with one another as dramatic figures is significant in evaluating the relative places of philosophy, sophistry, and rhetoric. I leave aside shorter works such as *Menexenus, Euthydemus,* and *Ion* that focus on particular forms of oratory, such as poetry, funeral oration, or eristics. In addition, the chapters that follow are not an exhaustive investigation of everything that Plato said about rhetoric, philosophy, or sophistry in any particular dialogue. Instead, I use each chapter to examine one particular set of problems about the intersection and divergence of philosophical and sophistical rhetoric. The unity of my discussion is therefore thematic rather than systematic. I note, however, that Plato himself did not limit himself to addressing the nature of the philosopher, rhetorician, or the sophist systematically.

In chapter 2, I turn to Socrates' use of forensic rhetoric in the *Apology*. I first show that the *Apology* should not be assumed to be an historical reconstruction or record of Socrates' own trial but rather should be understood primarily as Plato's own rhetorical defense of Socrates. The *Apology* closely follows other works written in the forensic style and uses common forensic topics. Socrates adapts elements of *eikos* (probability argument) and *êthopoiia* (portrayal of character) in order to make philosophical claims about the nature of wisdom, courage, piety, and justice. However, Socrates' rhetoric distinguishes itself in its aim of making the citizens of Athens more virtuous. Instead of gratifying the jurors, Socrates deliberately arouses discontent and discomfort in order to encourage them to care for their souls. In addition, I note important parallels between Gorgias' *Defense of Palamades* and Plato's *Apology*. Plato not only defends Socrates' way of life in the *Apology*; he does so through imitating a genre frequently used by the sophists and rhetoricians. In doing so, Plato acknowledges the difficulty in separating philosophical from sophistical practice.

In chapter 3, I focus on the nature of Socratic questioning in the *Protagoras*. The *Protagoras* encourages its readers to reflect on the nature of a philosophical method on at least two different levels. First, the dialogue exhibits Socrates' practice of questioning a sophist, and especially how Socrates attempts to show Protagoras the inconsistencies both within the sophist's own ideas and between his ideas and his lived experience. Second, Socrates makes a number of explicit claims about the value of questioning and interpersonal discussion that imply that Socratic questioning has social and performative dimensions. The *Protagoras* reveals that there are significant rhetorical dimensions to Socrates' philosophical practice, even as it helps us to sort out philosophical from sophistical rhetoric.

In chapter 4, I examine a series of apparent abstract distinctions made between philosophy and rhetoric in the *Gorgias* and show that no single distinction made in that dialogue adequately characterizes the difference between philosophy and rhetoric. Each of Socrates' distinctions between philosophy and rhetoric raises additional questions about the nature and value of philosophy rather than clearly demonstrating the superiority of philosophy to rhetoric. The *Gorgias* shows that Plato is well aware of the failure of non-circular reasons for accepting the philosophical stand-point, if one remains only at the level of abstract reasoning. However, the *Gorgias* still elevates Socrates' philosophical practice over that of his sophistical and political opponents. First, Plato suggests that Socrates possesses the character traits of goodwill, responsibility for one's own speech, and a commitment to knowledge that Callicles at least affirms in words, while Gorgias, Polus, and Callicles lack some of these characteristics. Second, Socrates is willing to be self-critical about his own practice in ways that the others, when faced with the challenge of philosophy to their worldviews, are not – although they claim to value such openness. In other words, Plato shows that the others are not only inconsistent in their arguments but also inconsistent with themselves as human beings.

Chapter 5 looks at the presentation of the philosopher and the sophist in Plato's *Republic*. In particular, I focus on Plato's claim that the philosopher and sophist share a similar nature. The sophist occupies a "middle ground" between the philosopher and the ordinary citizen. The sophist is presented as an incomplete philosopher, skeptical of opinion (*doxa*), freed from the chains within the cave, but not yet oriented toward the forms. Since he is neither committed to public opinions nor to the forms, the sophist is the most dangerous sort of character for the city. Thrasymachus is a prime example of this danger: he is an intellectual who presents a potentially compelling theoretical alternative to Socrates' moral vision, but he does not accept the idea of a transcendent truth. Plato affirms the philosopher not primarily for his greater ability to reason or to practice dialectic but rather for his commitments to the forms and how his rhetoric is guided by that commitment.

Chapter 6 examines the discourse and character of the Eleatic Stranger in the *Sophist*. Noting that the *Theaetetus* takes place only one day before the *Sophist*, I compare Socrates' and the Stranger's ways of speaking with the youth Theaetetus. I argue that the Eleatic Stranger is deliberately presented as an enigmatic figure who may alternately be identified as a sophist or a philosopher. The Stranger's understanding of himself as a philosopher is inadequate from Socrates' standpoint. While the Stranger identifies philosophy with a method of division and collection, and especially with applying that method to metaphysical questions, Socrates emphasizes self-knowledge and knowledge of the human soul and its good as central to philosophical practice. Socrates requires courage, curiosity, and humility on the part of his interlocutor, while the Stranger is relatively indifferent to the state of his interlocutor's soul.

Chapter 7 turns to the *Phaedrus'* description of good rhetoric. I argue that Socrates' rhetoric in the *Phaedrus* is not reducible to the method of collection and division that he outlines there. Both Socrates' use of myth in the *Palinode* and his prose description of rhetoric are oriented toward the persuasion of Phaedrus, a lover of sophistical speeches. Socrates deliberately uses rhetorical strategies in order to lead Phaedrus away from the sophistical rhetoric of Lysias and toward the rhetoric of philosophy. Love is not coincidentally the topic of the *Phaedrus*. Philosophical rhetoric is primarily concerned with love of two sorts: love of those with whom one speaks and love of the forms. While the sophist denies the reality of the love of the forms, and so denies a fundamental aspect of humanity, the philosopher affirms both the love of forms and of his fellow human beings.

2

Elements of Gorgianic Rhetoric and the Forensic Genre in Plato's *Apology*

I.

The *Apology* is a dialogue that at first blush seems to separate Socrates from the sophists with ease. After all, he denies that he is a teacher, while the sophists claim to teach. Socrates says that he teaches neither natural science nor excellence (*aretê*); although he has followers, he does not take any payment from them (19d–e). Certainly, these elements separate Socrates from the sophists. However, the *Apology's* account of the differences between philosophy and sophistry – particularly between philosophical and sophistical rhetoric – is far more nuanced, for Socrates uses common forensic *topoi* in his speech, seemingly giving credence to the prosecution's insinuation that he is a "clever speaker" (*deinou ontos legein*) (17b).[1] Moreover, as I argue herein, Plato's own rhetoric as the author of the dialogue follows closely in the footsteps of his sophistic predecessors. In particular, several elements of Plato's *Apology* closely mimic Gorgias' *Defense of Palamades.*[2]

In this chapter, I examine how Plato as the author of the *Apology* uses elements reminiscent of the sophists in order to *separate* Socrates from them. While philosophical rhetoric bears many superficial similarities to sophistic rhetoric, it has a distinctive set of aims. My discussion of

---

[1] Throughout this chapter, I use Grube's translation of the *Apology*. See Plato, "Apology," *Five Dialogues.* Trans. G. M. A. Grube (Indianapolis: Hackett Publishing Company, 1981), 23–44.
[2] Portions of this chapter were presented at the University of Arizona Colloquium in Ancient Philosophy, Tucson, AZ, in February 2006. I am grateful to audience members there for their comments, particularly Enrique Hülsz for his excellent commentary.

the differences between Socratic and forensic rhetoric falls into three main areas. First, Socrates' questions are aimed at making those whom he questions more virtuous. Because excellence cannot be taught, the most Socrates can do is to attempt to promote a kind of intellectual and emotional disequilibrium in the souls of those to whom he speaks, with the hope that his audience will emerge from this disequilibrium with a commitment to seek the truth. Socrates is rhetorical insofar as he attempts to influence the emotions of his jurors, and not only their intellects. However, rather than gratify and win the approval of the jurors, he deliberately inspires discomfort and even anger in order to promote greater self-knowledge in the jurors. Socrates' rhetoric is subjugated to the demands of virtue. Second, Socrates adapts elements of *eikos* (probability argument) and *êthopoiia* (portrayal of character) in order to make philosophical claims about the nature of wisdom, courage, piety, and justice. While Socrates portrays himself as embodying traditional Greek virtues, he shows that philosophical questioning also displays these virtues. Socrates attempts to locate in philosophical questioning many of the virtues that his fellow Athenians already value, while subtly reformulating those virtues to place philosophical questioning at the center of them.

While many commentators take Plato's *Apology* to be an historical document that attempts to approximate the trial of Socrates in content and style, there is good reason to question whether all of the content in Plato's version is historically accurate.[3] First, the very fact that Plato wrote numerous Socratic dialogues that are constructed dramas rather than historical

---

[3] I am largely in agreement with William Prior here, who argues that we suspend our belief as to whether the historical Socrates said exactly what the Platonic *Apology* says. See Prior, "The Historicity of Plato's *Apology*," *Polis* 18 (2001): 41–57. As Prior argues, Plato's Socrates is quite different than the Socrates of Xenophon's *Apology*. While they are not incompatible pictures, Plato and Xenophon each emphasize different traits of Socrates for different purposes (Prior, 45). For another excellent discussion of the historicity of the dialogue, see Brickhouse and Smith, *Socrates on Trial* (Princeton, NJ: Princeton University Press, 1989), 1–10. See also R. F. Allen, *Socrates and Legal Obligation* (Minneapolis: University of Minnesota Press, 1980), 3–35; Mark McPherran, *The Religion of Socrates* (University Park, PA: Pennsylvania State University Press, 1996), chapter 4; and Emile de Strycker, SJ, and S. R. Slings, *Plato's Apology of Socrates* (Leiden: Brill, 1994), 1–8. M. F. Burnyeat, in his "The Impiety of Socrates," *Ancient Philosophy* 17 (1) (spring 1997): 1–12, suggests that the differences between Plato's and Xenophon's *Apology* and the fact that Xenophon mentions in the plural authors that wrote about the defense show that this trial was a subject taken up by multiple authors. As Prior has argued, even Thucydides the historian did not claim to report exact words but rather wrote that speakers say "what was demanded them on the occasion"; see Prior, "Historicity," 52.

events ought to predispose us to consider whether the *Apology* is at least in part a construction of Plato's. If dramatic dialogues featuring Socrates at other points in his life are assumed to be Plato's own fictional constructions, we cannot safely take the *Apology* to be exceptional among the dialogues for its historicity.[4] Second, Xenophon's *Apology* presents a quite different picture of Socrates' trial, suggesting that one or both are, at a minimum, interpretive if not outright constructed.[5] Isocrates' *Antidosis* also picks up on elements of Plato's *Apology*, suggesting the possibility of a tradition of literary "apologies" that make reference to one another. Third, at least one stylometric analysis has placed the *Apology* as late as 386, many years after the date of Socrates' trial[6]; this later date suggests that Plato did not write the dialogue as a memorial of the exact events of the trial but rather took up the topic of Socrates' defense for some other purpose. Fourth, resemblances between Plato's *Apology* and Gorgias' *Palamades* imply that at least some of the *Apology* is a literary construction of Plato's. While it is perhaps surprising to suggest that Plato defended his teacher against sophistry by adopting elements of a sophistic text, Plato's propensity to borrow from and to allude to other genres in his own dialogues makes such a choice in keeping with the rest of his work.[7] Here, I do not deny that *some* elements of the *Apology* may be historical in origin. I only wish to emphasize the specific connections between the text of the Platonic *Apology* and that of Gorgias' *Palamades* and other forensic works in order to illuminate Plato's own rhetoric in defending his teacher.

Before examining the parallels between the *Apology* and the *Palamades*, a brief summary of the similarities between Socrates' speech and other

---

[4] Guthrie, for example, treats the *Apology* as entirely historical while asserting that other dialogues are Plato's own constructions. See Guthrie, *History*, 327–333. But not only Xenophon and Plato present Socrates differently from one another. Socrates is portrayed comedically in the *Clouds*, and we know of a sophistic work by Polycrates in which Anytus acts as an accuser against Socrates (*Socratous Kategoria*), now lost. See Anton-Hermann Chroust, *Socrates, Man and Myth* (London: Routledge, 1957), 69–100, for more on Polycrates' work. If these accusations of Socrates are fictional, then it is equally plausible that Plato's defense of his teacher is in good part his own construction. See also Blondell, *Play*, 33–37, who argues that Plato presents many of his characters, including Socrates, with some degree of fluidity.

[5] See Prior, "Historicity," 45.

[6] See G. R. Ledger, *Re-Counting Plato* (Oxford: Clarendon Press, 1989). Ledger places the *Apology* at around 386 BCE along with the *Gorgias, Menexenus, Charmides, Phaedo*, and *Laches*. Hathaway argues that style is not enough to show a precise date, as Plato might choose his style according to context. See Ronald Hathaway, "Law and the Moral Paradox in Plato's *Apology*," *Journal of the History of Philosophy* 8 (2) (April 1970): 127–142. Regardless, we cannot be certain that the *Apology* is one of Plato's first works.

[7] See Nightingale, *Genres*.

contemporary forensic speeches is in order. Both the overall construction of Socrates' defense speech and many of his particular techniques imitate a long line of defense speeches made in Athenian courtrooms. The overall structure of the first speech in the *Apology* follows the common structure of many extant court speeches. Socrates begins with a prooemium in which he describes how he will go about defending himself (17a–19a); follows with a narrative and argumentative *logos* (19b–35d); and ends with an *epilogos* (epilogue; 35e–42a). This overall structure is typical of the courtroom speeches written by courtroom logographers such as Lysias and Antiphon. Within each of these sections of Socrates' speech, we find parallels to other forensic speeches in Athens. Socrates also includes a second and third speech after each of the votes for his guilt and penalty. Additionally, the parallels between Gorgias' *Palamades* and Plato's *Apology* are more specific and striking than their use of general forensic topics (*topoi*). (In using the term *topic*, I mean the term as Aristotle uses it, as strategies of argument.)

The purpose of the prooemium was not only to introduce the speech but also to establish the goodwill of one's audience.[8] We find, for example, in Lysias' composition, "The Killing of Eratosthenes," the following plea:

> I should much appreciate it, gentlemen, if you would adopt the same attitude to me as jurymen in this case as you would towards yourself if you faced a similar experience; for I am sure that if you were to hold the same view about other people as you do about yourselves, not one of you could fail to feel indignation at what has happened, but all of you would regard as small the penalties imposed upon men who engage in such practices (1).[9]

Here, the speaker (Euphiletus) defends himself against the charge that he unjustly murdered his wife's lover. Lysias opens this speech with a plea for sympathy: the jurors are asked to put themselves in the same place as the defendant, who goes on to argue that he is a simple man who responded in the heat of the moment as would many victims of adultery. He appeals to the jury's natural sense of injustice at adultery, a crime that juries often punished by death or other penalties left to the choice of the cuckolded husband. Such a plea to the jury to see the defendant as a victim rather than a perpetrator of a crime is a common *topos*. Other familiar

---

[8] See Robert J. Bonner, "The Legal Setting of Plato's *Apology*," *Classical Philology* 3 (1908): 151.

[9] I have used Edwards and Usher's translation for Lysias' and Antiphon's works throughout. See M. Edwards and S. Usher, eds., *Classical Texts Series: Greek Orators, Vol. 1* (Warminster: Aris and Phillips, 1985).

topics in forensic prooemia include the sanctity of oaths, the greatness of Athenian law or Greek civilization, the seriousness with which jurors ought to take capital cases, and the rhetorical ability or inability of the defendant himself.[10] Socrates takes up the latter topic in the *Apology*:

I do not know, men of Athens, how my accusers affected you; as for me, I was almost carried away in spite of myself, so persuasively did they speak. And yet, hardly anything of what they said is true (*alêthes*). Of the many lies they told, one in particular surprised me, namely that you should be careful not to be deceived by an accomplished speaker (*hôs deinou ontos legein*). That they were not ashamed to be immediately proved wrong by the facts, when I show myself not to be an accomplished speaker at all, that I thought was most shameless on their part – unless indeed they call an accomplished speaker the man who speaks the truth. From me you will hear the whole truth, though not, by Zeus, gentlemen, expressed in embroidered and stylized phrases like theirs, but things spoken at random and expressed in the first words that come to mind, for I put my trust in the justice of what I say, and let none of you expect anything else (17a–c).

Here, Socrates denies that his speech is premeditated (i.e., that it is written or otherwise preplanned for its rhetorical effectiveness). He then associates, on the one hand, artificiality of speech with persuasion and lies and, on the other, spontaneous speech with truth and justice. Persuasion and truth are held in opposition: Socrates thus implies that speaking the truth need not mean that the jury will be persuaded and that persuasive rhetorical ability might even lead the jury to believe in unjust lies.

However, none of these claims is unique to Plato. Other forensic introductions also attempt to arouse the jury's suspicion of clever speech. For example, Antiphon's "On the Murder of Herodes" opens with the defendant's claim that he wishes that his powers of speech were as great as the misfortunes that have lately befallen him. He, too, states that many poor speakers were disbelieved because they told the truth, while many able speakers were believed although they told lies. The defendant then claims:

I request this of you, that if, on the one hand, I make some mistake in speaking, you will pardon me and attribute the error to inexperience (*apeiria*) and not to dishonesty (*adikia*); and if on the other hand, I express something well, you will attribute this to truthfulness (*alêtheia*) and not to skill (*deinotês*) (5; Edwards and Usher, eds.).

Here, Antiphon opposes inexperience and truthfulness to cleverness and dishonesty.

---

[10] See Bonner, "Legal Setting," 154.

Of course, Antiphon's speech, like Socrates', is carefully planned. Both utilize antithesis and parallelism at the very moment that they deny that they possess rhetorical ability. Both oppose the truth to lies and claim that they will be truth-tellers, even as they acknowledge the possibility that clever speech can lead others into lies. Both imply that the prosecution possesses clever rhetorical ability, while they as defendants lack it. Perhaps most cleverly of all, both Socrates and Antiphon use rhetorical devices in order to deny that they use rhetorical devices! While such a move might have gone unnoticed in Antiphon's own time, by the time that Plato writes, this device has been used over and over again (see Antiphon 1 *Stepmother* 1; 3 *Second Tetraology* b1–2; Lysias 12 *Eratosthenes* 3; Demonsthenes 27 *Aph. i.* 2; and D.H. *Is.* 10–11).[11] Plato must have expected Socrates' own use of the device to be noticed by a careful contemporary reader. Immediately, then, the speech raises questions as to whether Socrates' rhetorical skill undermines his claim to speak the truth or asserts a more complicated relationship between rhetoric and truth.

A second device in Socrates' opening is to claim that the origin of the accusations against him lies in slander (*diabolê*, 18d; 19b; 20e). Others, impossible to name (with the exception of Aristophanes), have falsely accused Socrates of studying things in the sky and below the earth and making the weaker argument the stronger. Socrates suggests that the real origin of this false accusation stems from his questioning of others in response to the command of the oracle at Delphi. Socrates felt obligated to refute the oracle's proclamation that no one was wiser than he is and so asked questions that led others to be angry with him, when they ought to have been angry with themselves (*Apology* 23c–d). Socrates' mention of slander here suggests that it is not he but his prosecutors who are guilty of the greater crime. Other Athenian forensic speeches also take up this *topos* of suggesting that it is the accuser who has done the more serious wrong, and not the defendant. For example, Antiphon in "On the Murder of Herodes" suggests that the prosecution had acted violently and illegally in pursuing the case (8–19). Lysias' "For Manthitheus" opens with the claim that his opponents desire "to harm me by every possible means" (1), while his "For the Invalid" accuses his accuser of slanderously taking him to court for monetary gain (2). In each of these cases, the defendant responds to his attackers with a counterattack designed to raise questions about the motives of the prosecutors.

[11] See Edwards and Usher, *Classical Texts*, 68.

Slander was a prosecutable charge in Athenian courts, although it was limited to those who had spoken ill of others in a public setting.[12] The prosecutor in Lysias' speech, "Against Theomnestus I," claims that although going to court for slander is usually considered inappropriately litigious, because he has been accused of patricide, the charge is so great that it would inappropriate to stand aside and do nothing (2). Lysias associates the desire to fight against egregious slander as a point of honor and virtue. Socrates, however, suggests that he could *not* have gone to court over the slander against him, for his accusers are so numerous and persuasive that it would be like fighting with shadows, cross-examining when there is no one to answer (18d). Socrates reworks the *topos* of accusing one's prosecutor into a more general accusation of Athenian society at large, a move that is both strategically risky and philosophically compelling. Even at this early point in the defense, Socrates makes clear that he is defending his whole life against the accusations made by *Athens* and not only by the named prosecutors.

The body of Socrates' defense of himself against the charges of impiety (*asebeia*) and corrupting the youth is also typical of forensic speech in its broadest strokes. Socrates calls witnesses in his defense, cross-examines the prosecution, and attempts to defend his character and the value of his contributions to the city. Socrates begins his narrative at 19b, stating the slanderers' charges, which Socrates says are more important than those expressed by Meletus. He does not formally call up individual witnesses, as would be typical in a defense, but does claim that the jurors themselves are already witnesses to the fact that he does not have any part in the sorts of sophistic enterprises presented by Aristophanes in his comedy (19c–d). He also calls upon Chairephon as an indirect witness; while hearsay evidence was usually disallowed in the Athenian courtroom, exceptions were made for the witness of the dead.[13] Most important, Socrates uses the oracle of Delphi as a witness in his favor. Much of Socrates' defense against the informal charges or slanders rests on his use of the oracle as a witness. As I discuss further in this chapter, this use of an oracle in lieu of human witnesses attempts to link Socrates' piety and his devotion to philosophical questioning. By claiming that the oracle at Delphi is the source of Socrates' mission of questioning, Socrates attempts to bridge a perceived gap between piety and philosophy. For Socrates, philosophical inquiry is

---

[12] For details on the nature of prosecutable slander, see Douglas MacDowell, *The Law in Classical Athens* (Ithaca, NY: Cornell University Press, 1986), 126–130.

[13] See Bonner, "Legal Setting," 186.

the embodiment of a certain kind of piety rather than an activity set in opposition to it.

Socrates also cross-examines one of his prosecutors, Meletus, a common practice in courtroom settings. Here, Socrates takes up his defense of himself against the formal charges of the indictment, that he corrupts the youth, does not believe in the gods in whom the city believes, and believes in other new gods (24b–c). Nearly all of Socrates' response to those formal charges takes place during this cross-examination of the prosecution (24b–27b). Socrates' main strategy in proving his innocence is to go on the attack against the prosecution. Again, this is not an altogether unusual ploy in forensic speech. Other orators cross-examined their opponents, usually about matters of fact about which there was some dispute (cf. Andocides I 14; Isaeus xi 5; and Denarchus 1 83). What is unusual here is that Socrates' approach in this cross-examination might lead him to appear to be like a sophist at the very moment that he is claiming not to be one. Rather than concentrating on arguing about factual matters, Socrates attempts to show that Meletus is inconsistent in his own views about the education and care of the young.

In his narrative, Socrates also addresses the question of whether he is useless to the city and ashamed of his past actions – in particular, his practice of philosophy. Throughout this section of his defense, Socrates' overall emphasis is on the portrayal of character (*êthopoiia*). Socrates compares himself to Achilles, who did what was right rather than act in response to the fear of danger. He alludes to his courage in battle at Potidaea, Amphipolis, and Delium and emphasizes his own piety in obeying the god at Delphi (28e; 29d). He denies that his philosophical practice is useless, emphasizing his contribution to the city as its "gadfly," biting those who are asleep in order to rouse them to care for excellence (31d). Many forensic orators used this technique of *êthopoiia* in order to win the favor of the jurors; Lysias was particularly talented in this respect. For example, in Lysias' speech, "Defense against a charge of subverting the democracy," the speaker claims that he is not only innocent of responsibility for any of the city's disasters but also has brought "many benefits to the city both physically and fiscally" (4). Like Socrates, the defendant emphasizes that he did not harm his city either under the oligarchy or under the democracy and refused to take office under a tyranny even when he had the opportunity (7–11; 14). The defendant goes on to list financial donations to the city, taxes paid, and battles fought in the city's defense (12–13). Other forensic speeches commonly make mention of ways in which the defendant is a benefactor. (For another excellent example, see Lysias, "Against Erastosthenes," 20.)

Socrates' claim that he will offer proof of his commitment to justice not in words (*logoi*) but in deeds (*erga*) is also commonplace in forensic oratory. Socrates tells his jurors: "A man who really fights for justice must lead a private, not a public, life if he is to survive for even a short time. I shall give you great proofs of this, not words (*logous*) but what you esteem, deeds (*erga*)" (32a). But other Athenian defendants draw a comparable contrast: Lysias' "Against Eratosthenes" tells the defendant that the jury must "pass its verdict on your deeds (*ek tôn ergôn*) rather than your words (*ek tôn logôn*)" (33). Antiphon criticizes his prosecutors using the same opposition: "Other men prove statements (*tous logous*) with facts (*tois ergois*) but the prosecution seeks to discredit the facts (*ta erga*) with statements (*tois logois*)" ("Murder of Herodes," 84). Socrates ends the main body of his speech by saying that he will not parade around his family in order to gain the jurors' pity but instead will rely upon his ability to teach and to persuade the jurors in order to gain his acquittal (34c–35c). He ends his plea for acquittal with the claim that he believes in the gods as none of his accusers do (35d). The jury, however, votes that Socrates is guilty of the charges. Socrates goes on to give two more speeches; because there are no comparable speeches in the extant literature, I reserve my discussion of them until later.

II.

Beyond the numerous ways in which Socrates' speech is in continuity with ancient Athenian forensic speech in general, there are also a number of more specific ways in which the *Apology* bears similarities to Gorgias' *Apology of Palamades.* These similarities extend beyond the ways in which both speeches reflect generic forensic *topoi.* The *Palamades'* subject is a fictional defense of the character of Palamades from the myths about the war at Troy. In most ancient accounts of Palamades, Odysseus has framed Palamades to appear as though he has been a spy for the Trojans, and Palamades is innocent of the charges. Gorgias' *Palamades* is an argument that rests on probability (*eikos*) and the construction of character (*êthopoiia*), designed to show that it is unlikely that Palamades could have committed the crime of betraying the Greeks. Palamades cannot give any direct proof that he has not been acting as a spy; he says that he is perplexed as to how to address such an unsubstantiated charge (4). Instead, he must indirectly show that he could not have committed treason. He emphasizes that acting as a spy could be of no financial or personal benefit and is contrary to his character and past virtuous actions. Palamades then attacks his accuser and asks that the jurors take their responsibilities seriously and vote for his acquittal rather than acting on the basis of the slander that they have heard.

Relatively few commentators have noted the parallels between Plato's *Apology* and Gorgias' *Palamades*.[14] However, Socrates and Palamades both make particular claims whose remarkable similarities go beyond those common to forensic *topoi*. That is, I argue that they are not simply relying upon the same forensic *topoi* but more that Plato's defense of Socrates is intended to be reminiscent of Gorgias' *Palamades* in particular. First, both Palamades and Socrates begin their defense with the claim that they lack the means to commit the crimes of which they are accused and next claim that they could not commit these crimes because of their civic loyalty. Second, each offers as proof of their civic devotion ways in which he has acted as a benefactor to the city. Each defendant claims that the best witnesses for the truth of what he is saying are the jurors themselves rather than any formal witnesses. Third, Socrates and Palamades make startlingly parallel moral assertions. Each accuses his attacker of lacking knowledge of the matter in question. Each argues for the "justice" of what he says. Each refuses to supplant his arguments about justice with an appeal to pity. Each defendant claims to prefer death to dishonor. Each claims that no one does evil willingly, using nearly identical phrasing at one point in the argument. Most strikingly, Socrates adds that he would be delighted if, upon reaching the underworld, he could converse with Palamades and others who have died unjustly to compare their ordeals (41b).

To begin, both Palamades and Socrates deny that they had the capability to commit the crimes of which they are accused. Both offer a kind of probability argument (*eikos*) at the beginning of their defense. Probability arguments attempt to show that it is unlikely that the defendant could have committed the crime rather than offering direct proof that the defendant did not do so. Palamades later explains why he cannot offer a direct proof: "For it is quite impossible for what has not happened

---

[14] See, as notable exceptions, Kenneth Seeskin, "Is the *Apology* of Socrates a Parody?" *Philosophy and Literature* 6 (1982): 94–105; James Coulter, "The Relation of the *Apology* of Socrates to Gorgias' *Defense of Palamades* and Plato's Critique of Gorgianic Rhetoric," *Harvard Studies in Classical Philology* 68 (1964): 269–303; and D. D. Feaver and J. E. Hare, "The *Apology* as an Inverted Parody of Rhetoric," *Arethusa* 14 (1981): 205–216.

to be testified to by witnesses, but on the subject of what has happened, not only is it not impossible, but it is even easy, and not only is it easy, but even necessary" (23). Palamades can give evidence of his utility to the city but in his first section, he must rely on probability arguments to show that he did not commit the crime. Palamades emphasizes that he is not capable of committing this act of treason (6). He says that he would have needed to meet with the Trojans to plan the treason before he could commit it and yet could not have met with the enemy unless a messenger of some sort wrote a note to arrange it and to deliver it. But no such messenger is known (6). Alternatively, if he were to have done it all through his own speech, how could he, a Greek, have communicated with the barbarians? Again, no known translator was present (7). Palamades goes on to offer numerous other practical obstacles to his having committed treason, such as the fact that it is not likely that the Trojans would trust a Greek to take their side; the difficulty of transporting the money; problems with committing the treason with so many guards present; and the lack of any clear motive for Palamades to take the side of the Trojans against his fellow Greeks (9, 10, 21).

Socrates, too, offers practical considerations at the beginning of his own defense: he emphasizes that he does not occupy himself with the study of things in the sky and under the earth, as Aristophanes' play had portrayed him doing; he does not even discuss these things (19b–d). Socrates lacks the ability to be a sophist occupied with things in the natural world. In addition, he also lacks the knowledge to be a sophistic teacher of moral and political matters. While he would "pride and preen" himself (*autos ekallunomên te kai hêbrunomên*) if he were an expert in human excellence, as Evenus and other sophists claim, he lacks such knowledge (20a–c). He does not even take money for his teaching, as is evidenced by his modest way of living (19e; 30a–c; 36b–c). Palamades, too, emphasizes his modest finances (15).[15] Like Palamades, Socrates emphasizes his lack of means to commit the accused "crimes"; this culminates in his general claim that his only wisdom lies in knowing what he does not know (20c–21c). Socrates argues that he is different than the sophists in occupying himself with different subjects than they do; he is incapable of sophistry because he is ignorant of the things that the sophists teach. In these ways, Socrates also offers a modified version of a probability argument. In their use of probability argument, both Socrates and Palamades are drawing upon a common *topos* found not only in extant forensic

---

[15] See Seeskin, "Parody"; Coulter, "Relation of the *Apology*," 279.

speeches but also in works of literature and drama (e.g., Sophocles' *Oedipus Rex*).[16] However, when one examines the details of Palamades' and Socrates' choice of words and subject matter, the parallels between the two works are even stronger. Of particular interest is the way in which both Palamades and Socrates assert the limitations of *logos* and criticize ordinary courtroom rhetoric (while at the same time drawing upon it) in ways that ordinary forensic speeches generally do not.

In the opening to his speech, Palamades emphasizes that the jury has the power to kill him, a power which he entirely lacks, while he possesses the power to be just: "justice is up to me, roughness is up to you" (2). He implies that if his speech triumphs, it will be due to its justice alone and not to any skill with words. Socrates also emphasizes the "justice of what I have to say" near the beginning of his speech, adding that the excellence of a judge lies in concentrating his attention on the justice of what the defendant has to say (18a). Both Palamades and Socrates name the limitations of the spoken word as a potential obstacle to the success of their own defense. Palamades claims that he is somewhat perplexed and at a loss in his own speech in attempting to make his defense (4), although he knows that he has not committed the crime (5). Similarly, Socrates says that he realizes how dangerous (*deinos*) his opponents are (18c) but that he must speak as the law obligates him to do so (19a). Both figures are at a bit of a loss as to what to say in making their defense and yet realize that they are left with no other alternative.[17]

Both Palamades and Socrates claim that they are of such character that they could not be the perpetrators of such crimes. In doing so, each defendant appeals to the jurors themselves as the best possible witnesses.[18] Palamades says, "I shall offer my past life as sure evidence that I am speaking the truth, and you be witnesses to the witness, for you are my companions and thus know these things" (15). Socrates also says that he calls upon "the majority of you as witnesses" of the fact that he does not pursue study of natural phenomena (19c). His claim that he is in court because he has angered the politicians, poets, and craftsmen through his aggressive questioning relies upon the jury's own knowledge of his public behavior. Socrates, like Palamades, does not call upon living witnesses to offer testimonials but instead attempts to construct for the jurors a

---

[16] See George Kennedy, *A New History of Classical Rhetoric* (Princeton, NJ: Princeton University Press, 1994), 25.

[17] See also Seeskin, "Parody."

[18] See Feaver and Hare, "Inverted Parody," 208.

picture of his own character and virtue. As material for this reconstruction of character, Socrates relies upon what the ordinary person knows of his questioning activity, even as he attempts to reinterpret this activity in order to give it new meaning.

In painting a picture of his character for their jurors, each defendant entreats his jurors to keep in mind the ways in which he has been a benefactor (*euergetês*) to the city (*Palamades* 30; *Apology* 36d).[19] Palamades' claims are quite remarkable as he says that he has benefited not only the Greeks but also all of mankind, including those yet to come (30). Palamades is reputed to be an inventor. Palamades credits himself with the invention of military equipment, written laws, letters, measures and weights, numbers, and draughts (30). He suggests that if he has busied himself with such enterprises, that it would be inconsistent for him also to betray the Greeks, as "it is impossible for one applying himself to the latter [useful enterprises] to apply himself to this sort of thing" (31). Socrates, too, takes on the question as to whether he has been a benefactor to the Athenians, claiming that he is a gadfly to the city, awakening it from its slumber (30e). Socrates describes himself as a "gift" from the gods to the city (30e), and he addresses the question of his "uselessness": he claims that his devotion to the city is clear from the fact that he has neglected his own affairs and lives in relative poverty (36b–c; 30a–c). Socrates says that he is a benefactor to the city insofar as he persuades others not to care for any of his belongings over caring for the wisdom and goodness of his own soul, never caring for the city's belongings over the good of the city itself (36c).

Socrates also claims that he has lived a life devoted above all to virtue, whether under a democracy or oligarchy, as when he voted against trying the ten generals as a group or refused to kill Leon from Salamis (32b–d). Like Palamades, Socrates emphasizes how his current activities will be beneficial to the city's future (39d). Both Socrates and Palamades present themselves as citizens more occupied with public than private or personal affairs. One important distinction between Socrates and Palamades is that Socrates' activity is morally ambiguous, while Palamades can state with

---

[19] See Seeskin, "Parody"; Feaver and Hare, "Inverted Parody." Coulter's approach is somewhat different: he emphasizes Socrates' contrast between truth and the tactics of sophistry, arguing that Socrates' persuasion rests on "truth rather than illusion" (297). See Coulter, "Relation of the *Apology*." However, precisely what Coulter means by "truth" is unclear. The claim to speak the truth is common to both Palamades and Gorgias. De Strycker is dismissive of any relationship between the *Palamades* and the *Apology*; see de Strycker, *Plato's Apology*, 374–375.

confidence that his fellow Greeks understand the value of the activities by which he has benefited them. As I discuss in section III, Socrates' reconstruction of both his own character and his philosophical questioning is central to his defense. The value of Socrates' activity of asking questions is controversial, while Palamades' inventions are not.

After defending his character, Palamades turns to address his own accuser, Odysseus. Palamades attacks Odysseus, asking him what sort of person he is to accuse someone such as himself (22). He questions whether Odysseus' accusation stems from knowledge or from imagination and asks whether Odysseus possesses knowledge of the time, place, or details of the treason, if he knows of them directly (22). He says that since Odysseus has not furnished witnesses to support his case, he must lack knowledge and have only an opinion (24). Palamades emphasizes the importance of this contrast between knowledge and opinion:

> But surely it is open to all men to have opinions on all subjects, and in this you are no wiser than others. But it is not right to trust those with an opinion instead of those who know, nor to think opinion more trustworthy than truth, but rather truth than opinion (24).

Socrates also addresses his own accuser in his cross-examination of Meletus. There, too, he argues that Meletus claims to be concerned with things about which he does not really know or care (23d; 24c). Meletus has not given much thought either to the question of how to teach the young to be virtuous or to what belief in the gods entails. Socrates also emphasizes the importance of wisdom and truth over other goods (29e). Making a pun on Meletus' name, Socrates says that Meletus must "know" (*oistha*) who improves the young, if he cares (*melon*), and then argues that Meletus does not really care about education (24d).

Socrates and Palamades both refuse to appeal to the jurors for pity or to take advantage of their friends in order to extricate themselves from this situation (cf. Seeskin 1982). Palamades states:

> For the rest, my speech is to you and about you; when I have said this I shall end my defense. Appeals to pity and entreaties and the intercession of friends are useful when a trial takes place before a mob, but among you, the first of Greeks and men of repute, it is not right to persuade you with the help of friends or entreaties or appeals to pity, but it is right for me to escape this charge by means of the clearest justice, explaining the truth, not deceiving (33).

Palamades refuses to dishonor himself by using unjust means to win the trial, and stands on the principle that he will persuade by simply explaining what is true. Socrates, too, repeatedly says throughout his defense that he must speak the truth (17b; 18a; 22a; 31e), even if it angers the jurors. He, too, says that he will not do what many others do, such as bringing in his children and parading them in front of the jurors, as such actions would contradict his reputation and bring disgrace upon him (34e). Socrates does not call upon his friends for aid, although many were present and he could have done so. He is insistent that he will not do anything that he does not consider to be good, just, or pious, saying that he believes in the gods as none of his accusers do (35d).

Both Palamades and Socrates insist that they prefer death to dishonor (*Palamades* 35; *Apology* 28b–d; 38d–39b).[20] Palamades begins his speech with a statement of the relative value of honor over avoiding death:

Prosecution and defense are not a means of judging about death; for Nature, with a vote which is clear, casts a vote of death against every mortal on the day on which he is born. The danger relates to honor and dishonor, whether I must die justly or whether I must die roughly with the greatest reproaches and most shameful accusation (1).

Socrates uses similar words in the *Apology* when he claims, "You are wrong, sir, if you think that a man who is any good at all should take into account the risk of life and death; he should look only to his actions, whether what he does is right or wrong, whether he is acting like a good or a bad man" (28b). A good man in the right position of service to his city must "remain and face danger, without a thought for death or anything, rather than disgrace" (28d). Later, again, Socrates argues that it is not difficult to avoid death but much more difficult to avoid wickedness (39a–b). Like Palamades, Socrates emphasizes the mortality of all human beings. What is more important than how long we live is how well we live; virtue is more significant than the length of life.

Both Socrates and Palamades claim that no one chooses to do evil (*Palamades* 13–14; *Apology* 25d–e).[21] Palamades introduces the idea as part of his probability argument: he argues that he has no motive to be wicked without any reason of reward, and that the prosecution has supplied no clear motive for attributing this crime to him; no one would choose to do what is most wicked (13). Socrates, too, argues that he could have no motive for harming the young, asking whether "I have reached such a pitch of ignorance that I do not realize this, namely that if I make one of my associates wicked, I run the risk of being harmed by him so that

---

[20] See Seeskin, "Parody," 97.
[21] See Seeskin, "Parody," 97.

I do such a great evil deliberately, as you say?" (25e). Later, Palamades'
phrasing is remarkably close to that of Socrates'.[22] Socrates says, "Either
I do not corrupt the young, or if I do, it is unwillingly, and you are lying in
either case (*all' ê ou diaphtheirô, ê ei diaptheirô akôn, hôste su ge kat' amphotera
pseudei)*" (25e–26a). Palamades' words, similarly, are: "If therefore I am
wise, I have not erred; if I have erred, I am not wise. Thus in both cases
you would be lying (*ei men oun eimi sophos, oux hêmarton. Ei d'hêmarton, ou
sophos eimi. Oukoun di' amphotera an eis pseudes)*" (26). Both Socrates and
Palamades claim that either they are in error and so cannot be accused
of being clever or they are wise and so could not have chosen to commit
a wicked act.

Socrates even directly compares himself to Palamades when he suggests that death might not be such a bad thing if he were able to keep on
conversing with others in Hades:[23]

> Again, what would one of you give to keep company with Orpheus and Musaeus,
> Hesiod and Homer? I am willing to die many times if that is true. It would be a
> wonderful way for me to spend my time whenever I met Palamades and Ajax, the
> son of Telamon, and any other men of old who died through an unjust conviction,
> to compare my experience with theirs. I think it would be pleasant (41a–b).

What is striking about the mention of Palamades is not simply that his
name arises in the dialogue as an example of an unjustly convicted man
but that he sees Palamades as a possible partner for philosophical conversation. In writing the *Palamades*, Gorgias defends a character consistently
portrayed in the myths as innocent. By having Socrates mention Palamades by name, Plato reminds his own audience of Socrates' own innocence. But here, Socrates adds the novel idea that nothing – not even
death – will deny him the pleasure of philosophical conversation. Along
similar lines, while Xenophon's version of the trial has Socrates mention
Palamades only as an example of a man who has been unjustly convicted
(*Apologia* 26), Plato's emphasis on Palamades is as a potential partner for
a philosophical discussion about unjust conviction. In the next section,
I take up the question of how Plato's *Apology* is distinct from that of the
Palamades and other forensic works and how these differences help to
illuminate Plato's philosophical rhetoric.

For the moment, we can see in Plato's positive use of elements of Gorgianic rhetoric both a defense of Socrates as a teacher and the adaptation

[22] See Feaver and Hare, "Inverted Parody," 207–208; Coulter, "Relation of the *Apology*,"
272.
[23] See Seeskin, "Parody," 97; Feaver and Hare, "Inverted Parody," 208–209.

of traditional rhetorical devices in support of philosophical values. Plato willingly argues from probability to show that Socrates cannot reasonably be believed to have willingly corrupted the youth. After all, how could a man who professes that his only wisdom lies in knowledge of his own ignorance, who claims not to teach anyone, and who never takes a fee or concerns himself with material gain be a sophist? This is not a direct proof of his innocence but rather an attempt to show how unlikely it is that Socrates could corrupt when he makes no claims to know anything positive. Plato also relies upon *êthopoiia* in order to reconstruct for us a new Socrates, different than his accusers' portrayal of him as a threat to the city. Instead of being a corruptor, interested in destroying the city's values and replacing them with his own, Plato suggests that Socrates is both pious (in his obedience to the oracle at Delphi) and devoted to the good of the city (in his acting as the gadfly of Athens). Meletus' character is set in contrast to that of Socrates': while Socrates cares for learning about virtue above all, Meletus is portrayed as both indifferent and care-less about these matters. Socrates values virtue more than a longer life and just speech more than persuasive speech.

But valuing justice over persuasion clearly does not mean indifference toward rhetoric or its active rejection. Quite to the contrary, Socrates' use of *êthopoiia* and use of other forensic *topoi*, such as the antithesis between truth and mere persuasion, the difficulty of fighting against slander, and counterattacking the prosecution, reveal a conscientious use of tradi-tional rhetoric in order to defend philosophy. Socrates' use of rhetoric is distinctive precisely in its subjugation to the demands of virtue. His char-acter and his unwavering commitments to justice and care for the soul are always the centerpiece of his use of these rhetorical devices. Rather than centering its values on the persuasiveness of rhetoric, good philosophical rhetoric requires commitment to the traditional Greek virtues of justice, courage, piety, and wisdom.

III.

Why, then, does Plato compare Socrates to Palamades and use elements from the work of a well-known sophist in his *Apology*? I suggest that Plato knew that Socrates was easily confused with the sophists. Certainly, Aristo-phanes' *Clouds*, to which Socrates alludes in the *Apology*, portrays Socrates as a sophist. In the *Clouds*, Aristophanes does not even treat the category of the philosopher as distinct from that of the sophist. Instead, his com-edy lumps together scientist, rhetorician, philosopher, and we might say "intellectual" in general into the rather broad category of corrupting "sophist."[24] Perhaps Plato's inclusion of Aristophanes here is meant to raise a more general question about the power and danger of *logos*. In various ways, many of Plato's predecessors, such as Parmenides, Zeno, Aristophanes, and Gorgias, were concerned with both the power and limitations of speech. This suspicion of *logos* seems also to be shared by the ordinary Athenian, who seems to have been influenced by Aristophanes' fears that some forms of *logos* are potentially a threat to tradition and the well-being of the *polis*. If the Athenians did not cleanly separate the sophist from the philosopher, then crucial to Plato's defense of Socrates would be acknowledging ways in which he might appear to be sophistic. Commentators such as Seeskin, and Feaver and Hare view the *Apology* as a "parody" of the *Palamades*. Seeskin sees Plato as concerned with the truth, while Gorgias cares only about probability. Along similar lines, Feaver and Hare argue that Socrates' use of rhetoric is ironic. However, I do not see Plato's main purpose here as parody or irony. Rather, Plato seems to be acknowledging ways in which Socratic rhetoric *does* draw upon sophistic rhetoric and is in continuity with it, while at the same time Socratic rhetoric refashions rhetorical devices for distinctly philosophical purposes. Socrates does not reject sophistic rhetoric altogether but instead takes up elements of it to be used in service of a higher moral purpose.[25]

The following discussion focuses on two themes. First, while Socrates uses rhetoric to affect the emotions of his jurors, he does so for the purposes of encouraging them to take up virtue. To encourage them to care for their souls, Socrates does not attempt to please or to flatter his jury but instead does the opposite. He deliberately angers and upsets them but for the purpose of awakening them to the importance of caring for virtue and knowledge above other goods. Second, Socrates uses the conventions of probability argument and *êthopoiia* in order to reformulate the jury's opinion not only of himself but also of the virtues. Socrates uses these forensic *topoi* to connect philosophy to traditional Greek notions

---

[24] Aristophanes presents the sophists indiscriminately as teachers of rhetoric and as natural scientists, criticizing both as threats to tradition. Those who study natural science attribute to natural forces what used to be considered the domain of the gods, while those who make the weaker argument the stronger promote their own self-interest. Aristophanes presents both as threats in their antitraditionalist use of *logos*. I argue here that Socrates attempts to connect philosophy back to an older tradition of the virtues.

[25] See Seeskin, "Parody"; and Feaver and Hare, "Inverted Parody."

of courage, wisdom, piety, and justice since the jurors treat philosophical questioning as a vice.

First, what is notable about Socrates' use of rhetoric is its subjugation to the demands of virtue. Socrates' main purpose is to encourage his jurors to become better people. It is not a lack of rhetoric that distinguishes Socrates from the sophists, or others who are "clever speakers," but rather his commitment to use rhetoric in order to cultivate virtue.[26] Socrates is not exclusively interested in getting an innocent verdict but rather in trying to encourage excellence in the jurors, as unlikely as success may be.[27]

Socrates' claim that he will speak what is just and true, while his opponents do not (18a–19a), is not especially unusual. Neither does his appeal to slander set Socrates apart. What is unusual is Socrates' open identification of his slanderers with the entire Athenian public rather than his specific prosecutors alone. Ordinarily, identifying one's prosecutors as slanderous is a move designed to lead a jury to be suspicious of the prosecution's motives. A defendant claims that his prosecutors are slanderous in order to remind the jury that they would not want to be the victim of slander either and so to gain their sympathy. While Socrates does claim that the slander started with a smaller, unidentifiable group of people, he adds that the jurors *themselves* have been so persuaded (18d). He tells the jurors that they are easily persuaded of untruths (18d), believe themselves to be wiser than they really are (22a–23a), are worthy of reproach and questioning (29e–30a; 30e), are likely to read false irony into what Socrates says (38a), and are not easily persuaded of the truth (38a–b). Socrates implicitly criticizes the jury as slanderers. While Palamades emphasizes that he would be ashamed to say anything untrue, Socrates suggests that it is the jury and the Athenian public who ought to be ashamed. Socrates even claims that a good man will not long survive public life, implying that the politically active among his jurors are not good (32e). He adapts the *topos* of speaking the truth by opposing his

---

[26] Cf. de Strycker and Slings, *Plato's Apology*; Seeskin, "Parody."

[27] I do not wish to imply that Socrates is uninterested in winning the case – only that winning is a secondary aim, subordinate to his project of encouraging the jurors to become more virtuous. While persuasively arguing for his innocence might be one way of making them more virtuous, Socrates takes risks in his defense that do not guarantee an innocent verdict. That is, winning his case is not simply a special case of convincing the jurors of the truth. For example, it may well be that the rhetoric and argument that persuades some of the jurors of the virtues of philosophy will also anger others and turn them even farther away from Socrates. Or an argument that initially leads to Socrates' conviction might become meaningful or persuasive to the jurors later in their lives.

truth not only to the untruths of the prosecutors but also to the untruths of the very lives of the jurors.

Socrates' aim is to improve the jurors through subjecting them to his demand that they inquire into the state of their own souls. He asks individuals to question themselves, their beliefs, and even their capacities to reason. Socrates' questions demand that his interlocutors ask about *themselves* and not only particular beliefs that they hold to be true.[28] Socrates notes that most people who are confronted with this sort of questioning become angry with him instead of with themselves (23c–d). Socrates anticipates the outbursts that occur among the jurors at several points in his speech (i.e., when he remarks upon the pronouncements of the oracle of Delphi (21a); when he questions Meletus (27b); and when he claims that he would continue with the same course of action, even if he were to face death many times (30c)). The jury's anger at Socrates during the trial mirrors the anger and defensiveness of the politicians, poets, and craftsmen whom Socrates questions. Rather than flattering his audience, Socrates forces the jurors to identify with those whom he questions so that they might judge the value of his questioning activity. This is in distinct contrast to the picture of the sophists we find in the *Gorgias* as flatterers (464c) or in the *Republic* as those who wish to tame the *demos* (493a–c). Socrates is interested neither in taming nor in flattering but instead in enlightening his jurors about the values of wisdom and the virtues. He says that he will not please or obey the jurors and will instead obey the god of Delphi alone (29d).

Socrates does not use the *prooemium* to win over the jurors' goodwill but instead uses it to prepare them to be questioned.[29] Socrates cannot directly teach others to be virtuous; he thinks that this is impossible. The most that he can do is attempt to affect their emotions and promote a sort of disequilibrium in the souls of his audience that might lead them to further examine themselves. While Socrates is often presented as if he were solely concerned with logic or argumentation, here Socrates uses traditional Greek rhetorical devices in order to affect the emotions of his jurors. However, instead of attempting to gratify and please them, Socrates' aim is to anger and upset them.[30] Although Socrates hopes that

[28] See Gordon, *Turning*, 30.

[29] As Sallis notes, Socrates uses the phrase "men of Athens" rather than the more common "judges" in his opening, reflecting his care for them as human beings. See Sallis, *Being and Logos*, 28–29.

[30] Note that Thucydides praised Pericles in part for the same quality to his rhetoric, noting that he refused to flatter the demos and often preferred to anger them through the use

they will be angry with themselves and not with him (23c), all Socrates can do is to use his rhetoric as a biting fly that attempts to arouse those who listen to him from their listlessness (30e). Socrates is interested not only in a conversion of his audience's belief but also in each member of his audience's taking up action to commit himself to the work of care of the soul. Socrates' rhetoric affects the emotions of his jurors and not only – or even primarily – their intellect but with the moral purpose of encouraging greater self-knowledge.

Socrates also uses probability argument (*eikos*) for entirely different purposes than does Palamades. While Palamades' aim is clearly to be found innocent, Socrates' main concern is to inspire the jurors to take up philosophy and to pursue virtue:[31] "For I go around doing nothing but persuading both young and old among you not to care for your body or your wealth in preference to or as strongly as for the best possible state of your soul" (30b). Insofar as Socrates claims that he cannot have corrupted the youth since he lacks the means to teach either natural science or excellence, his speech bears strong similarities to Palamades' probability arguments. However, more important to Socrates than the fact that his ignorance shows his innocence is the very admission *that* he is ignorant. While Palamades shows that he lacks the means to commit a crime, Socrates' statement that he lacks knowledge is an existential declaration. When Socrates says that his wisdom lies in knowing that he does not know (21c–d), he wishes to do more than to prove his own innocence. Instead, Socrates admits his own ignorance in the apparent hope that members of his audience will imitate him and also admit theirs. This ignorance is universal to all human beings; Socrates wants others to identify with his own condition, to sympathize with him, not qua defendant but qua human being. Probability argument is elevated from a demonstration of the defendant's lack of means to commit a crime to an admission of an existential "lack" that is common to all human beings.

---

of contradiction (Thucydides 2.65). See Harvey Goldman, "Reexamining the 'Examined Life' in Plato's *Apology of Socrates*," in *The Philosophical Forum* 35 (2004): 1–33.

[31] Seeskin argues that while Gorgias was more concerned with probability arguments, Socrates was concerned with the pursuit of truth and not only probability. However, in the *Apology*, the dispute over Socrates' activity is not a disagreement about the facts so much as about the value of his upsetting the traditional order through aggressive questioning. Seeskin claims that Gorgias' aim was to delight and to persuade, while Socrates sought to teach and to persuade, a distinction that Seeskin sees also in the *Gorgias* ("Parody," 100). But here, Socrates denies that he teaches, and yet he does clearly attempt to persuade his jurors, at a minimum, of the value of philosophy.

Socrates' claim that no one does wrong willingly also expresses this existential idea, while Palamades' similarly worded claim does not. Palamades uses the claim that no one would voluntarily choose to do what is wicked as part of a longer argument asserting that the prosecution has not given him any clear motive for committing this act (13–21). Socrates, in contrast, asserts the more fundamental and controversial claim that no human being ever chooses to do what is wrong and so must be educated rather than punished for his mistakes. While Socrates makes a philosophical claim about human nature, Palamades makes only the much more limited claim that no one does what is bad without some other motive (e.g., wealth, prestige, or other goods). Similarly, Palamades' contrast between wisdom and error seems to be designed to trip up his opponent: the prosecution could not accuse him of cleverness if he is making a mistake, and yet surely wickedness must be a mistake on his part: therefore, he cannot be both clever and wicked (26)! Palamades' argument sounds a bit like a showpiece of rhetoric at this point; he is a clever and playful speaker who can turn his opponent's argument on its head. Socrates' claim that no one willingly does evil, despite its controversial nature, has an utterly serious tone. For Socrates' claim is situated in the larger context of the dialogue's claims about the importance of care for one's soul. Because Socrates' encounter with Meletus is set in the midst of claims that care of the soul is essential, that Socrates' life is dedicated to encouraging such care, and that life is not worth living without philosophical questioning, we as readers naturally impart the claim with greater seriousness than one is inclined to grant to Palamades.

Similarly, Socrates does not use *êthopoiia* simply to build up his own character, in order to win the case and be set free. (After all, Socrates is surprised that he receives as many innocent votes from the jury as he does; cf. 36a.) When Palamades uses the device of *êthopoiia*, he offers as his examples of his courage and devotion to the city widely accepted instances of those virtues. He reminds the jurors that he has fought bravely in battle, has not been overly concerned with money, and has provided the city with many useful inventions. All these examples are ones that the jury will easily identify with examples of excellence and benefit to the city. But Socrates' goal here is not merely to assert that he has been courageous, just, and devoted to the city but also to declare philosophical questioning to be virtuous when ordinary Athenians might consider it vicious. Socrates does not only show how he fits into his jurors' preconceived notions of excellence but also uses *êthopoiia* to link philosophical questioning to justice, courage, wisdom, and piety. While the predisposition of the jury is to identify philosophy with the overturning of traditional Greek virtues, Socrates attempts to heal the rift between virtue and philosophy. Socrates uses *êthopoiia* to build up not only his own virtue but also a new ideal of virtue itself.

Socrates takes up the virtues of wisdom, courage, justice, and piety and transforms each one through linking them to philosophy. Wisdom, of course, is transformed through Socrates' description of it as being different than positive knowledge or political skill. Socrates uses the oracle of Delphi to relate this new picture of wisdom to an ancient religious tradition. Rather than presenting wisdom as positive knowledge, Socrates describes true wisdom as knowledge of one's own ignorance. Most Athenians understand wisdom to be positive knowledge of some subject matter (whether politics, poetry, or crafts) and themselves to be its possessors (21b–22e). But Socrates identifies his own distinctive wisdom as the fact that he is wiser "to the small extent that I do not think I know what I do not know" (21d). In presenting his view of wisdom as self-knowledge rather than as knowledge of other objects, Socrates effectively distinguishes himself from the sophists. Socrates disassociates himself from those sophists who claimed to be wise through suggesting that his wisdom (*sophia*) is of an entirely different kind. While Palamades emphasizes his positive knowledge as an inventor, Socrates emphasizes the poverty of his knowledge.[32] Socrates also links wisdom to piety by situating human wisdom in the oracle's prophecy; here, too, he sets himself apart from sophists such as Protagoras, who were atheistic or agnostic. Some of the inscriptions on the wall at Delphi have now become closely associated with Socrates himself: "Know thyself" and "Nothing in excess" are two of the most famous, but others less often repeated, such as "Hate hubris," "Bow before the divine," and "Observe the limit," make clear that Delphi is a place in which the human being was supposed to be aware of his limitations as a human being in face of the divine. The appeal to the oracle of Delphi is used to support Socrates' claim that even the Greek tradition holds learning of one's own ignorance and limits to be a virtue.

Socrates also links his life as a philosopher to traditional Greek ideas of courage, particularly bravery on the battlefield. Part of the effectiveness of Socrates' association of philosophy with courage takes place by using uncontroversial examples that identify Socrates with a traditional model of courage. Just as Palamades emphasizes his courage in battle, Socrates reminds his jurors that he, too, has fought bravely at Potidea, Amphipolis,

---

[32] See Coulter, "Relation of the *Apology*," 277–278.

and Delium (28e). Socrates proclaims, "You are wrong, sir, if you think that a man who is any good at all should take into account the risk of life or death; he should look to this only in his actions, whether what he does is right or wrong, whether he is acting like a good or bad man" (28b). He then goes on to compare himself to Achilles in his willingness to face danger and death (28c–d). All of these are uncontroversial examples of courage. But then Socrates also attempts to locate philosophy within this scheme of traditional Greek manliness: he reminds the jurors of the times in battle when he did not abandon his station and then compares his role as a philosopher to a god-given "station" (*tou de theou tattontos*) that he cannot abandon (28e). In addition, Socrates' term for exhortation here, *parakeleuomai*, was commonly used to describe the exhortation of soldiers before battle.[33] By linking the language of the battlefield with the practice of philosophy, Socrates associates philosophy with traditional ideas of courage. He then links this courage to justice: his courage in standing up for philosophy is not only for the sake of his own soul but also for the sake of the entire *polis*. For Socrates, philosophical activity includes courage and devotion to the city's defense. Since most sophists were non-citizens who entered and left countries with the aim of making money but had no strong commitment to the cities in which they resided, Socrates distinguishes himself from them by his courageous commitment to care for the good of the city at his own expense. His courage is not the personal courage of an Achilles bent on maintaining his honor but rather the civic courage of a man loyal to his own city's good.

Socrates also spends a considerable amount of time discussing the justice of his own actions. First, Socrates clearly associates his own lack of concern with money with his commitment to justice. While the sophists took money for their teachings but offered nothing of themselves to the city other than what they gave in private and often exorbitantly expensive lessons to their students, Socrates claims that his whole life has been about his devotion to justice and not money (19d–20c; see also *Hippias Major* 282b). Moreover, Socrates separates himself from orators who took payment for writing courtroom speeches (for a time, this practice of taking money for speechwriting was forbidden by law).[34] By emphasizing that his aim has never been to make money, Socrates effectively argues that he is not the sort of character who places his self-interest above civic duty.

---

[33] See Goldman, "Reexamining the 'Examined Life' in Plato's *Apology of Socrates*," in *The Philosophical Forum* 35 (2004): 1–33.
[34] See Bonner, "Legal Setting," 206.

In this respect, Socrates' conception of justice is in keeping with Athenian forensic tradition. However, Socrates also departs from the Athenian ideal of justice in at least one important way. While most Athenians under a democracy would certainly have associated justice with politics, Socrates separates the two. He tells the jurors, "A man who really fights for justice must lead a private, not a public, life if he is to survive for even a short time" (32a). This division of justice and politics must have seemed strange to the Athenian jurors, for under the pure democracy in Athens, every adult citizen was responsible for the governance of the city. Politics was not the responsibility of a select few but a universal responsibility of all adult male citizens. Socrates' claim that justice is separable from politics implies that Socrates lives according to a higher standard than the one set out by the city. Socrates does not think that democracy is the ultimate standard against which to measure justice. Instead, justice is independent of and on a higher plane than the sphere of politics.

Aside from wisdom, piety is the Greek virtue that perhaps gets the most explicit attention in the dialogue, no doubt because Socrates was being accused of impiety (*asebeia*). Key to Socrates' defense and reconstruction of his own character is his reliance upon the oracle of Delphi. The oracle of Delphi serves as a link between Socrates' piety and his philosophical questioning. While most Athenians would have perceived his questioning as impious and as undermining the stability of the city, Socrates uses the oracle story to show that piety is not only compatible with philosophical questioning but also, in fact, demands it. As in the case of each of these other virtues, Socrates does not only associate philosophy with a traditional Greek virtue but also transforms what is intended by the virtue itself by linking each one to philosophical questioning. Socrates' use of the oracle of Delphi as his sole witness differs from ordinary uses of witnesses in forensic speeches insofar as he literally calls a god as his witness!

The appeal to the oracle of Delphi as part of political speech has at least one precedent. For example, Themistocles argued that the oracle of Delphi prophesied that the "wooden walls" of the Athenian fleet alone could save them from the Persians (cf. Herodotus, *History* 7.140–144; Aristotle *Rhetoric* Book One, chapter 15, sections 13–17). This appeal to the oracle was understood by the Athenians to be in part responsible for the eventual battle and victory over the Persians at the battle of Salamis. However, Socrates' reliance upon an oracle as his witness is unique to the extant forensic literature.[35]

---

[35] See McPherran, *The Religion of Socrates*, 115.

Another unusual element of Socrates' use of testimony is that his "witnesses" cannot be tested or questioned; it remains entirely in Socrates' hands to shape their testimony as he wishes. Normally, hearsay "evidence" would be excluded from the Athenian courtroom since it could not be known to be reliable.[36] One of few exceptions is if the witness were dead; because Chaerephon has died, Socrates is allowed to introduce his testimony about the oracle's pronouncements. Ancient witnesses, like modern ones, could also be questioned as to their truthfulness. Prosecutors could bring a case for a false witness (*pseudomarturion*) if they wished to challenge his truthfulness,[37] but, of course, this too is impossible since Chaerephon is dead and the oracle cannot be brought into the courtroom. It is clear from the jury's outrage that they had not previously heard Socrates' claims about the oracle (21a). By bringing in only the testimony of the dead and then asserting that Apollo cannot speak falsely since it is not "lawful" (*themis*) for him to do so (21b6–7), Socrates insinuates that anyone who might challenge this hearsay testimony is *himself* impious. The jury cannot have missed Socrates' rhetoric here, and they might very well have seen Socrates' appeal to the oracle as a case of manipulatively using "loopholes" in the law for his defense. Such a move on Socrates' part potentially increases the jury's perception that he is a sophist bent on winning his case. Such difficulties have led some commentators to claim that Socrates is merely ironic when he mentions the oracle.[38] But, as Brickhouse and Smith point out, if Socrates fabricates the oracle story entirely, then he is guilty of dishonest rhetoric when he promises from the outset of his speech to speak the truth.[39]

Socrates might easily have claimed to be pious and loyal to the gods of the city by noting festivals and sacrifices of the city at which he had been present. In Socrates' Athens, worship according to the laws of the city was a duty of each citizen that had political and not only private significance. The cult of the city was also its political foundation. Socrates' impiety is a perceived political threat. His defense against the charge of impiety might have been expressed in political as well as religious terms. Had Socrates argued that he is a pious man by demonstrating that he participated in the religious–civic festivals of Athens, he might easily have shown that he is not a threat to the city. But rather than appeal

---

[36] See Bonner, "Legal Setting," 186.

[37] See MacDowell, *Law in Classical Athens*, 244.

[38] See Burnet, "Legal Setting," 107; I. G. Kidd, "Socrates." In *Encyclopedia of Philosophy*, Edwards (ed.), VII. London and New York: MacMillan, 1967, 482.

[39] See Brickhouse and Smith, "Oracle," 658.

to the regularity of his political–religious participation, Socrates appeals exclusively to the oracle of Delphi. In doing so, Socrates' main aim is not to show that he is pious according to Athenian standards but rather to refashion the concept of what it means to be pious. Socrates resolves the apparent tension between piety (and so also loyalty to the city) and philosophical questioning by claiming that questioning and piety are harmonious. Socrates' divine mission, as given to him by the oracle, *is* to call into question the traditional ideas of the city. For Socrates, the most pious act is to ask whether the political values of his day really do embody the most virtuous practices.[40] His process of questioning is not a display of impiety but is instead an expression of piety and respect for the god, Apollo – who is, after all, the god of reason.[41]

Some commentators have denied that Socrates' story about the oracle was true or that his piety was genuine.[42] While Socrates says he tries to "refute" the oracle (21c),[43] Socrates in practice does not attempt to refute the oracle per se but only his own initial interpretation of its most obvious *meaning*; that is, he initially attempts to refute its apparent implication that he is a wise man in some positive sense. But Socrates never claims that the oracle ought to be ignored or disobeyed. His obedience to the oracle and his self-imposed demand to submit himself to the truth of the oracle – at least until it is shown to be otherwise – is a display of genuine piety on Socrates' part. Once Socrates discovers that rational sense can be made of the oracle's proclamation that no one was wiser than Socrates, his commitment to the oracle's binding power is only deepened. For Socrates, piety and questioning are not at odds, for piety does not mean a blind acceptance of the city's religious and cultural institutions but rather includes an attempt to understand them rationally. In the case of Socrates' testing of the oracle, it means using rationality to seek out and understand the meaning of a divinely revealed

---

[40] In other ways, Socrates calls into question elements of Greek piety; as Mark McPherran argues, Socrates is critical of the idea that the gods are responsive to human sacrifices in a way that focuses on material rewards. See McPherran, "Recognizing the Gods of Socrates," *Apeiron* 30 (4) (December 1997): 125–139.

[41] As Gordon argues, Socrates' commitment to dialectic exhibits a kind of faith in the power of dialectic to give him the means to be committed to his beliefs, even as he remains open to the possibility of their revision in light of new discussions. See Gordon, *Turning*, 40–41.

[42] See Vlastos, "Socratic Piety"; McPherran, *The Religion of Socrates.*

[43] John Burnet, for example, argues that Socrates attempts to prove the god wrong and that Socrates is predisposed against the god. See Burnet, *Euthyphro, Apology of Socrates, and Crito* (Oxford: Oxford University Press, 1977), 92.

truth. In a certain sense, Socrates' commitment to "refute" the oracle turns out to be a refutation of himself – for what Socrates discovers is not that the oracle was wrong but only that he was mistaken in what he originally thought that the oracle meant. Again, Socrates offers himself to the Athenians as a model for discovery of one's own ignorance and limitations in admitting that his initial understanding of the oracle was incomplete.[44]

Socrates' appeal to the oracle serves a positive purpose in his use of *êthopoiia*. By appealing to a divine rather than a human witness, Socrates already asserts what he will say later in the *Apology*: that he lives according to a divine rather than a human standard and that his philosophical activity is grounded upon this divinely instituted mission (29d). Many commentators have rightly pointed out that Socrates' philosophical questioning could not have begun with the oracle's pronouncement since it seems that he knew of his own ignorance already through questioning, and so this activity must have preceded the question to the oracle.[45] Still, his identification of that activity as a divine *mission* results from Chaerephon's question at Delphi. Now Socrates works "according to the god" (*kata ton theon*; 22a4; 23b5) and in service (*latreia*) to him (23c1). Socrates' connection of that philosophical activity to a religious call seems to be triggered by the oracle's answer.[46] This connection of the oracle's claim to philosophy is Socrates' own interpretation and not from the oracle. The oracle's original statement does not give Socrates any mission; it only makes a claim about Socrates' state of wisdom and not what he ought to do about it.[47] Socrates alone makes the sweeping claim that he is obligated to philosophize as work on behalf of the god, intertwining human reasoning and divine revelation in his activity of philosophizing.

---

44 I agree with Brickhouse and Smith, "The Origin of Socrates' Mission," *Journal of the History of Ideas* 44 (1983): 664, that Socrates already believes before the oracle's pronouncement that piety demands obedience to the gods, but that he did not yet understand fully what this entails.

45 See de Strycker, *Plato's Apology*, 78–79; C. D. C. Reeve, *Socrates in the Apology* (Indianapolis: Hackett Publishing Company, 1990), 25–26.

46 See McPherran, *Religion*. As Brickhouse and Smith argue in "The Paradox of Socratic Ignorance in Plato's *Apology*," *History of Philosophy Quarterly* 1 (1984): 125–131, Socrates' certainty in the goodness of his mission to philosophize is logically distinct from his proclaimed knowledge of ignorance about the virtues. His belief in his divine mission is grounded in the oracle's proclamation but likely received additional confirmation when Socrates began to practice philosophical questioning.

47 See de Strycker, *Plato's Apology*, 80.

The difficulty with effectively persuading the jurors of these links is that Socrates' use of the divine witness is simultaneously a call to avoid hubris and an elevation of his own activity as divine. Socrates conveys the paradoxical nature of his activity of questioning others: while it is intended to encourage humility, it can also be perceived as arrogance. The paradoxical claim that Socrates is both the wisest man in all of Athens and also one who is ignorant is amplified in the nature of the oracle story as both a sign of Socrates' unique divine call and also of his utter humility. Socrates must have been aware of the danger of using the oracle example in this way. A juror can choose to either condemn Socrates for elevating himself as a person on a divine mission, as one who thinks of himself as the wisest of all men, or he can keep in mind that his mission is a humble one in principle available to everyone. Either way, a juror's focus will have to be on whether Socrates' philosophical activity is in its essence pious and not whether Socrates attended the right festivals, went to the appropriate sacrifices, and so on. Socrates' risky choice to appeal to the oracle story forces each juror to make a choice: he must decide whether Socrates' philosophical activity is a moral and even religious virtue. If the mention of Delphi successfully convinces the juror that philosophical questioning can be an exhibition of piety and humility, then Socrates has not only won his case but also contributed further to his mission to the city. He has then succeeded in overcoming the perceived gap between piety and philosophy. However, this strategy demands that the jurors understand Socrates' piety in terms of his practice of philosophy. For this reason, a juror's response cannot be guaranteed to go in Socrates' favor. What *is* clear is that Socrates does not use *êthopoiia* to build up only his own virtue but also to build up a new idea of the virtues in relation to philosophy.

Socrates' cross-examination of Meletus helps to demonstrate how Socrates' questioning examines a person as well as an issue. One important difference between Palamades' and Socrates' prosecutors in the two works is that Meletus is given a voice in the Platonic *Apology*. Odysseus is entirely silent in Gorgias' *Palamades*. In the *Palamades*, there is no reason to bring Odysseus into the written work, for the point of Palamades' leveling accusations against Odysseus is only to raise doubt as to the veracity of the charges. However, the cross-examination of the person of Meletus and the philosophical examination of the issue of who teaches the young to be virtuous are not separable elements in Socrates' questioning. His cross-examination of Meletus is simultaneously an exhibition of dialectical exploration of a philosophical problem ("Who teaches virtue?") and a cross-examination of his prosecutor's character ("Who is Meletus?").[48] As Gordon describes it, "Dialectic is a philosophical way of life as well as being a philosophical procedure."[49] Socrates is not interested merely in the intellectual enlightenment of his interlocutors over a particular issue – although he may hope that Meletus will see the inconsistencies in his own thought. He is interested in the transformation of the whole person. Socrates wants each person to care for his own soul and for virtue above all other goods. Making such a commitment requires more than simply admitting the inconsistency of a particular point of argument. Socrates here relies upon the public shaming of Meletus as a means for members of his audience to examine themselves and their own relative valuation of other goods over the good of their souls.

Socrates' cross-examination of Meletus also serves as an opportunity for the implicit cross-examination of each juror in his audience. Socrates does not ask questions of specific fact, such as whether Meletus saw Socrates last Tuesday asking questions in the *agora*. Each of Socrates' questions is one that any juror can answer internally for himself. (The same holds true for Plato's own audience of readers of the dialogue.[50]) Socrates is acting as the gadfly of Athens, doing political work as well as offering a forensic defense. Perhaps this is also the reason that Socrates addresses the informal charges in his defense rather than focusing on the formal charges: his ultimate aim is to defend his way of living against the conventional way of life represented by Meletus. By questioning Meletus' commitments, Socrates promotes self-knowledge in his entire audience, potentially inspiring it to recognize how philosophy promotes greater self-understanding.

Plato's *Apology*, too, departs from Gorgias' *Palamades* in its link to the historical person of Socrates. Gorgias' work is a set piece, perhaps meant to be memorized by students and used for practice in developing one's rhetorical skills. It is also a piece of epideictic rhetoric: Gorgias manages to pack into one speech a number of elaborate forensic *topoi*, where

---

[48] Louis André Dorion argues persuasively that in a number of authors before Plato, the term *elenchus* is used to describe a line of questioning used to reveal the lies or to put to shame others assumed to be guilty of deception. Here, too, Socrates seems to be interested in revealing Meletus' shortcomings as a human being and not only in showing the logical inconsistency of his ideas. It is doubtful that Socrates intends to persuade Meletus to stop prosecuting him. See Dorion, "La Subversion de l'elechos juridique dans l'Apologie de Socrate," *Revue Philosophique de Louvain* (October 1990): 311–344.

[49] See Gordon, *Turning*, 32.

[50] As Burnyeat, "Impiety," 2, argues, each of Plato's readers is also a potential juror.

presumably one could locate a variety of lines of argument that could be used in future speeches. In this sense, the *Palamades* can be understood as a collection of forensic arguments used to show off Gorgias' skill as a rhetorician. The *Apology*, however, defends the life of a real person who was brought to trial and later put to death. This historical reality of Socrates' life and death is always present in the background of the dialogue and imparts a seriousness that is lacking in the Palamades. Palamades' defense is always fictional and exists for the sake of studying rhetoric. In the *Apology*, it is Socrates' life and commitments that Plato seems to want us to study and emulate. Plato writes a work of *epideixis*, but this *epideixis* is an encomium to Socrates, as well as a set of forensic arguments and philosophical arguments. If Gorgias' *Encomium to Helen* is a forensic piece disguised as a piece of encomium, perhaps Plato's *Apology* is an encomium disguised as a piece of forensics.

Socrates' most striking departures from forensic *topoi* come at the end of his speech. Socrates' second and third speeches (after the guilty vote and penalty vote) have no precedents in the surviving forensic genre, and we do not have any other surviving counterpenalty proposal.[51] In his second speech, Socrates famously proposes as his counterpenalty free meals in the Prytaneum, as befits a hero (36c–d). A more common counterpenalty would have been a lesser punishment, such as exile or fines. But Socrates lays out a number of reasons why other counterpenalties that he might propose as an alternative to death are problematic: exile will not help because he will continue to philosophize elsewhere and every community will reject philosophy in the same way; money is insufficient because he has none and will go back to his old practices anyway. Eventually, his friends persuade him to offer a counterpenalty of thirty minae (38b). By this time, however, Socrates had undoubtedly raised the ire of his jurors.

After the jurors vote for the penalty of death, Socrates responds to the jury by offering to prophesy (*chrêsmôidêsai*). He claims that vengeance (*timôria*) will come upon those who voted to kill him (39c). More young people, whom Socrates has held back from testing others in public, will come forward after Socrates' death. He suggests that being tested is inescapable, and the best that one can do is attempt to be as good as possible (39c–e). As de Strycker has argued, the topics he pursues in this speech are remarkably similar to those in Thucydides' account of

---

[51] See Bonner, "Legal Setting," 169.

Pericles' *Funeral Oration*.[52] Just as Socrates discusses death, immortality, and the care of his children, Pericles treats all of these subjects in his praise of the dead. He tells the Athenians: "For this offering of their lives made in common by them all they each of them individually received that renown which never grows old and for a sepulcher, not so much that in which their bones have been deposited, but that noblest of shrines wherein their glory is laid up to be eternally remembered upon every occasion on which deed or story shall call for its commemoration" (43). He also comforts those who have lost relatives and promises that the state will take on the father's role of educating the children of the dead at public expense (44–46). A variety of funeral orations by Lysias, Demosthenes, and Hyperides all discuss fame and immortality in praise of the dead as well (Lysias' *Funeral Speech* ii 77–81; Demosthenes' *Funeral Speech* 32–34; and Hyperides' *Funeral Speech* vi 41–43).[53] In essence, Socrates offers us a kind of miniature funeral oration for himself in advance of his own death. As Pericles argues that the citizens of Athens must sacrifice themselves for the sake of the city's excellence and freedom (41–42), Plato argues that Socrates sacrificed himself for Athens' sake. Isocrates in the *Evagoras* says that we can eulogize others in order to lead us on to mimic their deeds (77); perhaps Plato uses these final two speeches of Socrates to eulogize Socrates and attempt to inspire his own audience to take up philosophy. In this sense, the *Apology* is both an encomium and an exhortation. In including more than one genre here, Plato's dialogue goes well beyond usual forensic speeches (whether constructed or historical) in serving as a defense, an encomium, and an exhortation to philosophize all at once.[54]

Socrates at the very end of his speech adds on that he is willing to stay around the courtroom a bit longer, as long as the court officers are able to remain, to discuss the meaning of what has occurred (40a). He goes on to reflect upon death once more, as well as the need for his sons to be reproached and questioned as they grow to be adults (41e–42a). As Plato has written this final segment of Socrates' speech, Socrates' forensic speech has no definite conclusion; instead, he gradually shifts away from

---

[52] See de Strycker, *Plato's Apology*, 235–239.

[53] See de Strycker, *Plato's Apology*, 236.

[54] See de Strycker, *Plato's Apology*, 10–15, who points out that the ancient author of "On Figured Speeches" writes that Plato's *Apology* is (1) an *apologia* of Socrates; (2) an accusation of the Athenians for bringing such a man to court; (3) an encomium to Socrates; and (4) an exhortation, *paraggelma*, of what sort of person a philosopher ought to be. See also Burnyeat, "Impiety," 5.

his formal reply to the jurors and into a more informal discussion of the meaning of death and education. Socrates returns to his old practice of discussing philosophy "in the marketplace" and other public spaces, even if this time that space is the courtroom. This forensic speech leads naturally into Socrates' ordinary philosophical conversations.

What distinguishes Socrates from the sophists in the *Apology* is neither rhetoric-free speech nor a precise philosophical method. Instead, Socrates and Plato are both rhetorical in the sense of being willing to draw upon the techniques of orators and sophists in order to persuade their own audience. These rhetorical elements constitute part of their arguments and cannot be artificially separated from them. The difference between Socrates and other orators, including the sophists, is not that Socrates separates philosophy from rhetoric. Instead, Socrates' use of rhetoric is at the service of the virtues of wisdom, justice, courage, and piety. But part of Plato's argument in the dialogue is to establish that these virtues arise from and are intimately connected to Socrates' commitment to philosophy as a way of life. In this sense, Plato's *Apology* is simultaneously a defense of Socrates and of philosophy itself.

3

The Rhetoric of Socratic Questioning in the *Protagoras*

I.

Exploring the purpose of Socratic questioning in the dialogues is a crucial part of making sense of Plato's approach to philosophical and sophistical rhetoric.[1] Superficially, Socratic questioning seems to share something in common with sophistic eristic. Socrates often asks questions that seem to lead his opponents toward conclusions that do not necessarily follow from the premises. Perhaps Adeimantus puts it best when he speaks to Socrates about this common perception of philosophers in the *Republic*:

> [H]ere is how those who hear what you now say are affected on each occasion. They believe that because of inexperience at questioning and answering, they are at each question misled a little by the argument; and when the littles are collected at the end of the arguments, the slip turns out to be great and contrary to the first assertions. And just as those who aren't clever at playing draughts are finally checked by those who are and don't know where to move, so they too are finally checked by this other kind of draughts, played not with counters but speeches, and don't know what to say (*Rep.* 487b).[2]

Here, Adeimantus suggests that the experience of being questioned by Socrates feels akin to being tricked in a game of checkers. This image of a game particularly emphasizes the possibility that Socrates is interested

---

[1] As Harold Tarrant has argued, the term *elenchus* is a metaphor and not a technical term for a single Socratic method. See Tarrant, "Naming Socratic Interrogation in the *Charmides*," in Robinson and Brisson (eds.), *Plato: Euthydemus, Lysis, Charmides, Proceedings of the V Symposium Platonicum* (Sankt Augustin: Academia Verlag, 2000). I prefer the term *Socratic questioning* here rather than *elenchus*.

[2] Bloom's translation.

in being the victor in a competition rather than in seeking the truth. While Adeimantus goes on to express confidence that Socrates pursues the truth, most of Socrates' partners in speech have somewhat less confidence.

As we have seen in the *Apology*, Socrates frequently speaks of his devotion to knowledge and virtue, a devotion that his opponents do not always share. Socrates emphasizes the centrality of both the love of wisdom and of self-knowledge, particularly of one's own limits. Socrates loves not only arguments but also the good. The puzzle for a commentator, then, is to make sense of how to reconcile the Socrates who devotes himself to the truth and humbly acknowledges his own ignorance with the Socrates who skillfully questions his opponents. In other words, how does Socratic questioning differ from the eristic questions or epideictic displays of the sophists with whom he is frequently in opposition?

I address this question through examining how Socrates questions his sophistic opponents in the *Protagoras* and the *Gorgias*. These chapters on the *Protagoras* and the *Gorgias* look at two quite different ways in which Socrates asks questions of his interlocutors. Socrates does not take the same approach in questioning Protagoras, Gorgias, Polus, and Callicles because his interlocutors are different sorts of human beings. In the *Gorgias*, we see a significantly more aggressive and critical Socrates who seems interested in shaming his opponents. In the *Protagoras*, Socrates is somewhat friendlier, even as he and Protagoras are mutually frustrated in their attempts to speak with one another. Socrates asks questions that are designed to help uncover many of Protagoras' ideas about courage, knowledge, and other virtues.

Traditionally, many commentators have seen Socrates' questions as primarily constructive or as promoting a positive doctrine or Socratic teaching. For example, commentators frequently take the *Protagoras* to advocate the unity of the virtues, an art of measurement in ethics, and/or hedonism.[3] The *Protagoras*, understood in this way, is a battle between Socrates, who has a well-developed philosophical teaching that centers around the importance of precise measurement in living well, and

---

[3] Authors who take the hedonism argument to be a positive Socratic teaching include Thomas Brickhouse and Nicholas Smith, "Socrates and the Unity of the Virtues" *Journal of Ethics* 1 (4) (1997): 311–324; I. M. Crombie, *An Examination of Plato's Doctrines*, volume I (London: Routledge and Kegan Paul, 1962); John Cronquist, "The Point of Hedonism in Plato's *Protagoras*," *Prudentia* 12 (1975): 63–81; R. Hackforth, "The Hedonism in Plato's *Protagoras*," *Classical Quarterly* 22 (1928): 38–42; and Terence Irwin, *Plato's Moral Theory: The Early and Middle Dialogues* (Oxford: Clarendon Press, 1977).

Protagoras, who is variously presented as advocating a more traditional, democratic Greek understanding of political *aretê*; as defending a more pragmatic and contextual view of the good; or as merely interested in winning a verbal battle in order to gain more students.[4] For some commentators, the difference between philosopher and sophist is reducible to a conflict between two different intellectual standpoints – a claim that minimizes the rhetorical dimensions to Protagoras' expression of his ideas.[5] Others have claimed that there is a clear difference in the method of the two, in which it is generally presupposed that Socrates attaches himself to some rational ideal of rhetoric-free argumentation, while Protagoras extols a rhetorical ideal opposed to that model of rationality. On this view, there is a fundamental gap between the approaches of the sophist and of the philosopher that can be characterized by excluding rhetoric from philosophy or rationality from sophistry.[6] On nearly all accounts, Socrates is the "winner" who represents the Platonic – and more defensible – view.

---

[4] Understandings of Protagoras' position vary widely. Levi, for example, sees Protagoras as having a non-relativistic understanding of human nature, in which justice and shame are central. See A. Levi, "The Ethical and Social Thought of Protagoras," *Mind* 49 (1940): 284–302. S. Moser and G. L. Kustas emphasize the political functionality of excellence. See Moser and Kustas, "A Comment on the Relativism of the *Protagoras*," *Phoenix* 20 (1966), 111–115. A. E. Taylor sees Protagoras as a relativist, who saw moral education as the indoctrination of students into the city's morals. See Taylor, *Plato: The Man and His Work* (New York: Meridian Books, 1960), 246. Arthur Adkins sees Protagoras as deliberately equivocating in the argument in order to answer Socrates' questions, while Kerferd maintains that Protagoras gives a perfectly consistent account of the teachable nature of excellence. See Adkins, "Arete, Techne, Democracy, and Sophists: *Protagoras* 316b–328d," *Journal of Hellenic Studies* 93 (1973): 3–12; and G. B. Kerferd, "Protagoras' Doctrine of Justice and Virtue in the *Protagoras* of Plato," *Journal of Hellenic Studies* 73 (1953): 42–45. David Roochnik also argues that Protagoras deliberately equivocates as part of his rhetorical practice. See Roochnik, *The Tragedy of Reason: Toward a Platonic Conception of Logos* (New York: Routledge, 1990), 58.

[5] Edward Schiappa argues that by contemporary standards, Protagoras would be considered a philosopher. See Schiappa, *Protagoras and Logos: A Study in Greek Philosophy and Rhetoric*, 2nd ed. (Columbia: University of South Carolina Press, 2003). Kerferd takes a similar view, writing "Both Socrates and Protagoras believe in education as the key to all social and political problems. They differ radically about its content, but that is all." See Kerferd, *Sophistic Movement*, 138.

[6] Gregory Vlastos puts the distinction in terms of a greater precision on Socrates' part than on Protagoras' part. See Vlastos, *Introduction to Plato's* Protagoras (New York: Liberal Arts Press, 1956), xvii. An assessment of an even deeper philosophy–rhetoric split can also be found in Roochnik, *Tragedy of Reason*, especially chapter 1, who argues that Protagoras values power and views Socratic *logos* as a barrier to the pursuit of that power. Charles Griswold, "Relying on Your Own Voice: An Unsettled Rivalry of Moral Ideals in Plato's *Protagoras*," *Review of Metaphysics* 53 (1999): 533–557, argues that the philosopher values self-reliance, responsibility, and accountability to reason while the sophist does not. See also Patrick Coby, *Socrates and the Sophistic Enlightenment: A Commentary on Plato's Protagoras* (Lewisburg, PA: Bucknell University Press, 1987).

However, the contrast here between Socratic questioning and sophistic rhetoric is not so straightforward. The confrontation between Socrates and Protagoras is neither simply a contest between two different intellectual positions nor a philosophical argument presented by Socrates to Protagoras, for Socrates himself does not evaluate his defeat of Protagoras in the debate as a triumph of a particular view of excellence, wisdom, or teaching. Instead, Socrates notes that *both* his own and Protagoras' understandings of excellence are confused and require further exploration. While at the beginning of the dialogue, Protagoras states that excellence is teachable and that he is a teacher of it (319a), and Socrates expresses strong doubts that it can be taught (320b), by the end their positions seem to be reversed. Socrates says that a person listening to them might say,

How absurd (*atopoi*) you are, Socrates and Protagoras. For you, having at first said that excellence is not teachable, are now going against yourself, trying to show that all things are knowledge (*epistêmê*) – justice, soundmindedness, and courage – the best way to show that excellence appears to be teachable (361a3–b7).[7]

Protagoras' position has also shifted in an equally extreme manner. Socrates concludes that their state is one of "terrible confusion" that can only be adequately addressed by going back to further examine the nature of excellence (361c4). That is, Socrates explicitly says that neither the nature of excellence nor its teachability has been discovered. In addition, Socrates emphasizes that he wants Protagoras to state his own beliefs in answers to questions (331c–d). If the conversation is about the beliefs of the interlocutor, then the *aporia* at the end of the dialogue might be understood as revealing a problem in either the line of questioning, or the answers, or a combination of both. Moreover, Protagoras and Socrates never have a conversation that is satisfying to them both. As Griswold has argued, there is a fundamental incommensurability between Socrates' approach and that of Protagoras.[8]

Plato's highlighting of the gap between Protagoras and Socrates suggests that part of Plato's aim in the dialogue is to show the value of question and answer as a positive philosophical mode of speech; more specifically, I argue that question and answer is a form of philosophical rhetoric. That is, Socratic questioning in the *Protagoras* is a mode of speaking in which the form of the speech is as important as its content.

---

[7] Translations throughout are Plato, *Protagoras*, revised edition. Translated with notes by C. C. W. Taylor (Oxford: Clarendon Press, 1991).

[8] See Griswold, "Relying on Your Own Voice."

I focus on two rhetorical elements of Socratic questioning in the *Protagoras*. First, I argue that Socrates asks questions designed for his particular interlocutor, Protagoras, rather than offering a universal argument that is detached from any concerns about audience. I focus on the hedonism section of the dialogue and argue that Socrates' questions there can be understood as an *ad hominem* argument. Socrates wishes to show flaws in Protagoras' understanding of excellence; at the same time, Socrates also contributes his own concerns and ideas in the development of the conversation.[9] Second, I examine Socrates' more explicit statements as to the value of question and answer between two people in the pursuit of truth. Socratic questioning is deeply rhetorical insofar as Socrates' philosophical questioning has significant social and performative dimensions. The discovery of truth and its expression in language takes place between two people whose ideas inform how that truth is articulated and understood. In addition, the very act of questioning and of listening to others embodies the philosopher's self-knowledge. Plato is not interested in the wholesale rejection of the rhetorical tradition so much as in reshaping that tradition's meaning in light of the aims of philosophy.

II.

The nature of Socratic questioning in the dialogues has been an issue of tremendous debate. Perhaps most influential has been Vlastos's well-known account in "The Socratic Elenchus." According to Vlastos, Socrates shows an interlocutor that a belief he holds is fundamentally incompatible with some of his other beliefs. Vlastos suggests that Socrates means to do more than only refute a faulty proposition (p); he often takes the refutation of such a proposition to prove the opposite (not-p). While recognizing that the refutation of p does not, of course, logically prove that not-p is true, Vlastos explains that in Socrates' view, further inquiry will always show that a false belief entails a set of inconsistent beliefs, while Socrates'

---

[9] Portions of this chapter are republished here with permission from *Ancient Philosophy*. See Marina Berzins McCoy, "Protagoras on Human Nature, Wisdom, and the Good: The Great Speech and the Hedonism of Plato's *Protagoras*," *Ancient Philosophy* (spring 1998): 21–39. For others who claim that this is some version of an *ad hominem* argument, see M. Dyson, "Knowledge and Hedonism in Plato's *Protagoras*," *Journal of Hellenic Studies* 96 (1976): 32–45; Scott R. Hemmenway, "Sophistry Exposed: Socrates on the Unity of Virtue in the *Protagoras*," *Ancient Philosophy* 16 (1996): 1–23; Daniel C. Russell, "Protagoras and Socrates on Courage and Pleasure: "Protagoras 349d," *Ancient Philosophy* 20 (2000): 311–338; and Roslyn Weiss, "Hedonism in the Protagoras and the Sophist's Guarantee," *Ancient Philosophy* 10 (1990): 17–39.

beliefs are self-consistent and cannot be refuted.[10] More recently, commentators have questioned the constructivist nature of Vlastos' model. As Benson has argued, refutation of a belief *p* does not imply that *not-p* is true but only that *p* is incompatible with some other belief to which the interlocutor has assented. But it might be that this other belief *q* is faulty or that some third alternative not yet on the table is a better answer to the question at hand.[11] Still others have asked whether refutation might not have purposes well beyond the refutation of belief, such as increasing an interlocutor's understanding of his own state as a person, and not only as a thinker or believer of propositions.[12]

Here, I do not attempt to make general claims about all instances of Socratic questioning, as his approach to questioning varies depending upon the person with whom he is in dialogue. Here, I look at the hedonism section of the dialogue and argue that Socrates' questions to Protagoras are intended to bring out problems inherent in Protagoras' own ideas; that is, they are a modified version of an *ad hominem* argument. The hedonism section of the argument is not reducible to Socrates' own views on the nature of pleasure and wisdom. Neither does it simply reveal what Protagoras already thinks about these topics. Instead, Socrates' questions first develop aspects of Protagoras' views already articulated in the Great Speech and then show the limitations of these further-developed views about pleasure, knowledge, and courage. His questions are rhetorically oriented toward producing a state of confusion in Protagoras about the ideas that he had set out earlier in the Great Speech; Socrates' aim seems to be for Protagoras to become aware of the limitations of his own views rather than to teach a positive doctrine. At the same time, Socrates' questions arise from his own concerns about the virtues as well. The outcome of their conversation is a result of each of their contributions to the discussion at hand.

That Socrates' questions about hedonism are designed to bring out something in Protagoras' views is not immediately obvious. Near the start

---

[10] See Gregory Vlastos, "The Socratic Elenchus: Method Is All," in Vlastos, *Socratic Studies*, ed. Myles Burnyeat (Cambridge: Cambridge University Press, 1994), 4. Passages that insist on the importance of an interlocutor using only his own beliefs include *Protagoras* 331c5–9, *Crito* 49c–d, *Gorgias* 500b, *Meno* 84a, and *Republic* 346a.

[11] See Hugh Benson, "The Problem of the Elenchus Reconsidered," *Ancient Philosophy* 7 (1987): 67–85; and also Benson, "Problems with Socratic Method," in Gary Scott (ed.), *Does Socrates Have a Method?* (University Park, PA: Pennsylvania State University Press, 2002), 101–113.

[12] See Scott, *Does Socrates Have a Method?*

of the hedonism section, when Socrates asks whether the pleasant life is the *same* as the good life, Protagoras gives a qualified yes: so long as one takes pleasure in praiseworthy things. Protagoras seems to maintain a distinction between noble and base pleasures. Socrates presses him on the point: Isn't something also good insofar as it is pleasant? Protagoras suggests that they investigate: if Socrates' questions lead to the conclusion that pleasure and the good are equivalent, then Protagoras will agree; but if not, he will disagree. Although Socrates gives Protagoras the opportunity to ask questions, Protagoras insists that Socrates lead the discussion. He reminds his potential critics, "it is fitting for you [Socrates] to lead, for you brought up the idea" (351e10–11). Protagoras' resistance suggests that Protagoras is uncomfortable being publicly associated with a hedonistic position.

Still, I want to claim that Socrates' questions in the hedonism section are primarily intended to draw out aspects of Protagoras' own thinking from earlier sections of the dialogue and not to present Socrates' ideas alone. The responses that Protagoras gives to Socrates' questions are strikingly harmonious with the ideas that he sets out in the Great Speech and in his definition of the good as the beneficial. In the Great Speech, Protagoras values precisely the kinds of goods described in the hedonism section of the dialogue: survival, pleasure, and other physical goods.

According to Protagoras' Great Speech, human nature is "layered." Unlike the animals, whose formation came about in two steps at most (the formation of the physical substratum and the addition of specific qualities), human beings were formed in four steps. The process of human formation is as follows: first, the gods make the underlying material "stuff" of all mortal beings; second, the human being is supposed to have been given unique defenses by Prometheus and Epimetheus but is left metaphorically and literally naked; third, human beings receive the arts and fire from Prometheus; and fourth, they receive justice and shame from Zeus.

Let us examine the most elemental aspect of human nature, before the reception of the arts (*technai*), justice (*dikê*), and shame (*aidôs*). Human beings are wholly material in origin.[13] The gods make humans out of earth and fire – later strongly associated with technical skill (*Protagoras* 321d) – and their compounds (320d). The next step in the formation process is also entirely focused upon making the physical body: Epimetheus determines what sorts of defenses from aggression the animals are to

---

[13] See Roochnik, *Tragedy of Reason*, 61.

possess (e.g., strength, speed, claws); how they are to protect themselves
from the elements; and what sorts of foods will be necessary to sustain
their bodies. In his description of the formation of animals and human
beings, Protagoras never mentions the idea of a soul or nonmaterial component. The physical, the bodily, composed in a purely technical fashion,
is the earliest and most basic component of human nature.

In addition, human beings have no purpose other than to survive.[14]
Protagoras' story lacks an account as to why the animals were made.
Mortals were not brought into being in order to please the gods; rather, it
is as if the genesis of mortals were some predetermined part of the world's
existence to which even the gods are subject (320c8–d3). The purpose
of human and animal life from the point of view of the gods is merely to
continue to exist. The exclusivity of survival as the human purpose is not
lost with the invention of the arts in the next stage of human formation,
for the existence of physical weakness motivates Prometheus to steal fire
and technical skill from the gods (321c8). It is *only* because Epimetheus
failed to give human beings claws, speed, or other means of protection
before he exhausted his resources on the other animals that we possess
uniquely human abilities at all; they are a huge mistake.[15]

Significantly, in the first stages of creation, the human being's desire
for survival is entirely centered on himself. Like the capacities of other animals, our pre-political rationality does not compel us to consider others'
interests just because the gods have species survival in mind. Although
the speed of deer exists to promote the survival of the species, the individual deer desires only to preserve its own welfare when running away;
similarly, pre-political human beings also sought their individual interests even as the gods looked to species survival. When humans possessed
only the arts but not shame and justice, Protagoras says that they lived
"scattered" and came together into larger groups only to avoid destruction by beasts. Because they treated one another unjustly, they scattered
again (322b–c). At this stage of human existence, social and political
interactions were forced by circumstance and short-lived because of the
selfishness of human nature. For Protagoras, humans are not naturally
social beings but rather forced to rely upon one another because of physical weakness.

Do Zeus' gifts of justice and shame fundamentally alter human nature
or merely serve to further the same end of survival that characterized prior

[14] See Roochnik, *Tragedy of Reason*, 62.
[15] See Coby, *Socrates*, 55.

stages of human existence? Nussbaum has argued for the former position: Protagoras presents the introduction of the gift of justice as a new capacity that makes human nature "political."[16] Her evidence is threefold. First, she argues that human survival is no longer separate from the survival of the *polis*. The gifts of Zeus are clearly presented as central to the survival of the *polis*. Second, Nussbaum says that Protagoras wants to teach others to be "good citizens," indicating Protagoras' own belief that being a good citizen is fundamental to the good life. Third, Protagoras' language indicates that the human being has a natural tendency toward justice, as in his comparison of moral education as that which makes a person "better" (325a), like the straightening of bent wood (325d).[17]

Nussbaum correctly recognizes Protagoras' desire to harmonize the communal good – the city's survival – with the survival of individuals prior to the reception of the gifts of justice and shame. Indeed, Protagoras does present the political art as fundamental to the human condition – we are not solitary animals, now that political life is a real possibility. However, Nussbaum's claim that human nature is fundamentally political according to Protagoras is too strong. For Zeus gives human beings justice and shame in order to ensure species survival; political virtue is a means rather than an end in itself. Individuals might wish for and promote the survival of others but only as a means to their own survival. There is no clear indication that the ends or purposes of human existence have been fundamentally altered. It is also important to note that it is Socrates, and not Protagoras, who introduces the idea of making others "good citizens" (319a4–6) as a recapitulation of Protagoras' description of his teaching as prudence (*euboulia*) and as teaching others to be the most capable or powerful (*dunatotatos*) in the city. Socrates shifts the terms of the discussion from political management to moral education. Moreover, Protagoras in no way implies that there is a natural tendency to be just, which requires gentle training, for the "straightening of the wood" image suggests correction through beating and violence. On the contrary, the image suggests that human beings naturally are a little "warped" with respect to virtue. Protagoras even says that "this sort of excellence" does not "come by nature or luck" (323c4–6). We might contrast this to Socrates' claim in the *Apology* that if he has been unjust, he should be instructed rather than punished (26a).

---

[16] See Martha Nussbaum, *The Fragility of Goodness* (Cambridge: University of Cambridge Press, 1986), 102.

[17] See Nussbaum, *Fragility*, 102–103.

In addition, there are at least three places in Protagoras' Great Speech that suggest that justice and shame are naturally weaker than more primal self-centered human tendencies and that the city's survival remains a means of survival rather than an end in itself. First, even the average citizen who possesses justice and shame is aware of his ultimate *interest* in possessing them, as a means of self-preservation. Protagoras emphasizes that the good man will teach his sons to be virtuous so that they will not suffer the confiscation of property, exile, or death (325b–c). The motivation for teaching one's children to be virtuous is not that virtue is intrinsically pleasurable or a good in itself but rather that one might lose other goods if one lacks virtue. Second, the idea of punishment dominates Protagoras' view of conventional education (325c7–d9).[18] His recognition that people feel compelled to correct bad behavior through punishment ought to make us wonder how deeply ingrained in our nature justice and shame are. Like a twisted and bent piece of wood, the child is "straightened out" by blows from his educators. While self-interest is natural, the capacity to consider others' well-being must be taught through violence.

Protagoras describes the social expectation that every individual at least publicly proclaims his own justice (whether he is in fact just or not) as evidence that everyone possesses at least a minimal amount of justice. He says:

With respect to other abilities, just as you say, if anyone says that he's a good flute player or good at any other art when he isn't, they laugh at him or are angry with him, and his relatives come and treat him like a madman. But in the case of justice and the other political virtues, even if they know someone is unjust, if he himself tells the truth about it to everyone, though they called it good sense (*sôphrosunê*) before, they call this truthfulness madness and they say that it is necessary for all to appear to be just whether they are or not, and that anyone who doesn't pretend to be so is mad. For everyone must share in it to some extent, or else not be among men at all (323a7–c1).

What does Protagoras mean in calling even the unjust man "just"? Protagoras suggests that even the unjust have a *capacity* for justice, but one not fully brought to fruition by teaching. Even the person whom we consider unjust enough to punish with a fine is more just than a person who had been raised in the wild; at a minimum, for example, he must know what justice is well enough to dissemble. Nonetheless, the sensible person hides his injustice, raising the question as to whether and how Protagoras unifies the virtues. Although this section is ostensibly about why

---

[18] See Coby, *Socrates*, 64.

justice is universal, it shows that an expectation of *good sense* (*sôphrosunê*) is universal: any person foolish enough to admit his own unjust behavior is deemed mad, presumably because an admission of wrongdoing is tantamount to seeking out punishment. There is a natural tension between justice, which regulates the well-being of the city, and *sôphrosunê* (understood as self-interested prudence), which regulates the well-being of one's self. The tension between these virtues reflects the conflict in Protagoras' understanding of human nature itself, between the ability to belong to the *polis* and to please others in it and a more fundamental desire to pursue one's own interests.

Later sections of the *Protagoras* seem directed toward examining this tension and bringing it out. Among the questions that Socrates asks that seem to be oriented toward showing the unity of the virtues are a series of questions cut off by Protagoras from 333d1–e2. Socrates has already brought Protagoras to admit that good sense and wisdom are identical. Now, he takes up the question as to whether some people who act sensibly also act unjustly. Protagoras is uncomfortable with this line of conversation but, rather than denying the claim altogether, is willing to say so for the sake of argument (333d4). Socrates asks a series of questions that link acting unjustly to acting sensibly, acting sensibly to planning well, and, finally, planning well to doing what is good (333d–e). That is, Socrates seems to be leading Protagoras to the conclusion that to act unjustly is to act in a way that is good! Given Socrates' well-known commitment to the goodness of justice, it is difficult to believe that he is arguing for the goodness of unjust behavior. Instead, Socrates seems interested in drawing some of the ideas hidden in the Great Speech so that its full implications might be addressed.[19]

Protagoras avoids having to contend with such a conclusion, however. He interrupts the stream of thought by suggesting that not all good things are beneficial. Socrates asks whether he means that some good things are not beneficial at *all* or not beneficial to *man*? Protagoras responds:

> I know of many things that are useless to men, food and drink and drugs and countless other things, and others that are beneficial. Some are not for men, but for horses; some are only for cattle, or for dogs. . . . Oil, too, is totally bad for all plants and destructive of the hair of animals other than humans, but in the case of humans it is helpful, and also for the body. So multifaceted and varied a thing is goodness (*agathon*), that here the same thing is good for the outside of the body, but bad for the inside (334a–c).

---

[19] See Hemmenway, "Sophistry Exposed," who makes the case for the influence of Protagoras' views on the direction of the unity of virtues argument.

Protagoras' examples of goodness all concern physical benefit. Protagoras speaks of goodness not with reference to bravery in battle or other noble acts but rather with reference to food, drink, drugs, and cosmetics. He conceives of the good in narrow, corporeal terms.

Protagoras' view of the good as the beneficial is entirely consistent with psychological hedonism for on his view, all creatures naturally pursue that which benefits them physically.[20] To the objection that we sometimes act in ways that are self-defeating or that cause us pain, Socrates shows that the hedonist can make sense of apparent *akrasia* through the notion of miscalculation. Socrates gives three examples of apparent *akrasia*: being conquered by the desires for food, drink, and sex (353c7). His choice of these examples in particular is telling, for they are all pleasures of the body. Nowhere does Socrates mention any pleasures of the soul such as intellectual pursuits. Protagoras never objects that these examples are too focused on the physical, but this should come as no surprise to us, given his description of the good in terms of physical benefit.

Socrates asks Protagoras, who acts as a representative of the many, whether we call certain pleasures "wrong" because they are pleasurable or because they later lead to other physical problems, such as disease and poverty. Protagoras answers that most people would say the latter. It is because disease and poverty cause pain or deprive one of pleasures that these are evils. Conversely, when the many say that painful things are good, what they really mean is that a short-term pain leads to other good conditions, such as when an uncomfortable medical treatment produces health. Again, the absence of the goods of the soul is underlined by Socrates' choice of examples: he mentions health, good bodily condition, the safety of the city, rule over others, and wealth (354a3–b5), *precisely* those goods which Protagoras favors. He values wealth, for he takes payment as a sophist; he believes rule over others to be a good, for he teaches political prudence (*euboulia*); and in the Great Speech, he explicitly mentions the safety of a city as its primary good. All indications here are that Socrates' argument is *ad hominem* and not the expression of his own views (for Socrates is neither wealthy, a teacher, nor a ruler). Socrates does not explicitly adopt hedonism as his own position. Nowhere does he say that he believes that pleasure is the good, although he willingly affirms other controversial ideas in the dialogue – for example, that wisdom is sufficient for virtue.

[20] See Dyson, *Knowledge*, 32–45.

Furthermore, this view of pleasure as the good sits well with Protagoras' ethics. In his view, the purpose of human beings, like all species, is simply to continue to exist. This is precisely what Socrates seems to take as the purpose of the hedonistic calculus. At six different places in the text, Socrates refers to the advantage of the calculus as promoting our survival: he says it will "save our lives" (356e; 357b); "save us" (356e); or "preserve our lives" (356e; 357a). Although Socrates says that pleasure is the aim for the individual (354b), pleasure is perfectly compatible with survival in at least two ways: understood as pleasure in the long run, pleasure promotes survival and, furthermore, survival is necessary for us to enjoy more pleasures. For example, eating food is necessary to survival, and survival is necessary for the experience of further pleasures, including eating. An intense pleasure which would harm one's chances for survival would not be desirable, since in death one would lose other pleasures associated in living. Similarly, in some cases, painful actions that promoted survival might be desirable, as in the case of a medicinal treatment that produced discomfort but promoted health. One might even argue that existence itself is pleasurable. In many cases, then, the ends of pleasure (i.e., a package of pleasures and pains considered as a whole) and individual survival are compatible. Perhaps, then, Socrates is trying to delve deeper into how Protagoras understands the good – what he *means* by saying it is the "beneficial."

Socrates himself clearly leaves open the possibility of some other understanding of the good, asking whether:

[t]hese things are good because of the fact that they result in pleasure and in the relief of and avoidance of pain? 'Or do you have some other criterion in view, other than pleasure and pain, on the basis of which you would call these things good?' They [the many] would say no, I think (354b8–c2).

Protagoras answers, "And I would agree with them" (354c3). Socrates a second time asks whether enjoyments could be called bad for any other reason than that they are painful and claims that the many could not give any other criterion of the bad. Protagoras once again agrees: "I don't think they'll be able to either" (354d1–4). Socrates reiterates a third time, "But even now it is still possible to withdraw, if you are able to say that the good is anything other than pleasure or that the bad is anything other than pain" (354e8–355a4). Socrates pushes home the point that none of his interlocutors – neither the many with whom he is in imagined dialogue nor Protagoras – can provide any alternative account of the good. Socrates implicitly suggests that there is another way of understanding the good, but Protagoras' inability to suggest an alternative indicates that *he* has no other criterion for what makes something good than that it is pleasurable. Perhaps Socrates is suggesting that Protagoras' understanding of the good as the beneficial can be more systematically articulated in terms of hedonism, for Protagoras has no way of distinguishing "beneficial" acts from other acts except on the basis of the quantity of pleasure produced.

However, Protagoras is not happy with the results of the hedonist line of thinking once they are applied to the nature of courage. Protagoras wishes to maintain a distinction between noble and base pleasures. He clearly believes that courage is neither reducible to mere animal daring nor to exacting technical calculation of what is beneficial for oneself (see, e.g., his description of courage at 350c–351b). He openly admires those willing to go to war and disparages those who avoid it (359e–360a). He values the courage of those who are ready to fight against what most other men fear (349e). Still, Protagoras' understanding of the virtues as instrumental and the good as the beneficial are insufficient for expressing his ideas about courage. More generally, Socrates will go on to show that Protagoras' particular understanding of human nature makes an argument for just action in the face of personal danger difficult if not impossible. For courage under the hedonism model is defined as "wisdom about what is to be feared and what isn't," and the criterion by which one judges the fearful is the relative quantity of pleasure and pain that the actor will experience as a result.[21] However, this means that the courageous person is he who knows how to avoid pain and suffering, hardly Protagoras' own picture of the courageous man. Protagoras is so upset by the conclusions to which he is being led that he first gives short answers, then only nods, and eventually refuses to answer (360d). Socrates evokes not only intellectual confusion but also an emotional response in Protagoras. Socrates' hope is that this confusion will lead Protagoras to consider further the nature of the virtues and wisdom. To this extent, Socrates seems to be unsuccessful, as Protagoras continues to see their conversation as a verbal contest in which Socrates has performed well (361e).

The hedonism section of the dialogue, then, is not an argument designed to express Socrates' own views, nor even to expose Protagoras' explicit belief in hedonism, but rather to sharpen the focus upon what is implicit (and lacking) in Protagoras' understanding of justice, virtue,

---

[21] See Weiss, "Hedonism," 17–24, for an exposition of the way in which Socrates reduces courage to technical knowledge.

and the good. Put somewhat differently, the hedonism section is not really the "view" of either Protagoras or Socrates before that series of questions and answers takes place; rather, it arises from Socrates' emphasizing particular elements of Protagoras' ideas as he has expressed them so far and reiterating some of those ideas as questions to see whether Protagoras will modify, accept, or reject those ideas as Socrates restates them.

Socrates' questions in the hedonism section seem to have two purposes. First, they show Protagoras that implicit in what the sophist has already said is a view that apparently supports the centrality of knowledge above other virtues: knowledge cannot simply be one among many virtues on Protagoras' own account. Socrates implies that Protagoras does not know how to make sense of his own claims to wisdom as a teacher. Second, Socrates shows that Protagoras' account of the good is not rich enough to account for some of the ideas about courage to which Protagoras is already committed. Protagoras values the nobility of courage. Socrates does not offer a solution to these difficulties but rather encourages Protagoras to go back and rethink the nature of excellence, virtue, and wisdom. His questions are designed to bring out problems in Protagoras' own thinking in order to encourage Protagoras to revisit these issues.

Still, Socrates is a participant in the conversation: he clearly sees certain insufficiencies in Protagoras' thought and directs the question toward bringing out what Socrates sees as problematic. For example, Socrates conveys his own concern with the centrality of knowledge in living well by focusing his questions on the role of wisdom rather than, for example, which habits parents and teachers develop in children. Socrates focuses upon the relationship of the virtues to one another rather than upon how effective Protagoras is at persuasion. In this sense, the questions *do* also reflect Socrates' concerns.

Their conversation, then, is a product of two active participants rather than a straightforward expression of either Socrates' or Protagoras' own views. On the one hand, Protagoras has an intellectual standpoint – a particular view of the world, of human nature, and of the virtues – that informs how he answers his questions. He is not "merely" a rhetorician with an interest in winning the argument or shaping the responses of his audience; he has commitments to certain ideas about goodness, excellence, and human benefit. On the other hand, Socrates asks questions with attention to what he finds interesting or puzzling in Protagoras' thinking but not necessarily from a dogmatic standpoint. Socrates connects the rational to the rhetorical. He does not use questions to teach a well-formulated view. Instead, Socrates' expression of his own rationality takes place in the mode of questioning. As the next section shows, understanding Socrates' questions here as arising from the interaction of both Protagoras and Socrates is compatible with the more explicit statements Socrates makes about philosophical questions as a means of discovery of the truth.

III.

The interdependence of both partners in speech is visible not only in how Socrates and Protagoras interact but also in the more direct statements that Socrates makes about the nature of speech. There are two salient features to Socrates' descriptions of his method of questioning in the *Protagoras*. First, Socrates characterizes the aim of question and answer as discovery rather than winning the argument, a claim that Protagoras never seems fully to understand. But Socrates does not understand that process of discovery to be undertaken by an autonomous rational agent. He describes the process of philosophical discovery as a social one necessitated by the limits of individual reason. The evaluation of ideas – and the very expression of their meaning – takes place in conversation rather than at the level of abstract thought, logic, or writing. Philosophical question and answer has performative and social dimensions according to Socrates. Second, questioning as an activity exhibits some of the key virtues of being a philosopher. In particular, the very *act* of asking questions and of listening to others exhibits the philosopher's knowledge of himself as needy and limited as a human being.

Protagoras continually misunderstands the nature of Socrates' questions. Plato presents Protagoras as concerned with two main aims in his use of words: to gain admiration and to maintain his own safety. Protagoras cares most about whether or not his speeches make others admire him. For example, while Socrates does not care whether Protagoras speaks to Hippocrates and him in public or private, Protagoras chooses a public venue (316b–d), suggesting that the presence of an audience is important for Protagoras. A bit later, Socrates characterizes Protagoras as wanting to perform and to make himself look good in order to gain admiration (317c–d). When the discussion between Protagoras and Socrates begins to break down and Socrates demands that Protagoras speak only briefly, he replies: "Socrates . . . I've already undertaken many verbal contests (*agôna logôn*), and if I had done as you demand, and spoken as my

antagonist (*antilegôn*) demanded, I would never have appeared to be the
better, nor would Protagoras have become a name in Greece (335a)."
Protagoras never objects to Socrates' right to ask questions as he sees
fit; he only wants to be able to answer them any way he likes. But Protagoras also assumes that Socrates understands their conversation as a
verbal contest (*agôn*). We can see this when Protagoras suggests that it
does not matter what he thinks in answering Socrates' questions (331c)
or in his rather surprising concession to Socrates later that all the parts of
excellence are similar after all, except for courage (349d), when earlier
he had not agreed that Socrates' arguments were acceptable (e.g., 332a;
334a–b). Protagoras seems willing to "stipulate" his opponent's claims
as one might in a courtroom, confident that he will dominate by separating courage from the other virtues in the course of their argument.
When at the end Protagoras appears to have lost the debate, he applauds
Socrates' enthusiasm and way of arguing; but he also asserts that while
Socrates is pretty good for his age and might be famous some day, he
does not regard himself as a "bad man (*anthrôpos kakos*)" either (361d–e).
Protagoras views their conversation in terms of his own and Socrates' rep-
utation, and assumes that Socrates sees it all in this way too.

In contrast, Socrates says that his aim is to better understand what
troubles him. Consider Socrates' remarks to Protagoras at a moment
when the sophist is especially defensive:

Protagoras, please don't think that I have any other wish in our discussion
(*dialegesthai*) than to examine the things that are difficulties for me each time.
For I think that there is a lot in what Homer says: "Two go together, and one
saw (*enoêsen*) it before the other." For somehow we human beings are all more
resourceful (*euporôteroi*) this way, in each deed, word, or thought. "And if he sees
it alone," he straightaway goes around to search for someone to whom he can
show it (*epideixêtai*) and who will confirm it (*bebaiôsêtai*) (348c–d).

Socrates' goal is to examine the *aporia* in which he finds himself. Socrates
claims that an individual inquirer is without the resources to address
all of his questions: other human beings are needed to find what one
is looking for. For Socrates, philosophical inquiry is by nature a social
activity, spoken and not simply thought.

Socrates gives two reasons for why this is so: first, two people are more
likely than one to discover hidden truths. Here, Socrates is referring
to a passage from Homer's *Iliad* X.224–5. In this section of the *Iliad*, the
Greeks have recently suffered huge losses on the battlefield, while Achilles
continues to refuse to fight. As a solution to the Greeks' apparent strategic

disadvantage, Nestor has asked for volunteers to go into the Trojan camp, in order to see what the enemy has planned. While all the other Greeks lack the boldness for the task, Diomedes courageously volunteers for the job but then asks whether anyone might accompany him. His reasons are that he will have greater comfort if another person spies with him, and that a single individual's mind (*noos*) does not reach as far as two together (*Iliad* X.226). Diomedes chooses Odysseus for his shrewdness and courage. Diomedes speaks the line that Socrates quotes; Socrates then plays the part of Diomedes and Protagoras plays that of Odysseus.[22] Socrates' use of the comparison no doubt is intended to encourage Protagoras by insinuating that the sophist is as clever and able as Odysseus; however, it also suggests skepticism about the individual human being's ability to reason adequately on his own. For Socrates, question and answer promote the possibility that some positive discovery will take place; he suggests that philosophical discovery is a social process, emphasizing the ultimately cooperative nature of their debate over autonomy.

Another reason Socrates suggests that philosophical inquiry must be social in nature is that even if one person somehow does make an independent discovery, he cannot be certain that his discovery is adequate unless another person is there to confirm it. This is an extremely important claim for it suggests that whatever sorts of "discoveries" philosophy arrives at, these are not finally discoveries that the non-social, non-human world gives to us directly. Socrates does not hold that there is some independent, universal epistemic standard by which a person could judge whether his beliefs are adequate or inadequate (e.g., an argument grounded in self-evident propositions). If a person arrives at what seems to him, by the light of his own reason, to be a genuine discovery, he still cannot be certain of what it is that he has really found. For Socrates, philosophical discovery and what is "reasonable" have social and linguistic dimensions rather than being independent of social discourse. Socrates does not adhere to the idea that some particular epistemic test can automatically yield the truth. Otherwise, the person who made a "discovery" would not have to go to another human being to see what they think of it; independent confirmation would be possible.[23] Socrates' use of the image

---

[22] See also Coby, *Socrates*, 131.

[23] As Eugenio Benitez points out, Socrates' view of the social role of evaluating ideas is incompatible with the historical Protagoras' "man is the measure" doctrine, which emphasizes the individual percipient's role in evaluation. See Benitez, "Argument, Rhetoric, and Philosophic Method: Plato's *Protagoras*," *Philosophy and Rhetoric* 25 (1992): 222–252.

of "spying" as analogous to the pursuit of truth suggests the difficulty of uncovering the truth for human beings.

Socrates, then, claims that both the expression of ideas and their eval-uation take place in conversation; that is, philosophy is social in nature. With respect to their expression, the conversation "belongs" to neither Protagoras nor to Socrates alone but rather to both of them. Socrates asks questions that demand the articulation of ideas in ways different than Pro-tagoras had anticipated (e.g., asking how different virtues relate to one another), but his subsequent questions are also often guided by Protago-ras' ideas (as in the hedonism section). In an important sense, Protagoras does not even know what his own beliefs are (e.g., about the relationship between courage and wisdom) until he is forced to explain them aloud. Socrates' questions demand not only that Protagoras reveal his opin-ions to Socrates and to the audience but also to *himself.* But neither does Socrates fully understand these problems; Socrates acknowledges his own *aporia*, which fuels much of the dialogue. Socratic question and answer breaks down the absolute barrier between speaker and audience found in Protagoras' long speeches and in epideictic display.[24] Neither Socrates nor Protagoras is the speaker or audience – both are participants in the formation of the speech. Philosophical exploration is not the responsibil-ity of one speaker alone – both participants in a conversation are (ideally) responsible for the ideas.

The evaluation of the ideas is also social. Socrates draws out of Protago-ras' Great Speech certain elements (e.g., the emphasis on the material, on pleasure, on survival) and not others (e.g., the nurture involved in education, the mythical connections to the Greek pantheon, the role of shame in teaching). A different questioner might very well have been concerned with, or perplexed with, quite different concerns. Protago-ras at times objects to Socrates' framework and at times does not; where and when he objects guides the future of the conversation. Their dia-logue is not about determining the logical consistency of a preexisting set of propositions or ideas.[25] Rather, Socrates and Protagoras together

---

[24] Surprisingly, Socrates gives the longest speech in the dialogue when he offers his inter-pretation of Simonides' poem. As I have argued elsewhere, Socrates uses this speech to create an internal dialogue between different voices in the poem and between his own and others' voices. To this extent, even his long speech contains elements of Socratic question and answer. See Marina Berzins McCoy, "Socrates on Simonides: The Use of Poetry in Socratic and Platonic Rhetoric," *Philosophy and Rhetoric* 32 (1999): 349–367.

[25] Contrast this to the view taken by Christopher Gill, who writes, "In the *Protagoras* and other early dialogues, Socrates is shown as urging adolescents and adults alike to under-take an autonomous, rational assessment of received standards. His own, very distinctive

determine the shape of the expression and the evaluation of ideas for the rest of the dialogue. Philosophical discovery happens in conversation rather than prior to it.

This emphasis on the social nature of philosophy suggests that, for Socrates, philosophy has some performative elements. In rhetorical theory, "performative" has generally been used to mean an understanding of language that stresses the use of speech as a social act (especially between performers and audiences) rather than as the representation of ideas or thoughts; the multifaceted nature of speech's purposes; and the ways in which culture and history inform what words and speech acts "mean."[26] In some respects, Socrates would disagree with a purely performative understanding of language. He clearly values the real as existing beyond our social construction of it; he sees language as (ideally) connected to an individual's opinion, an opinion that cannot be reduced to a culturally determined understanding. Language is not only an act but also aims to represent or to imitate the real. However, philosophy also takes place in a conversation in which both questioner and interlocutor contribute to the meaning of terms and in which the meaning of one term (e.g., wisdom) inevitably inflects our understanding of other related terms (e.g., courage). The expression of human rationality takes place at the level of speech, not in thought alone (or at least not reliably there).[27] The particular conversation Socrates and his partner have determines how individual statements are integrated into a larger context of meaning. As Desjardins has written, for Plato, "... language does not transparently and unequivocally *mean*, just like that."[28] We have to interpret its meaning, and this interpretation takes place in a particular, temporal, philosophical

kind of dialogue, with its demand for full definition of terms and for logical consistency, is presented as an instrument to promote this activity." See Gill, "Plato and the Education of Character," *Archive für Geschichte der Philosophie* 67 (1985): 1–26.

[26] For an overview of this understanding of the performative, see Richard Bauman and Charles Briggs, "Poetics and Performance as Critical Perspectives on Language and Social Life," *Annual Review of Anthropology* 19 (1990): 59–88; and Bauman, "Performance," *International Encyclopedia of Communications*, vol. 3 (Oxford: Oxford University Press, 1989), 262–266. While those working in communications have been more interested in the performative aspects of speech, J. L. Austin has been particularly influential for his emphasis on speech as a social act rather than as representative of things. See Austin, *How to Do Things with Words* (Oxford: Oxford University Press, 1962). Bauman and Briggs use the term *performative* in a broader and more inclusive way than does Austin; it is their wider sense of the term that I use here.

[27] Isocrates makes a similar claim about the importance of language for thinking and action in his "Hymn to Logos," where he states that *logos* is used not only for persuasion but also for deliberation. See *Nicocles*, 5–9.

[28] See Rosemarie Desjardins, "Why Dialogues? Plato's Serious Play," in Griswold (ed.), *Platonic Writings, Platonic Readings* (London: Routledge, 1988), 116.

discussion rather than either at the levels of abstract reasoning, individual thought, or society or "culture" at large.

To take an example: in the *Protagoras*, the term *aretê* (virtue or excellence) does not have a single, obvious meaning before it is discussed. It is not clear that social-cultural explanations will suffice to explain its nature; readers can see that Protagoras' definition of what he teaches as *euboulia* and Socrates' restatement of this as the art of being a "good citizen" are both likely parts of the larger cultural understanding of excellence and yet not necessarily consistent with one another. Socrates wants to do more than anthropology; he wants to know what it is to live well in the face of many competing claims to authoritatively answer this question. So, cultural ideals alone will not do. But neither can individual definitions solve the problem, for it is not clear that Protagoras the individual fully understands what *aretê* means, even for himself – for example, what definition would be adequate to explain it, what examples would best express its activity, and so on. Until he is asked about the relationship between the virtues or his ideas about whether and how courage is taught, his ideas about these matters may not even have yet come into being. Socrates also does not know whether his own ideas about excellence indicate that it is teachable or not teachable. Both cultural ideas and individual ideas require further interpretation and deeper expression of content if they are to contribute to the project of living well, and Socratic question and answer is the realm in which this further interpretation and creation of meaning takes place.

"Creation" of meaning in philosophical conversation is not here meant to imply either "arbitrary" or inflexibly constructed by the larger society; after all, Socrates asks Protagoras to say what he really believes in an attempt to ground the discussion in something real, if yet undefined and undeveloped. However, the simple dichotomy of performative/social in *opposition* to philosophical/rational is not easily applied to Socrates; he would not see the division in this way. Reason and social discourse are not at odds for Socrates; reasoning is always both social *and* striving for a truth beyond socially constructed truths. Conversely, Socratic conversation also makes clear that the fullness of belief has not yet fully come into being before being articulated in conversation. In his reference to Homer, Socrates *explicitly* associates discovery of the truth with conversation and the activity of a community of (at least) two. Truth and conversation are intertwined. Along similar lines, the Stranger in the *Sophist* describes thinking as "the soul's inner conversation with itself" (*Sophist* 263e). Even the solitary reasoning of a person includes an implicit conversation with an "other," in which the self artificially constructs an alternative voice with which to be in dialogue. Plato's dialogues, too, include multiple voices; in this respect, the dialogues are both a conversation of Plato with himself and with his potential readers. By including opposition in the dialogues, Plato anticipates the kinds of conversations that can take place between authors and audiences. Contemporary neo-sophistic commentators who present Plato as possessing an abstract and extremely detached understanding of reason often overlook these performative aspects in Plato's writing.[29]

Perhaps because conversation is crucial for the pursuit of truth, Socrates emphasizes the importance of listening, a seemingly ordinary and commonplace activity but one that Socrates presents as both rare and valuable. Socrates says that if you ask most public speakers a question,

> Just as copper, once struck, rings and goes on until someone takes hold of it, so too these rhetors, if asked a little question, stretch out their speech into a long course. But Protagoras can give not only long and beautiful speeches, as is clear here, but when questioned he can also answer briefly, and when he asks one himself he waits and listens (*apodexasthai*) to the answer, which few are prepared to do (328e–329b).

Socrates' comments are interesting for he associates the value of questioning with the ability to listen (*apodexasthai*) to what has been offered. Socrates claims that the ability to listen is a rare phenomenon. Given that any discourse even of the most basic sort requires listening, Socrates must mean more than listening at a superficial level. Socrates' use of the term *apodexasthai* suggests that the sort of questioning Socrates has in mind is being receptive in some way to that which a speaker offers. True listening on Socrates' account requires being able to "accept" what another says. This need not, of course, mean that one ultimately adheres to the view of the other person. Rather, it suggests a willingness to seriously consider the possibility that the other is correct (and, if the other's view is different, that one's own view falls short). This sort of listening requires sympathetically putting one's self in the place of the other: if I listen to you, for the moment, I do more than just try to understand the meaning of your

---

[29] See, e.g., Bruce McComiskey, *Gorgias and the New Sophistic Rhetoric* (Carbondale, IL: Southern Illinois University Press, 2002), who writes, "For Plato, the rational is based on certain knowledge of immutable truth; it is to an eternal image or form, discoverable only through negative dialectic, that arguments may be compared in order to determine their rational or irrational character."

words. Rather, I try to accept what you say from your own perspective even if it is not something to which I will ultimately commit. To listen fully to another human being requires a sort of temporary suspension of the self and openness to the other person. Socrates' implication is that long speeches are reflective of a preoccupation with the self insofar as they only express an answer, while short speeches allow for the possibility of a concern for the other's views and so provide for the conditions for genuine learning.

Protagoras seems not to listen to Socrates in the sense outlined herein. Protagoras' interest in reputation suggests that he is ultimately more interested in himself than in Socrates. We do, however, have in the dialogue two examples of "good" listening. One instance of good listening is that of the friend (*hetairos*) of Socrates to whom most of the story of the *Protagoras* is narrated. The prominence of listening is emphasized in their brief interchange: Socrates three times mentions the importance of listening (*akouô* and its derivatives; cf. 310a1; 310a5; 310a6). When the friend says that he will be grateful to hear about the story, Socrates says that it is a "favor on either side" (310a6); that is, both Socrates and his friend will benefit from the telling and from the listening. Second, listening is a prominent feature of the conversation between Socrates and the youth Hippocrates. While Hippocrates is initially excited, even impulsive, in his desire to see Protagoras, he also listens with care to Socrates. Socrates draws an analogy between other arts and sophistry in the course of asking why Hippocrates wants to study with Protagoras. He claims that most students who study a particular art do so in order to become practitioners of that art (e.g., studying with a physician in order to become one). If this is true in medicine and in other arts, then, Socrates suggests, perhaps Hippocrates wants to study with a sophist in order to become a sophist. He next asks, "Wouldn't you be ashamed to present yourself to the Greeks as a sophist?" (319a5–6). Hippocrates admits that he would be and blushes just as day breaks.

Hippocrates' blush is important because it is the turning point in the conversation when he moves from a clear interest in studying with Protagoras to a state of confusion over what he really wants. But Hippocrates has not been convinced of any particular positive claim. Socrates' questions to Hippocrates are not primarily oriented toward finding a better account of Protagoras' teaching. Instead, they are designed to affect Hippocrates' spirit (*thumos*).[30] Before Socrates' questions, Hippocrates

---

[30] There may be a cognitive component to shame, but shame is not purely intellectual. For the association of shame with *thumos* and the emotional nature of shame, see Douglas

is prepared to go visit Protagoras before dawn and to spend all of his own and his friends' money on an education with him (310e–311a). Afterwards, Hippocrates listens to and takes seriously Socrates' contention that an education with Protagoras might not be desirable and needs to be evaluated rather than hastily embraced. Socrates' reawakening of Hippocrates' sense of shame moderates his impulsiveness and excessive enthusiasm. But it is only because Hippocrates first listens to Socrates in a way that opens himself to criticism that he can experience shame. Socrates is not only interested in getting Hippocrates to hold a particular proposition intellectually, such as "I know that I do not know what the sophists teach," but also to be in a different thumotic state. Hippocrates feels both intrigued by the prospect of working with a sophist and ashamed of it; he is not just unsure of what he *thinks* but also of how he *feels* about sophistry. But his sense of shame is indicative of a positive ability to be self-critical. When Hippocrates admits to his shame, he also shows his honesty and openness about what he really believes. Protagoras' unwillingness to be revealed is a crucial part of Plato's criticism of him. Hippocrates exceeds Protagoras in his willingness to listen to Socrates, even if it embarrasses him or reveals a personal shortcoming.[31]

Still, Plato presents philosophers as easily confused with sophists in another passage about listening. Socrates and Hippocrates stop at the door in front of Callias' house in order to finish their conversation. However, the doorman, having overheard (*katêkouen*) them, at first believes them to be sophists and shuts the door on them (314c–e); this suggests that, to some extent, sophists and philosophers sound alike. The dramatic movement of slamming the door closely parallels a similar scene in Aristophanes' *Clouds* where the sophists slam the door shut on Strepsiades when he visits their "thinkery" (130–135). While in Aristophanes' version Socrates is inside and presented as among the sophists, Plato places Socrates on the outside while the true sophists are within, dramatically separating him from them. Perhaps one point of separation is this ability to listen with genuine openness to others.

Socrates is emphatic that his questions examine a person and not only a thesis. In describing his questioning to Protagoras, Socrates compares himself to a doctor uncovering his patient's body in order to better assess the health of his patient (352a–b). He implies that his questions are

Cairns, *Aidos: The Psychology and Ethics of Honor and Shame in Ancient Greek Literature* (Oxford: Clarendon Press, 1993), especially 5–14.

[31] See Walter Brogan, "Plato's Dialectical Soul: Heidegger on Plato's Ambiguous Relationship to Rhetoric," *Research in Phenomenology* 27 (1997): 3–15.

therapeutic, designed to benefit his interlocutor, the person rather than
only the ideas being discussed. When Protagoras suggests that it does not
matter whether he thinks that there is a difference between justice and
holiness and says that they can go ahead and say that they are the same,
Socrates stops him: "'Oh, no,' I said. 'I don't want this "If you wish" or
"If you think so" to be examined (*elegxesthai*), but instead you and me. I
say "you and me" thinking it best to examine the argument by getting rid
of any "If's"' (331c5–d1)." Here, Socrates suggests that it is the person
rather than the thesis that is being examined. Socrates' main concern
is with the person being asked rather than with theses abstracted from
persons.[32]

A bit later, Socrates seems to say the opposite. When Protagoras says
that he would be ashamed to assent to the claim that the unjust man acts
sensibly in being unjust, Socrates says that they can still argue about the
point in question-and-answer format if Protagoras will only take on the
role of the many. Socrates says,

> It doesn't matter to me, as long as you answer, whether you believe these things
> or not. It is mostly the argument (*logon*) that I am testing, but it all the same may
> end up testing me, the one asking the questions, and the one answering (333c).

Here, the priority is apparently reversed: the thesis is most important, to
the point that it no longer even matters whether Protagoras believes what
he is saying. Socrates shifts from a concern for what the person answering
questions believes to a concern for an abstract thesis.

However, this second passage also subtly reconnects the examination
of an abstract thesis to the examination of a person. *Both* the passages
at 331c–d and 333c assert a close relationship between a thesis and the
person who asserts it. Examining a person allows us better to understand
his ideas but, conversely, examining a thesis helps us better to understand the person who put it forth: "It is mostly the argument (*logon*)
that I am testing, but it all the same may end up testing me, the one
asking the questions, *and the one answering*" (333c; my emphasis). That is,
Socrates claims that to question a thesis is *already* also to test the person
that holds it. This explains the common response of Socrates' interlocutors to his questioning them: they become defensive and hostile because
they (correctly) sense that the inadequacy of their ability to respond well
to questions also implies an inadequacy in their person.

---

[32] Dorion argues for the use of the term *elenchus* beginning with Pindar to mean the testing
of the self, not only a thesis. See Dorion, "La Subversion," 311–344.

More perplexing are Socrates' claims that the questioner is being examined as he asks questions. Something about the person who is asking the questions is revealed in the ensuing conversation. This is a somewhat surprising thing to claim because, after all, the psychological experience of being questioned is more difficult and apparently more self-revealing than the experience of asking questions: if Protagoras fails to respond adequately to the person who asks him a question, he is likely to be blamed and Socrates praised.

But Socrates is insistent that the very act of asking a question is a test. This might be true in several senses. At the simplest level, a questioner might learn something through the answers given to him by his partner in conversation; in learning something new, he discovers that what he thought he knew was mistaken or incomplete. Alternatively, the questioner might learn about himself through reflection upon the limitations of his own line of questioning. Socrates implies this possibility when he suggests that the internal harmony of beliefs is important at 333a–b. There, he tells Protagoras that there are two alternatives available to him now that their conversation has shown that wisdom and moderation are the same: Protagoras can either question the assumption that each thing has one and only one opposite or the idea that foolishness has two distinct opposites (333a–b) if he wants to avoid the conclusion. Protagoras does not object to the argument's premises aloud, but suppose that he had. Had he objected to the premise that each thing has one and only one opposite, then Socrates and Protagoras would have been forced to examine *that* fundamental assumption in greater detail. The possibility always exists that Socrates might have to revise the stated assumptions that his questions imply.

Third, a questioner might decide that the answers given by an interlocutor confirm the current state of his own ideas. If Socrates is already committed to a claim that he is investigating, and others are unable to refute it, then he has better reason to regard it as true than he did before. Unfortunately, taking most of Socrates' claims in the *Protagoras* as representative of his own beliefs seems unlikely, as Socrates claims *both* that excellence does not seem to be teachable and that if it is knowledge (and it seems to be), it should be teachable. Socrates acknowledges that one or the other of these beliefs will have to go, and it is not clear to the reader as to which idea is the better candidate.

Fourth, asking a question reflects one's self-understanding of one's existential state. Hyland has written extensively on the nature of philosophical questioning in relationship to the place of the human being in the world.[33] He characterizes Platonic philosophy as essentially an "interrogative stance," or a stance of wonder. Socrates understands himself as incomplete: he knows that he does not possess full wisdom but is aware that he lacks it. This lack is a genuine needfulness: the human being longs for and strives for the divine, even as he is incapable of becoming divine. Questioning is the form of discourse most appropriate to such a state because if we both lack and need knowledge, then only questioning reflects our true human condition. To ask a question as a genuine question – rather than, say, as a means of tripping up one's opponent – is to acknowledge a lack in oneself. But it is also an acknowledgment or a commitment to the idea that there *is* something that might complete what is lacking in us. If I already presuppose that there is no answer to a question that I might have, then there is no point in asking it other than as a means to some other end (e.g., to manipulate my audience when I give a speech). Socrates need not commit to the claim that complete and final wisdom is possible for the human being; however, unless there is something positive to learn or some step toward greater completeness is, in principle, possible, then a question also ceases to be a real question. A question asked with no expectation whatsoever of at least a partial answer is not a question any more but instead some sort of an assertion disguised as a question – perhaps an expression of nihilism, cynicism, or skepticism. In other words, Socrates the philosopher has a commitment to truths about the questions that he is asking that he values so highly that other goods we might normally seek (e.g., self-protection, closure in thought, autonomy, or avoiding shame) become subsumed to it.

Socrates' questions are rhetorical, then, in several senses. First, for him, philosophy takes place in conversation rather than in the realm of thought, logic, or systematic writing. Philosophy requires conversation between at least two people. The truth is best discovered through social discourse, not through autonomous inquiry, matching one's ideas against a preexisting universal standard, logical analysis, or even common opinions (*doxa*). Philosophy has performative elements to it insofar as meaning and its expression in a social context go hand in hand; the meaning of excellence, courage, and related terms is developed in conversation rather than prior to it. The fact that Socrates' speech is performative does not in itself separate Socrates' discourse from that of Protagoras. Both Protagoras and Socrates are interested in how language

[33] See Drew Hyland, *The Virtue of Philosophy* (Athens, OH: Ohio University Press, 1981).

affects their audiences; this sets both Protagoras and Socrates apart from philosophers for whom good discourse is not rhetorical (e.g., those who focus exclusively on the logical consistency of ideas or who separate philosophical discovery from its expression). However, Socrates displays a much greater interest in the mutual give and take of ordinary conversation than does Protagoras. While Protagoras makes a clear separation between the speaker, who is active, and the audience, who is passive, Socrates treats both the questioner and answerer as active participants in the conversation. A good questioner must really listen to the person to whom he speaks, and the one who answers him must willingly state what he really believes and display a considerable amount of courage in being willing to be confounded. Protagoras' speech relies upon an asymmetry between the speaker and his audience, while Socrates' question and answer is potentially more symmetrical (especially if both parties are willing to take turns as questioner and answerer). The traditional rhetorician's distinction between speaker and audience is not absolute: the speaker at one moment might become the audience in the next.[34] In addition, Socrates treats the results of conversation as much more than arbitrary expressions of cultural norms; question and answer might help us to arrive at *truer* accounts of the virtues. Socrates uses the language of discovery, not persuasion, in describing good conversation. Discovery and the cooperative expression and evaluation of ideas are not opposed for Socrates.

Second, for Socrates, good question and answer embodies the ability to be self-critical and to listen to others. These are not just character traits of instrumental value, prerequisites for reaching the correct conclusion; instead, asking questions and giving answers *embodies* what it means to be a philosopher.[35] These non-linguistic aspects of question and answer are part of what Socrates is after as he tries to persuade Protagoras to adopt his style of speech. Protagoras is not open to having his insufficiencies exposed, however, and frequently cuts off the conversation when he thinks it is going poorly for him.

---

[34] I do not mean to say that Socrates never acts as a more conventional speaker with an audience – his speech to the jury would be a prime example of a more conventional distinction – but Socrates seems to prefer a mode of discourse in which the separation of speaker from audience is less fixed and hierarchical.

[35] Francisco Gonzalez argues for a similar explanation of Socratic questioning in the *Cleitophon*, where questioning already embodies philosophical virtue rather than being only preparatory for it. See Gonzalez, "The Socratic Elenchus as Constructive Protreptic," in Scott (ed.), *Method*, 161–182.

Third, Socrates' questions are sometimes designed to get his interlocutors to experience certain emotions, such as shame or confusion. We see in the example of Hippocrates that the capacity to listen is related to an ability to grow in self-knowledge. Socrates' practice suggests that certain sorts of emotional or thumotic states, such as shame, self-doubt, and confusion, are part of what it means to be in a state of greater self-knowledge. Shame for Hippocrates is not just good preparation for later "serious" inquiry; rather, shame can be an appropriate constitutive part of being philosophical. These non-logical dimensions to Socratic questioning are crucial because Socrates is interested not only in how to *do* philosophy but how to *be* a philosopher.

4

The Competition between Philosophy and Rhetoric in the *Gorgias*

I.

Socrates' approach in questioning his opponents in the *Gorgias* is quite different than in the *Protagoras*. Here, we find a Socrates who is far more aggressive, critical, and angry with those whom he questions. Socrates upsets his opponents and even compares Callicles to a *kinaidos* (passive homosexual), an image that even the bold Callicles finds to be out of bounds (494e). While the conversation begins respectfully, by the dialogue's end we see what seems to be a verbal *agôn* between Socrates and Callicles. I suggest that Socrates' questions in the *Gorgias* have an agonistic character because Socrates is engaged in a real battle over the nature of the good life. Socrates' aggressive questions here underscore the tension between his and his opponents' understandings of a virtuous life.

In general, the assumption has been that Plato's aim in the *Gorgias* is to draw a sharp line of demarcation between the activities of philosophy and rhetoric, favoring philosophy over its obviously inferior opponent.[1] Commentators on the *Gorgias* have suggested numerous distinctions between philosophy and rhetoric: (1) philosophy requires the consistency of one's beliefs, while rhetoric consists of merely verbal refutation[2]; (2) philosophy requires a commitment to reason that the sophists

---

[1] A notable exception is Alessandra Fussi, "Socrates' Reputation of Gorgias," *Proceedings of the Boston Area Colloquium in Ancient Philosophy* 17 (2001): 123–145. See also James Arieti, "Plato's Philosophical *Antiope*: The *Gorgias* in Plato's Dialogues," in Gerald Press (ed.), *Plato's Dialogues.*

[2] See Vlastos, *Socratic Studies*; and Irwin, *Moral Theory.*

lack;[3] (3) the philosopher is committed to a different understanding of power – for example, the power to make others virtuous rather than domination over others;[4] (4) philosophers possess a refined self-knowledge that the rhetoricians lack;[5] (5) philosophy values technical knowledge while rhetoric does not;[6] or (6) philosophy is linked to a specific set of moral claims.[7]

However, although Socrates remains firmly committed to his principles, he fails to persuade any of his opponents. Their conversation ends with Socrates talking to himself in parodic fashion and offering a critical myth that seems aimed at Callicles. I argue that while Plato examines a variety of possible contrasts between the sophist and philosopher, he also questions the sufficiency of these initial points of contrasts, through the characters themselves and through the use of Platonic irony.[8] Rather than immediately revealing the fatal flaw of the rhetoric, the *Gorgias* reveals that the rhetorical standpoint is powerful despite being anti-philosophical. As Plato explores a number of possible differences between the philosopher and the rhetorician, still deeper questions are raised about the relative value of philosophy and rhetoric.

I suggest that Plato writes the *Gorgias* in this way because one of his aims is to examine critically philosophical speech, and not only to refute sophistic rhetoric. Because sophistic rhetoric is at the margins of philosophical speech, Plato puts the two together in order to explore further the nature and the value of philosophy. For example, competing notions of the rational and of what constitutes good argument are themselves questioned in the *Gorgias*. Here, I focus upon three different distinctions made between philosophy and rhetoric: (1) the contrast between art (*technê*) and rhetoric in the dispute with Gorgias; (2) the emphasis placed upon reliance on one's own beliefs in the section with Polus; and (3) the description of philosophy as unchanging and rhetoric as changing in the section with Callicles.

---

[3] See Jacques Bailly, "What You Say, What You Believe, and What You Mean," *Ancient Philosophy* 19 (1999): 65–76; J. C. Haden, "Two Types of Power in Plato's 'Gorgias'," *Classical Journal* 87 (4) (1992): 313–326.

[4] See T. J. Lewis, "Refutative Rhetoric as True Rhetoric in the *Gorgias*," *Interpretation* 14 (1986): 195–210. See also A. W. Saxonhouse, "An Unspoken Theme in Plato's *Gorgias*, War," *Interpretation* 11.2 (1983): 139–169.

[5] See Dan Avnon, "'Know Thyself': Socratic Companionship and Platonic Community," *Political Theory* 23 (2) (1995): 304–329.

[6] See McComiskey, *New Sophistic*.

[7] See Lewis, "Refutative Rhetoric"; and Nightingale, *Genres*.

[8] I distinguish the voice of Socrates and that of Plato. For a thorough explanation of various forms of irony in the dialogues, see Griswold, "Irony," 84–106.

I argue that there are two main differences between philosophers and the sophistical rhetoricians in this dialogue. First, Socrates possesses the character traits of goodwill (*eunoia*), responsibility for one's own speech (*parrêsia*), and a commitment to knowledge (*epistêmê*) that Callicles affirms as important to living well, while Callicles lacks these characteristics. Second, Socrates is willing to be self-critical about his own practice in ways that the others, when faced with the challenge of philosophy to their worldviews, are not – although they claim to value such openness. In other words, Plato shows that the others are not just inconsistent in their arguments but also inconsistent with themselves as human beings in important ways. Philosophical rhetoric is distinguished from sophistic rhetoric not by a precise method but rather by how Socrates' speech is informed by the presence of these key virtues.

II.

In the section of the argument against Gorgias, Socrates suggests that rhetoric is inferior to philosophy in three ways: rhetoric is not an art (*technê*); rhetoric creates persuasion apart from instruction; and rhetoric lacks knowledge of the subject matter about which it persuades. In contrast, Socrates implies that the philosopher is in possession of a political art and instructs on the basis of knowledge. However, if one examines Socrates' method in examining Gorgias, these boundaries between philosophy and rhetoric become questionable. Socrates does not instruct Gorgias in the way that practitioners of technical arts instruct their pupils. Neither does he claim to possess such an art or knowledge of political matters. There is a gap between Socrates' ideal picture of the practitioner of the political art and Socrates' own practice in the dialogue.

In his argument against Gorgias, Socrates advocates technical knowledge and instruction based upon such knowledge as superior to the mere persuasive opinion of the rhetorician.[9] When Gorgias defines rhetoric as a "producer of persuasion (*peithous dêmiourgos*)" (453a), Socrates draws upon the *technê* analogy in comparing rhetoric to painting, medicine, and mathematics.[10] Socrates asks Gorgias to state what specialized field of knowledge the rhetorician possesses, apparently hoping to show the

---

[9] McComiskey, *Sophistic Rhetoric*, takes Plato to associate technical knowledge and instruction with philosophy, and opinion and persuasion with rhetoric.

[10] I use Zeyl's translation for all extended quotes unless otherwise noted. Individual words are my own translations. See David Roochnik, *Of Art and Wisdom: Plato's Understanding of Techne* (University Park, PA: Pennsylvania University Press, 1996) for a thorough account of the *technê* analogy.

insufficiency of rhetoric if no knowledge supports its activity. Socrates presents the possession of technical knowledge as the foundation of good persuasion.

Socrates' refutation leads to what seems to be a serious contradiction in Gorgias' thought. Gorgias both claims (1) like some boxers, some students of rhetoric use the skill unjustly, but it is wrong to blame the teacher for the student's actions (457a); and (2) as a rhetorician, he teaches about just and unjust things (46oc). That is, Gorgias seems to suggest both that rhetoric is a value-neutral enterprise and that part of what constitutes rhetoric is teaching about justice and injustice.[11] Gorgias appears profoundly confused about what rhetoric is, while Socrates appears to advocate the possession of knowledge of justice above all else.

However, if examined closely, Socrates' argument against Gorgias does not necessarily indicate a true confusion on Gorgias' part, for it is Socrates who pushes Gorgias to answer whether he teaches about justice to his students if they do not come to him with such knowledge. Socrates corners Gorgias into choosing one of three alternatives: either Gorgias does not know about justice and injustice and only teaches his students to *appear* to know more than others; or he knows about justice but refuses to teach it (and so is responsible for his students' deficiencies); or he knows and also teaches about these things (459d–46oa). Gorgias chooses the last alternative.

Socrates goes on to argue as follows (at 46ob–c):

(1) Through using the *technê* analogy, Socrates shows that a technical expert is the sort of man that his expertise makes him.
(2) By analogy, a man who has learned what is just is just and does just things.
(3) An orator is "necessarily" (*anaykê*) just and will want to do just things.
(4) Therefore, an orator will never want to do what is unjust.

This contradicts Gorgias' earlier contention that some rhetoricians use rhetoric unjustly (a practice of which Gorgias does not approve). Socrates is correct in asserting that Gorgias gives no explanation of how he ensures that his teaching is not used unjustly. Gorgias seems to have no such guarantee. But, at the same time, it is Socrates and not Gorgias who

---

[11] See David Roochnik, "Socrates' Rhetorical Attack on Rhetoric," in *The Third Way: New Directions in Platonic Studies*, Francisco J. Gonzalez (ed.) (Lanham, MD: Rowman and Littlefield, 1995), 81–94.

introduces the idea that there is a "necessary" connection between good rhetoric and knowledge of justice in the previous argument. Up to that point, Gorgias consistently presents rhetoric and knowledge of justice as separable. At most, Gorgias loosely associates rhetoric with justice and the court system when he says that the rhetorician's speeches primarily take place in law courts and concern matters of justice and injustice (454b). Until 460a, Gorgias is clear that technical knowledge of particular subject matters (aside from the ability to persuade) is *not* part of rhetoric. And even when pressed by Socrates either to admit to not knowing or teaching about justice, or to knowing and teaching it, all that Gorgias really admits is this: "Well, Socrates, I suppose that if he [the student of rhetoric] really doesn't have this knowledge, he'll learn these things from me as well" (460a). While one might accuse Gorgias of slipping up when he agrees to the necessary connection that Socrates posits (at (3) herein) or not caring sufficiently about justice as part of his teaching, Socrates never shows that Gorgias' original position about the nature of rhetoric was incoherent. Gorgias views rhetoric as separable in principle from the knowledge of justice and sees no difficulty with treating rhetoric as a neutral skill like boxing.

Socrates' assumption that Gorgias must either know about justice and teach it or be held responsible for his students' appearing to know when they do not know is also questionable. There are, of course, other alternatives. One might know about justice oneself but be unable to teach it to others: consider the example of Socrates' failure to teach anyone present that the just life is always better than the unjust life in this very dialogue. Or one might believe that secure knowledge of justice is not possible or that it is conventional, for example (as some sophists seemed to believe).[12] Socrates asks leading questions in bringing Gorgias to a point where the rhetorician must either admit to lacking knowledge of justice or to teaching it. After Gorgias' defeat, Polus intervenes in the discussion and objects to Socrates' mistreatment of Gorgias, saying that he only claimed to teach about matters of justice and injustice because he was too ashamed to say otherwise (461b). While Gorgias' true view of justice remains unclear, Plato also draws his reader's attention to whether Socrates has been fair.

Moreover, in his longer explanation of rhetoric (456b–457c), Gorgias presents a coherent picture of the separability of rhetoric and other

---

[12] E. R. Dodds argues that Gorgias simply ought not have claimed to teach justice and thus could escape the argument. See Dodds, *Plato Gorgias* (Oxford: Clarendon Press, 1959).

areas of knowledge. A rhetorician is not concerned with knowing about the technical subject matter of his speeches; however, he does not need to be. For example, Gorgias claims that although he lacks knowledge of medicine, he can persuade a patient who will not obey his doctor's orders to take bitter medicine. Technical knowledge of the particular subject matter about which one is persuading is unnecessary. Instead, the rhetorician knows how to produce conviction apart from any specialized knowledge on either the part of the speaker or the one being persuaded. Whether the doctor or the rhetorician persuades, the practical effect is the same on his audience – in fact, even the epistemological effect is the same from the point of view of the patient, for whoever persuades, the person who takes the medicine will only have shifted his opinions. The difference is that the rhetorician is more effective at achieving his goal of persuasion. Gorgias does not deny that technical knowledge exists, but he denies that there is a necessary link between knowledge and good persuasion. When Socrates implies that technical experts are the best at providing advice on equipping the harbor or building the walls, Gorgias points out that it is orators who have always had the most success in persuading the assembly to pass the relevant laws, not the technical experts. Socrates does not disagree (456a). In short, Gorgias sees rhetoric as separable from knowledge, whether of technical or moral matters. In his eyes, this is precisely its strength.

Although the Gorgias of Plato's dialogue need not hold views identical to those belonging to the historical Gorgias, Gorgias' work, *On Non-Being*, is helpful to illuminate the coherency of his position here. According to Sextus Empiricus, Gorgias claimed that nothing exists; that even if it did exist, it could not be known; and that even if it could be known, it could not be conveyed to others through words (*logoi*). This is because *logoi* are as different from perceptions as auditory and visual perceptions are different from one another (DK 82.B.3). Words do not even belong to the same categories as objects of knowledge, if knowledge is possible at all. Gorgias attempts to show that there is a gap between being and perception and then again between perception and *logoi*. Therefore, words need not have any correspondence to the things that they sometimes pretend to imitate. However, words can persuade others to shift their opinions. Gorgias gives *logoi* almost unlimited power in this regard: words can change both the emotions and the opinions of those who hear them, essentially enslaving the listener to the power of the speaker. Gorgias even compares the power of *logoi* to a drug that can shape the soul of the one who listens (*Encomium of Helen* 14). According to Gorgias, rhetoric is more powerful than any view of the world that claims that knowledge is possible and can be taught.

While Gorgias in this dialogue acknowledges that doctors and others can have knowledge – or perhaps adapts his rhetorical strategy in order to suit his audience's needs – both the historical Gorgias and the character here agree that knowledge is irrelevant when it comes to the effectiveness of persuasion. Gorgias therefore can say, "with this ability you'll have the doctor for your slave, and the physical trainer, too"; in fact, all experts who lack rhetorical ability are less powerful than those who know how to persuade a crowd (452e). Gorgias presents a coherent picture of rhetoric that consistently denies the link between knowledge and good persuasion that Socrates attempts to set up. Moreover, Gorgias' praise of rhetoric as the source of freedom (*eleutheria*) in the city is suggestive of the greater practical importance of the ability to sway others than to teach them: Gorgias himself is in Athens to ask for military aid against the Syracusans. *Logos* is closely linked to political power for Gorgias but for him, the power of rhetoric to provide freedom is not just an abstract principle.[13] Rhetoric is a practical tool to aid Gorgias' own city and preserve its freedom; to this extent, he is indifferent to whether he possesses technical knowledge of justice. For him, his opinion that his city needs protection is enough. Socrates' argument at 459d–460c never addresses Gorgias' central claim that the rhetorician's persuasive ability is useful even though it takes place apart from technical knowledge of its subject matter.

Socrates' questions also seem closer to Gorgias' model of persuasion than to the paradigm of instruction or teaching on the basis of a political art that Socrates set out. Socrates does not imitate the model of the artisan who persuades through teaching what he knows. Instead, Socrates' aim seems to be to win the argument. Socrates seems determined to leading Gorgias into a contradiction that his original position did not necessarily contain. Socrates' refutative practice here subverts the ideal that good persuasion is simply instruction in technical matters. In the end, Socrates seems to act much more like the stereotypical picture of the sophist as verbal trickster, interested in verbal contradictions, while Gorgias seems interested in giving good reasons to defend the value of rhetoric as separable from knowledge.

---

[13] Note the similarity between Gorgias' statement about freedom here and Euripides' claim in the *Suppliant Women* (438–439) that freedom is having useful advice to set in front of the public. As Harvey Yunis notes, Euripides very nearly paraphrases the herald's opening cry at the Assembly. See Yunis, *Taming Democracy*, 49.

Second, Socrates does not claim that he possesses the necessary political knowledge for teaching in the Assembly or courtrooms, although he sets it out as an ideal. While Socrates says that there is a political art of which rhetoric is a mere imitator (464b–d), Socrates never claims that he or anyone else possesses such an art. In fact, in his later conversation with Callicles, Socrates says that one cannot point to anyone who has led the public according to such a craft (503d). Socrates says only that he is one of the few Athenians to "take up" (*epicheirein*) the political art (521d).[14] Socrates implies that he *pursues* knowledge of justice and injustice, but not that he is an expert in political matters the way that a doctor is an expert about matters of health. Socrates seeks such knowledge but still does not possess it. Third, Socrates' starting point in questioning here is not his own belief but rather his interlocutors' beliefs. Socrates says that each person ought to say what he really believes: he asks others not to listen to an expert in a particular craft but rather to state their own beliefs honestly.[15] The basis of the subsequent discussion is not knowledge or technical instruction but rather opinion.

By the end of the conversation between Socrates and Gorgias, it is clear that the difference between them is not that Socrates possesses knowledge that Gorgias lacks or that Socrates instructs others while Gorgias merely persuades. If there is any point of difference, it is that Socrates *seeks* a kind of knowledge to which Gorgias is indifferent. But Socrates never addresses Gorgias' claim that rhetoric has a more powerful practical effect than technical instruction. Socrates values knowledge not *because* it is more useful for persuading others but rather *despite* the fact that it is not. Socrates refuses to flatter the crowd, while the rhetoricians, like cooks, seek to please their audiences. Instead, Socrates seeks to make his interlocutors uncomfortable with themselves and their own ideas. But Socrates does not always succeed in improving them. This first section of the dialogue does not show the inferiority of rhetoric to philosophy but rather raises additional questions about the value of the philosophical valuation of knowledge over the practical efficacy of rhetoric. It presents the two competing worldviews of philosophy and rhetoric with entirely distinct goals and aims. Socrates has a passion to understand the truth about justice, but he does not possess nor can he promise to teach the political art that defines philosophy.

---

[14] See Roochnik, "Socrates' Rhetorical Attack," 91. Roochnik suggests that if Socrates is the only one who aims at this knowledge, but even he does not possess it, perhaps the *Gorgias* suggests that no one does.

[15] See Vlastos, *Socratic Studies*; and Bailly, "What You Say."

III.

In the section in which Socrates and Polus dispute the value of rhetoric, the question as to the role of belief also arises. Vlastos's well-known analysis of the elenchus focuses especially on Socrates' statements about belief in the *Gorgias*. Socrates seems to require at least two things from his interlocutors: they must state whatever they believe at the start of the discussion, and they must give up faulty beliefs if they are shown to be inconsistent.[16] According to Vlastos, Socrates possesses beliefs of which he can be confident – if only provisionally – because they have withstood refutation. One might then revise the distinction between philosopher and the rhetorician to something like this: the philosopher tests his own beliefs and is willing to be refuted, while the rhetorician irrationally rejects the consequences of arguments, more concerned with his own defeat than with the truths of reason. Some commentators see the conflict here as between those who acknowledge rationality and those who (irrationally) reject it. For example, Haden writes that in the *Gorgias*, Plato presents two visions of power: Callicles' vision of power as domination over the fellow human being and Socrates' vision of power as "surrendering oneself to the lucidity of reason."[17] Similarly, Bailly argues that there is another requirement for the elenchus: one need not only to say what you believe but also to believe what you say.[18] That is, if an interlocutor is led to particular conclusions through the elenchus, he ought to be willing to believe in those conclusions. According to this sort of approach, the philosopher subjects himself to logical consistency and rationality, while the sophist is unwilling to acknowledge the power of reasoned argument.

Indeed, Socrates does assert that it is crucial for those being questioned to state their own beliefs. Socrates says that Polus relies upon the witnesses of many people as key to a refutation, while Socrates cares only for what he himself thinks is true, even if he is a single witness against many: "Nevertheless, though I'm only one person, I don't agree with you. You don't compel me; instead you produce many false witnesses against me and try to banish me from my property, the truth" (472b). What matters to Socrates is not popular opinion but only one's own opinion, tested by philosophical discussion. However, Plato does not present Polus as unconcerned with reason but rather as having a *different* approach to the rational. Socrates says that Polus, like those who speak in the law courts, cares about what most "witnesses" would say about the subject at

---

[16] See Vlastos, *Socratic Studies*.
[17] See Haden, "Two Types," 326.
[18] See Bailly, "What You Say."

hand. His language about the two different understandings of refutation is surprisingly non-judgmental: Socrates says, "There is, then, this style of refutation, the one you and many others accept. There's also another one that I accept" (472b). Polus sees human opinion, particularly the opinion of large groups of people, as a reasonably reliable way of discerning what people truly desire (i.e., power and freedom).

If one developed Polus' view a little further, this conflict about method might easily be presented as a philosophical conflict about the relation between belief and knowledge. Aristotle, for example, places great emphasis on any good theory's taking account of ordinary beliefs about happiness: while *endoxa* cannot be taken at face value, a good theory should still account for them in some way. Polus is angry because Socrates never addresses ordinary beliefs at all; he simply rejects them out of hand. Polus cares about taking account of what most people say, but this is *constitutive* of his understanding of the rational rather than a rejection of rationality.

Furthermore, Polus also cares about whether Socrates the individual is really saying what he believes. On three occasions, Polus claims that Socrates is not stating *his* true opinion. The entire reason that Polus takes up the argument from Gorgias is because he does not believe that Socrates really believes the conclusions that have been reached about rhetoric. He exclaims, "Really, Socrates? Is what you're now saying about oratory what you actually think of it?," and then goes on to accuse Socrates of manipulating the questions in order to lead Gorgias into inconsistency for his own delight (461b–c). Later, after Socrates has seemingly led them to the conclusion that the tyrant who does as he sees as fit is still not doing what he wants, Polus is incredulous that Socrates can really believe the conclusion, stating that surely Socrates himself would want such power (468e). And, after a lengthy defense of the claim that the unjust man is unhappy, Polus again says to Socrates, "You're just unwilling to admit it. You really do think it's the way that I say it is" (471e). Three times Polus claims that it is *Socrates* who fails to live up to his own standard of believing what he says. (Later, Polus also brings in what the majority says, but from 461–471, his concern is for what Socrates believes.)

Polus does not reject the notion of the rational altogether. Rather, he connects the rational closely to opinion and to popular belief: if the conclusion of an argument is at odds with ordinary opinion and experience, then the argument is missing something. Consider the end of the argument where Socrates leads Polus to the conclusion that it is possible for the tyrant who does as he sees fit to not be doing what he really wants, if the tyrant lacks knowledge of what is really beneficial (467a–468e). Polus concedes that he has verbally contradicted himself but immediately afterwards asserts: "Really, Socrates! As if you wouldn't welcome being in a position to do what you see fit in the city, rather than not! As if you wouldn't be envious whenever you'd see anyone putting to death some person he saw fit, or confiscating his property, or tying him up!" (468e). The basis of Polus' belief that anyone, even Socrates, desires complete power and freedom to do as he wishes comes from empirical observation of what others say and do: Polus gives the examples of Archaleus, tyrant of Macedonia (470d; 471a-d); the King of Persia (470e); and the image of a man tortured on the rack (473c-d). Those people who do as they wish seem to be happy and feel no remorse, while those who suffer as the result of other's tyranny are miserable. Polus does not see rationality as equivalent to mere verbal consistency: part of the rational is what the evidence of ordinary moral actors points to, and Socrates has not given Polus any clear evidence that the man who commits an injustice will be unhappy on account of it.

In other words, Polus values consistency, too, but emphasizes whether a claim is consistent with ordinary motivations and actions. From Polus' point of view, accepting an argument's conclusion if it is still entirely disconnected from ordinary experience is the height of irrationality. He describes Socrates' conclusions as *atopa* – "absurd" or, more literally, "out of place" (480e)[19]; something is not quite right with such a counterintuitive conclusion. Polus is angry that Socrates seems to want him to say that he believes what he does not really believe even after their argument, and understandably so. Polus makes ordinary belief a particularly strong criterion, and if the conclusion of the argument with Socrates leads to an absurd conclusion, then he is perhaps rightly suspicious of the argument.

But neither does Socrates' method guarantee that one will arrive at the truth if one is only willing to submit oneself to his questions. First, the starting points of discussion are beliefs that are not independently argued for in advance of the argument and perhaps cannot be independently argued for. Socrates' approach is decidedly non-foundationalist. Second, it is important not to assume that just because a person's beliefs have been

---

[19] As Jeffrey S. Turner has argued, there is a gap between the dramatic success and the dialectical failure of the argument. See Turner, "'Atopia' and Plato's *Gorgias*," *International Studies in Philosophy* 25 (1) (1993): 69–77. See Blondell, *Play*, 74, on the use of the term *atopia* in the dialogues.

refuted that any positive conclusion has been reached.[20] For example, Socrates does not conclude after he has "refuted" Gorgias that Gorgias ought to have any positive view about whether rhetoric is good, bad, or neutral; instead, he suggests that the discussion must go on much longer: "By the Dog, Gorgias, it'll take more than a short session to go through an adequate examination of how these matters stand!" (461b). The direction in which they would next proceed is presumably open-ended. Third, while Socrates says, "What's true is never refuted" (473b), he is also committed to the view that one ought to begin a discussion with what one really believes. If Socrates and Polus were to begin the argument all over again, Polus' starting point could not be that unjust tyrants are unhappy even if he followed Socrates' standards because he still does not believe it. Authentic belief, not mere verbal assent, matters.

Their conflict in beliefs is further complicated by Socrates' introduction of the comparison between rhetoric and flattery. Just as cooking seeks only to please the palate without any knowledge of health, Socrates says that rhetoric is cooking's counterpart in the soul (465d). Rhetoricians seek only to flatter those to whom they speak but lack knowledge of the cause of each thing (465a). While rhetoric seeks to produce pleasure in those it addresses, philosophy as Socrates practices it with Polus admonishes its audience. However, Polus, like Gorgias, sees the aim of good speech as persuasion and not teaching. Polus and Socrates disagree about what ends are the best to pursue and not only the means by which to pursue those ends. Only in the discussion with Callicles will Socrates approach this question of ends as well as means.

We have then at the conclusion of the argument between Socrates and Polus a peculiar situation: Socrates continues to hold on to beliefs that he regards as true, both because he really believes them and because Polus has been unable to refute them. Polus has been refuted in argument but continues not to believe what Socrates believes; it seems too contrary to his own experiences. We can either conclude that Polus is an irrational man bent on winning the argument even when he sees that he is wrong, or we can take him at his word when he says that he finds the arguments unbelievable.

Socrates himself sees the problem as a gap between Polus' moral experience and his own: he says, "For the heart of the matter is that of recognizing (*gignôskein*) or failing to recognize (*agnoein*) who is happy and

---

[20] See Hugh Benson, "Problems with Socratic Method," in Gary Scott (ed.), *Does Socrates Have a Method?* (University Park, PA: Pennsylvania State University Press, 2002).

who is not" (472c–d). Polus looks at the world and does not see what Socrates sees. Polus sees the tyrant as someone who is fulfilling not only his but also anyone's real wishes, while Socrates sees the tyrant as someone who is deeply unhappy but does not even know it. Later in the discussion with Callicles, Socrates claims that if it were not for common experiences, it would be difficult for human beings to communicate with one another (481c–d). Polus and Socrates seem to have just such a difficulty communicating. Polus' and Socrates' experiences of the world seem to have little in common, and Socratic questioning does not overcome the gap.

Plato here raises an important question about the very nature of reason itself: what one person sees as reasonable, another person may not regard as rational. Part of what is at issue in the dispute between Socrates and Polus is the notion of the rational itself, a dispute that revolves in many ways around the notion of "recognition" of who is happy and who is unhappy as well as the appropriate role of common opinion. Polus interprets the inner world of the tyrant quite differently than Socrates. Stating that the philosopher is subject to reason while the sophist is not is an oversimplification. Plato presents a seemingly clear criterion for the superiority of philosophical activity – that the philosopher subjects his beliefs to the test of reason and accepts the consequences – only to raise further questions about the proper role of belief and the nature of reason in argumentation.

IV.

The conflicts that arose among Socrates, Gorgias, and Polus about the value of philosophical over practical knowledge and the nature of true happiness continue in the exchange between Socrates and Callicles. The issue at hand is whether the philosophical life is better than the political life that Callicles admires. Socrates seems incapable of defending his own life adequately in terms that Callicles would accept. Instead, their argument spirals into name-calling and eventually Socrates' speaking only to himself. In addition, Plato points out that to the outsider, Socrates might look like a corrupting influence as much as the sophists. There is no easy argumentative defense of philosophy to the non-philosopher. However, Plato suggests that Socrates possesses the characteristics of wisdom, free speech, and goodwill, while Callicles does not. Socrates is also more open to criticism and a lack of closure about his own ideas than the others.

Callicles, like Polus, finds Socrates hard to take seriously: he wonders whether Socrates is joking or serious (481c) and accuses him of trying to show off to the crowd (482c). In response, Socrates reflects on the nature of philosophy in his comparison of philosophy to his "beloved": Socrates says that he loves both philosophy and Alcibiades, just as Callicles loves both the demos and Demos, son of Pyrilampes. Socrates says:

I notice that in each case you're unable to contradict your beloved, clever though you are, no matter what he says or what he claims is so. You keep shifting back and forth. If you say anything in the Assembly and the Athenian *demos* denies it, you shift your ground (*metaballomenos*) and say what it wants to hear. Other things like this happen to you when you're with that good-looking young man, the son of Pyrilampes (481e).

In contrast, Socrates says of his own beloved, "As for that son of Cleinias, what he says differs from one time to the next, but what philosophy says always stays the same, and she's saying things now that astound you, although you were present when they were said" (482a-b). Again, we have what looks like a clear-cut difference: the rhetorician is willing to shift his opinions as whomever he wishes to influence demands it, while philosophy does not change its speech in response to its audience.

Socrates' descriptions are more or less accurate. Socrates seems consistent in what he believes, while Callicles shifts his stated beliefs according to whether he is winning or losing the argument. For example, Socrates consistently claims that the unjust tyrant is unhappy (and related moral claims such as that it is better to suffer than to commit an injustice). In contrast, Callicles shifts from claiming that the good is pleasure (495d) to the claim that there are some pleasures that are good and some that are bad (499b). However, Callicles gives reasons in defense of shifting one's approach: he explicitly states both that the practical benefits of rhetorical arguments are greater than the limited benefits of philosophical pursuits and that adapting one's speeches is necessary if one is to avoid punishment or death.

Earlier, Socrates implied that Gorgias is responsible for the corruption of his students if they use rhetoric unjustly. Now, Socrates asks whether anyone has ever become admirable and good because of his association with Callicles (515a). Here, Plato makes an unexpected allusion unknown to the characters but clear to the contemporary reader. Socrates' mention of his beloved Alcibiades and the latter's tendency to shift his views is a moment of great Platonic irony. For, consider the dramatic context of the dialogue: the entire dialogue takes place during the Peloponnesian

War.[21] Gorgias is in town to ask the Athenians for help in defending against the Syracusans. But, it is Alcibiades who will eventually give a speech to the Assembly encouraging them to send an expedition to Syracuse and then turn around to encourage the Spartans to defend Syracuse. Alcibiades is responsible for one of Athens' key losses, and Plato no doubt expects his contemporary audience to think of this when Socrates notes that Alcibiades is always changing what he says (482a).[22] Whereas Gorgias deploys rhetoric in the reasonable defense of his home, it is Socrates' beloved who uses arguments to achieve his own private ends at the expense of his own city. Although Socrates is determinedly committed to the belief that committing an injustice is worse than suffering it, Alcibiades was committed to the opposite. One might easily ask Socrates the same question he asks of Callicles: Has anyone become better through association with you?[23]

Callicles criticizes Socrates' attention to philosophy, claiming that being overly philosophical leads one to become inexperienced in matters of the law, public or private business, and human appetites and pleasures (484d). Callicles thinks of philosophy as impractical. Plato alludes to the eventual trial and death of Socrates when Callicles adds that Socrates would be unable to defend himself and would be put to death if he were brought before a court of law (486a–b). He emphasizes the necessity of flattery in speech because he finds it necessary in order to protect oneself (521b–c). Socrates agrees that the crowd is potentially dangerous but suggests that the length of one's own life ought not be attended to; his valuation of self-preservation and power in the city is quite different. The conflict over whether and how one's speeches ought to change is again connected to a deeper conflict over what sort of life is best.

This conflict between the life of the intellectual and of the practical man of politics is made even more prominent through the Gorgias' extensive reference to Euripides' *Antiope*.[24] In the *Antiope*, two brothers,

[21] See Saxonhouse, "An Unspoken Theme," 139–169.

[22] Alcibiades betrays Athens through the use of duplicitous speech. Isocrates specifically connects Alcibiades' destruction of Lacedaimonian power to his ability to persuade them. See Isocrates, *Philip* 60–61.

[23] See Gary Scott, *Plato's Socrates as an Educator* (Albany, NY: SUNY Press, 2000), on the question of why Socrates seems so often to fail to educate his followers. This question as to whether a teacher ought to be held responsible for his students is not confined to the Platonic dialogues. Isocrates praises himself for the good effects that he has had on his students and suggests that this is a good standard for evaluating the moral education offered by a teacher. See Isocrates, *Antidosis*, 99 and 220.

[24] See Arieti, "Philosophical *Antiope*," 197–214; and Nightingale, *Genres*, 60–92.

Amphion, a musician and intellectual who leads a private life, and Zethus, a public man concerned with practical affairs, argue over which is the best life to live. Zethus argues that the intellectual life cannot contribute to one's own material well-being and, in fact, leads to the neglect of city and household (fr. 8K). Amphion replies that the intellectual life is not only more pleasant but also more useful, since knowledge leads to the better management of the city (fr. 19k). While Zethus initially persuades Amphion to abandon his impractical life, in the end Hermes persuades Amphion to play his lyre, so that the music will lead the rocks and trees to build the walls of Thebes. The gods affirm Amphion's point of view. Here, Callicles compares himself to Zethus, saying that he feels rather like Zethus speaking to his brother when he reproves Socrates for his overzealousness for philosophy at the expense of more important practical matters (485e). Socrates embodies the life of the intellectual who puts little emphasis on practical matters; like the musician Amphion, Socrates is ever concerned with harmony, the harmony of the soul and the inner harmony of his own beliefs (482c).

What is really strange about Plato's use of the *Antiope* is that Amphion cannot win the public argument although he presumably has the "right" point of view from the divine standpoint. There is a weakness to the *logoi* of Amphion and seemingly also to the *logoi* of Socrates with his own interlocutors. No one seems persuaded by the end of the *Gorgias*: Callicles says that "the thing that happens to most people has happened to me: I'm not really convinced by you" (513c5). As was the case with Polus, Callicles hears all the words but does not accept the legitimacy of the arguments. Socrates and Callicles seem to have two very different views of the world that cannot be independently resolved through Socratic questioning, images, or speeches. By the end of the dialogue, Socrates is left speaking to himself, answering his own questions. He seems incapable of defending his vision of the good life to anyone.

Nightingale suggests that the final myth of the *Gorgias* serves as a sort of *deus ex machina* in order to affirm the Socratic standpoint when his argument fails to persuade (Nightingale 1995, 87).[25] The myth does play a comparable role in providing a "divine" standpoint. However, there are two key differences between the *Gorgias* and the *Antiope*. First, neither Callicles nor Socrates ever persuades the other to live differently. Callicles remains unconvinced of Socrates' moral standpoint, and Socrates' commitments also remain the same (while Amphion's change). Both the

[25] See Nightingale, *Genres*, 85.

philosopher and the politician/rhetorician fail to influence their opponents. Second, no actual divine being resolves the conflict in the *Gorgias.*
The *deus ex machina* of the *Antiope* is replaced in the *Gorgias* with a story
of Socrates' own making, but there is no independent resolution of the
conflict. The allusion to the *Antiope* does not resolve the seeming incommensurability of the conflict between Callicles and Socrates but rather
only heightens it, as we are left in the *Gorgias* without a divine judge of
who is right.[26]

We therefore have two problematic images of Socrates at work in this
section of the dialogue: Socrates as Amphion, the brother who is right
from the divine perspective but whose *logoi* cannot persuade others; and
Socrates the lover of Alcibiades who, despite his association with Socrates,
acts contrary to everything for which Socrates stands. In both cases, philosophy comes out looking weak in its influence on others. Plato seemingly acknowledges at least some of the charges that Callicles here levels
against philosophy – its uselessness, impracticality, and lack of persuasive
power. Whereas Socrates had earlier confronted Gorgias about the effect
of rhetoric on the soul of the one being persuaded, Plato raises similar
questions about Socrates' practice.

Socrates' rhetoric relies on both argument and images that might lead
others to envision the world differently, but there is no guarantee that this
will take place. When Callicles compares the soul of the restrained person
to a stone (492e), Socrates responds with his own image of the soul with
unrestrained appetites as being like a leaky jar (493b–c). Because neither
one is able to persuade the other to change his views through the use of
images, Socrates shifts to an argument for a distinction between pleasure
and the good. Still later, at the conclusion of the dialogue, Socrates uses a
myth to affirm the goodness of his vision of a just life. Socrates acts with
attention to *kairos*, a sense of knowing what sorts of *logoi* are called for
at different times in order to persuade his audience. He tries a variety
of approaches – questions, images, arguments, and myths – to persuade
Callicles that the just soul is better off; he is rhetorical and changes his
approach in different circumstances, although his moral stance remains
stable.

Plato's use of images is of especial interest here, for he treats images
as a *kind* of argument, as a species of explanation. That is, images are

---

[26] As Arieti has argued, Plato may be pointing out some of the insufficiencies of *both* Callicles
and Socrates: the non-philosophical politician *and* the apolitical contemplator. See Arieti,
"Philosophical *Antiope*," 197–214.

not merely imitations of a thing designed to teach or to persuade others what is already known through an independent philosophic argument; they constitute part of the argument between Socrates and Callicles. Both characters use images to highlight certain features of the soul of the just and the unjust man, in order that we might imagine the just and unjust persons in particular ways. Luxuriousness, intemperance, and freedom are excellence and happiness according to Callicles. Callicles suggests that Socrates' general claim that those who do not need anything are happiest is a mistake because if that were the case, stones and corpses would be happiest. If one were to take Callicles' mention of a stone or corpse as a literal, counterfactual example to a universal claim, his argument would be absurd: it is not even clear what it would mean to say that a stone or a dead body is "unhappy." However, Callicles' argument is provocative and interesting not as a counterfactual example but rather as a way of highlighting certain features of the just man in his audience's imagination. Callicles points out that the just man lacks passion, is passive, and is not lively. In other words, Callicles expresses a claim about human nature. For him, our nature is full of desires that are sought after, fulfilled, and then again expanded; anyone who lacks passionate desire of this sort is not fully human. His comparison to a stone or corpse is far more effective than the abstract claim ever would be: the natural revulsion associated with being dead or as dull as a stone evokes an imaginative and affective response in a way that an abstract concept cannot.[27]

Socrates' immediate response is not to ask a "what is x" question or to look into the consistency of Callicles' ideas; instead, he uses his own imaginative examples to show what the unjust soul lacks. Socrates compares the desiring part of the unjust soul to a leaky jar and the just man to the man of leisure who can afford to spend time as he pleases. Socrates then goes on to suggest that the unjust man is like the *kinaidos*, or passive homosexual (494e). That is, Socrates suggests that the most important feature of the unjust man is that his appetites have enslaved him and that he lacks manliness and self-control. The just man shares more in common with the traditional Greek warrior, who possesses courage and moderation, and the upper-class man of leisure. While Callicles is offended by these admittedly impolite images, Socrates is not simply associating the unjust with the *kinaidos* in order to win an argument. Again, his use of

---

[27] Gordon, *Turning*, chapter 6, takes on the larger issue of Plato's use of images in the dialogues. Particularly of interest is her claim that all language by its nature is an image; all *logos* interprets what is presented.

images is part of his argument. Plato treats these sorts of images as seriously as the later arguments that follow on the relationship among terms such as pleasant, good, knowledgeable, and courageous.

Near the beginning of his conversation with Callicles, Socrates highlights three characteristics of good speakers: wisdom, goodwill, and frank speech. I suggest that it is Socrates' possession of these virtues that sets Socrates' *logos* apart from that of his opponents. Socrates directly relates these characteristics of the soul to the ability to test one's ideas: "I realize that the person who intends to put his soul to an adequate test to see whether it lives rightly or not must have three qualities, all of which you have: knowledge (*epistêmên*), goodwill (*eunoian*), and frankness (*parrêsian*)" (487a). While Socrates somewhat ironically suggests that Callicles possesses all these qualities, he understands something quite different by each of these terms.

First, it is important to note that Socrates characterizes good inquiry as being willing to put one's *soul* to the test and not only one's ideas (487a). Socrates' remark suggests that he is not only testing specific propositions in this conversation but also testing himself. As even Callicles recognizes, Socrates' stated beliefs have profound implications for how he lives and, eventually, how he will die. Callicles is correct that Socrates will be brought to trial and even put to death if he continues to pursue philosophy instead of pleasing the crowd (486a–b), but this is a consequence that Socrates is willing to accept (508d–e). Socrates is open to the revision of his ideas, should he encounter a good objection, but is also strongly committed to living a life in accordance with his principles until a decisive objection comes along.

Second, Socrates indicates that he and Callicles understand wisdom differently. While Socrates says that Callicles is knowledgeable, he has overheard Callicles argue that one should not pursue philosophical studies "to the point of pedantry" but rather should be careful "not to become wiser (*sophôteroi*) than necessary and so inadvertently to bring yourselves to ruin" (487c–d). Callicles and his friends believe it wiser to shift their attention away from the abstract to more practical concerns. However, Socrates says of himself that he is ignorant and potentially in need of understanding whether his life is really worthwhile or not (488a); this is why he continues to pursue philosophy. Socrates' description of wisdom here is similar to the "human wisdom" of which Socrates speaks in Plato's *Apology*: he knows that he is wise insofar as he knows of his own ignorance, while others do not (*Apol.* 21d). By ignorance, Socrates cannot mean the simple absence of ideas about justice, for here he does make claims about the nature of justice. Instead, he seems to mean that his opinions could be mistaken; they do not qualify as knowledge in the strongest sense of the word and so must continue to be tested. While Socrates maintains his claim that the just life is a happier life than the unjust one, his certainty is tempered by his equal determination to seek the truth in light of his own ignorance. Although Callicles, Polus, and Gorgias do not, in fact, refute Socrates' position, Socrates suggests that he nonetheless is open to the possible revision of his beliefs, while Callicles is not. The wisdom that defines the philosopher here is not understood as the possession of specific doctrines but rather as a continual care for inquiry, premised upon the familiar Socratic proclamation that one must be aware of one's own ignorance.

Socrates suggests that *parrêsia* is also central to good inquiry: he describes *parrêsia* as a sense of shamelessness in how one speaks, or being responsible for one's own truthfulness. While Gorgias and Polus possess too much of a sense of shame to state what they really believe, Socrates claims that Callicles is different in this regard (487a–b). Socrates encourages transparency of one's belief that he hopes will allow them to get to the fundamental source of their disagreement; perhaps this allows Callicles the freedom to speak as he does about the happiness of the unjust man. Socrates' use of the term *parrêsia* also associates openness in philosophical conversation with a concern for the virtue of the city: *parrêsia* is a democratic political virtue associated especially with debate in the Assembly.[28] Callicles might share a commitment to this quality as a politician and a citizen. Callicles and Socrates initially appear to share the valuation of openness in speech.

However, while Callicles makes much of his willingness to be open about his controversial moral beliefs, he eventually concedes points to Socrates in order "to expedite your [Socrates'] argument and to gratify Gorgias here" (501c). Socrates then compares this same sort of gratification of one's audience to the sort of oratory that flatters its audience rather than attempting to improve it (501c–503b). He implies that Callicles is only interested in winning over the audience. This is, of course, also Socrates' primary criticism of rhetoric in the comparison of rhetoric to cooking: it is a "knack" that aims only at the pleasure and gratification

---

[28] See S. Sara Monoson, "Frank Speech, Democracy, and Philosophy: Plato's Debt to a Democratic Strategy of Civic Discourse," in J. Peter Euben, John Wallach, and Josiah Ober (eds.), *Athenian Political Thought and the Reconstruction of American Democracy* (Ithaca, NY: Cornell University Press, 1994).

of others rather than their good (462d–e). Both Socrates and Callicles are willing to speak openly, but Callicles chooses to be "open" in order to please his audience. In contrast, Socrates suggests that *parrêsia* is a virtue when it is connected to a genuine desire for the good of those to whom one speaks.

Socrates and Callicles also understand goodwill (*eunoia*) differently. Callicles does seem to possess goodwill toward Socrates, for in his comparison of himself to Zethus, he professes a brotherly concern for Socrates and claims that he regards him warmly (485e). Socrates remarks that since Callicles gave him the same advice that he overheard Callicles give to his closest friends – that is, not to pursue philosophy excessively – that he must have goodwill for him (487e). But Socrates then associates goodwill with a willingness to be honest in either holding onto or conceding a point in the course of their discussion: *parrêsia* and *eunoia* turn out to be interrelated. He claims that honesty in speech is required for friendship:

> If there's any point in our discussions on which you agree with me, then that point will have been adequately put to the test by you and me, and it will not be necessary to put it to any further test, for you'd never have conceded the point through lack of wisdom or excess of shame, and you wouldn't do so by lying to me either. You are my friend, as you yourself say (487e).

Socrates does not just want good feeling or warm regard from Callicles; he also wants Callicles to be completely honest about his own beliefs and his evaluation of Socrates' views. Friendship of this sort requires radical honesty. However, Socrates later claims that the completely unjust soul is incapable of friendship: only a just soul can be a good friend to other human beings and to the gods (507e). If Callicles is serious in his claims to value *eunoia* and to possess brotherly affection for Socrates, then he cannot believe that complete injustice and pursuit of one's own appetites at the expense of friendship is really the best life. In this way, the argument shows an inconsistency in Callicles' commitments, what he cares about, and not only in his stated propositions.

These characteristics of good inquiry are closely related to Socrates' description of the political art (521d). First, Socrates says that the aim of oratory is simply to flatter and to produce pleasure in one's audience (462c; 463b), while the political art aims at what is best for the citizens (521e). The practitioner of the political art must have goodwill for the citizens, especially the harmony of their souls, both in what he does and in how he speaks to them.[29] Second, Socrates characterizes the political art as open about its intentions, like the doctor who tells the truth about health to his patients; the rhetorician pleases his audience, like the cook who only pleases the palates of those who eat his unhealthy food (464d). Like Socrates, who is willing to speak openly about what he believes even if this eventually leads to his death, the practitioner of the political art practices *parrêsia* of an extreme sort. Third, those who pursue the political art value knowledge rather than persuasion alone and seek the cause of each thing (465a). This does not mean that the philosopher *possesses* full knowledge – Socrates explicitly denies it in his own case at 488a – but he does *seek* it. Practicing the true political art includes a commitment to the values of knowledge, goodwill, and frankness. But Socrates nowhere gives an abstract argument that grounds these values. Instead, he implies that Callicles is inconsistent with himself insofar as he claims to value these ends and yet does not embody them in how he speaks and lives. The contrast between Socrates and Callicles lies in what goods each person loves and how his commitments are reflected in speech and action.[30]

V.

We can now return to the question of why Socrates' conflict with his interlocutors is so much more hostile in the *Gorgias* than in the *Protagoras*. Perhaps Aristotle's claim in the *Rhetoric* that anger motivates action is relevant here. Aristotle defines anger as an impulse accompanied by pain in which the angry person desires revenge for being slighted (1378a32–35). In other words, anger is a state that stems from feeling hurt that gives impetus to a desire to relieve one's pain through lashing out at others. Certainly, this definition explains the hostility that Socrates often encounters as a result of his philosophical questioning. Socrates' interlocutors feel hurt and angry to the extent that his criticisms raise questions about themselves as human beings. However, Aristotle also suggests that anger has a positive purpose and, in fact, is a virtue when the anger is proportional to the offense and directed to the right person at the right time and place. For example, a general might give a speech to a crowd in order to increase their anger, thus inciting them to greater enthusiasm for a just war. Socrates' goal in angering his interlocutors seems to be to encourage

---

[29] Richard D. Parry, *Plato's Craft of Justice* (Albany, NY: SUNY Press, 1996), chapter 1.

[30] See Parry, *Plato's Craft*, especially 47–54, on similarities between Socratic questioning and the political craft.

them to be angry not with him but with themselves – as Socrates suggests in the *Apology* (23c–d) – so that they might admit their ignorance and throw energy into the pursuit of the truth. More often than not, however, his interlocutors keep their anger focused on Socrates. There seems to be no way in which to guarantee that a person speaking with Socrates will use his anger and frustration in a more productive way.

Socrates, however, might be a model of how to experience frustration and disequilibrium in the process of philosophical questioning. Socrates alludes to his own philosophical attitude at the beginning of the discussion with Gorgias. There, he suggests that part of his task is to question what seems obvious or clear. Several times he mentions the question of clarity. Socrates tells Gorgias, "But you won't be surprised if in a moment I ask you again another question like this, about what seems to be clear (*dêlon*), and yet I go on with my questioning – as I say, I'm asking questions so that we can conduct an orderly discussion" (454b–c). A bit later, Socrates returns to the issue of clarity regarding his own views: "For I am not yet able to perceive (*katanoêsai*) what I'm saying" (455b).[31] (The issue of clarity is also raised at 453c and 458a.) These remarks are peculiar since, throughout the dialogues, Socrates uses philosophical categories and distinctions that impose greater order on the phenomena being investigated. For example, in the *Protagoras*, Socrates explores the conceptual connections between the different virtues with Protagoras in a way that attempts to unify their disparate elements. In the *Gorgias*, he separates oratory from the political art through a series of oppositions that seem to bring more, not less, clarity to the topic.

However, I suggest that there are two ways in which we can understand Socrates as seeking a lack of clarity as much as clarity in the process of his philosophical explorations. First, Socrates encourages a willingness to explore popular ideas that are widely accepted as true and to find problems in commonly held opinions. He suggests that moral ideas that at first seemed to be obvious may turn out to be mistaken. The truth is best pursued through deliberately seeking to find problems in what seems on the surface unproblematic. In contrast, Polus thinks that Socrates is arguing about questions to which even a child knows the answers (470c), and Callicles sees his questions as trivial, petty, and useless (497b–c). Polus and Callicles cannot see the point of questioning what is clear and agreed upon by the majority. Socrates, in contrast, appears to prefer a lack of clarity in such matters.

---

[31] My translation.

Second, Socrates does not advocate closure on the philosophical ideas at which he or others arrive in the course of conversation. While it is true that Socrates is interested in the harmony of his own views, in rationality, and in irrefutability, he also maintains an openness to the probability that there is always something limited, or perhaps even gravely mistaken, about the views at which he has arrived. Socrates suggests that whenever one arrives at an apparently clear truth, the philosopher desires to explore the subject further, attempts to make the matter unclear again, in order to find a deeper understanding – or perhaps to find that one's views are untenable. The philosopher finds a kind of pleasure in disequilibrium and *aporia*. Socrates tells Gorgias that he gets more pleasure out of being refuted than refuting others:

> And what kind of man am I? One of those who would be pleased (*hêdêos*) to be refuted if I say anything untrue, and who would be pleased (*hêdêos*) to refute anyone who says anything untrue; one who, however, wouldn't be any less pleased to be refuted than to refute (*elegchthentônê elegxantôn*). For I count being refuted a greater good, insofar as it is a greater good to be rid of the greatest evil from oneself than to rid someone else of it. I don't suppose that any evil for a man is as a great as false belief about the things we're discussing right now (458a).

Although well known, Socrates' statement here is really remarkable: Socrates finds pleasure in being defeated. He actively seeks it. Socrates could have said that he finds pleasure in the stability of his beliefs or their irrefutability but instead identifies the primary pleasure in refutation and potentially even in change (so long as that change leads one toward the truth). Paradoxically, the same rhetoricians who are careful to change their public opinions and profess flexibility are deeply upset when their views are disturbed: Callicles proclaims that if what Socrates says about justice is true, then the whole world will be turned over (*anatetrammenos*) and everyone will have to do the opposite of what he does now (481c). This scenario bothers and angers him. Similarly, in the *Protagoras*, Socrates responds to the reversal of their initial positions with a rally to engage in further inquiry, but Protagoras ends the conversation (361d).

I suggest Socrates has in mind this sort of commitment to critical questioning when he suggests that there is another kind of rhetoric, aside from the one that Gorgias and his followers practice. Socrates asserts that a good orator will "always give his attention to how justice may come to exist in the souls of his fellow citizens and injustice be gotten rid of, how self-control may come to exist there and lack of discipline be gotten rid of, and how the rest of excellence may come into being there and evil may depart" (504d–e). Rhetoric is thus identified with a kind of care-giving of the soul. In this way, the *Gorgias* points ahead to the *Phaedrus'* discussion of rhetoric as the leading of souls, with the good as the object of the soul's desire. Socrates does not specify here how this caregiving of souls takes place. However, one possibility is that Socrates has in mind exactly the sort of activities that he practices here with Gorgias, Polus, and Callicles. He does not use one "technique" to accomplish this end but rather uses images, myths, short question and answer, and analogies to other arts as part of his argument. The common thread behind all of these means of persuasion is that each one forces the world of the inter-locutor to become at least a little bit unraveled. Socrates admonishes his audience and makes claims that are diametrically opposed to their own commitments. In other words, the self-critical stance that Socrates artic-ulates when he claims to find pleasure in disequilibrium is the same one that he encourages through his questioning of others.

But, if this is true, then one of the concepts always open to revision is the nature and value of philosophical activity itself. In the *Gorgias*, Plato seems to move between pushing together and pulling apart the philosopher and the rhetorician in order to make the unclear clear, but also the clear unclear again, in order to develop his understanding of philosophy. Part of the activity of the philosopher is to continue to explore the boundaries of philosophy in relation to other activities. Rhetoric is not merely a useful foil for drawing contrasts between it and philosophy. Plato sees rhetoric as sharing a sufficient number of characteristics with the philosophical, such that it also forces us to ask further critical questions about the nature of reasoning, the value of the intellectual life, the consistency of belief, and the like. There is no final or complete distinction between philosophy and rhetoric in the *Gorgias* because a key part of Platonic philosophical activity is to continue to test philosophy itself. The Platonic dialogue by its very structure retains opposition between different voices as part of its philosophical explorations. Its structure invites readers to test their own ideas about argument, persuasion, reasoning, the relevance of politics to philosophy, and so on. The diversity of characters and views within the dialogue allows all sorts of different readers – those more like Callicles but also those more like Gorgias, Polus, or Socrates – to further explore their own understandings of these topics, for each of these characters has someone else in the dialogue who opposes his views. In this sense, the dialogues promote a kind of open-endedness to philosophical inquiry at times lacking in contemporary academic writing, which generally seeks a strong sense of closure on philosophical topics.

Put somewhat differently, Plato here is less interested in finding a definition of philosophy vis-à-vis rhetoric than in critically exploring it as a practice. The *Gorgias* shows that philosophy shares many important dimensions with the practice of rhetoric. Both philosophy and rhetoric are interested in persuasion. Both are willing to use not only arguments concerned with the use and meaning of terms but also images and examples to persuade their audience. Both at times are willing to arouse the emotions of their audience in order to make a point. Both are concerned with the importance of opinion in good discourse. But Plato presents good philosophical rhetoric as distinguished by its commitments to goodwill toward one's partner in speech; frankness of speech; a love of knowledge, particularly of justice; and openness to self-criticism. The *Gorgias* does not reject rhetoric as such but instead connects good rhetoric to the possession of these philosophical virtues.

5

The Dialectical Development of the Philosopher and Sophist in the *Republic*

I.

The *Republic* is an excellent resource for drawing a contrast between the rhetoric of the sophist and of the philosopher. Its first book includes a dramatic conflict between the sophist Thrasymachus and the philosopher Socrates, while its middle books provide a detailed account of the nature of each. The dialogue contrasts and compares them through both its drama and abstract descriptions. In this chapter, I argue that Plato develops his presentation of the philosopher and the sophist dialectically.[1] The initial books deliberately set up Socrates to look a bit like a sophist and Thrasymachus to look a bit like a philosopher. While the middle books suggest that the philosopher and sophist stem from the same nature, Plato differentiates them by the philosopher's love of the forms and his possession of moral and intellectual virtues. However, because sophists do not even acknowledge that the forms exist, the philosopher is separable from the sophist only from the viewpoint of the philosopher. From the sophist's viewpoint, a philosopher is merely a deficient sophist. Philosophy is a normative rather than descriptive standpoint, grounded upon key moral and theoretical commitments.

This chapter proceeds in three main parts. First, I examine the way in which Book One presents Thrasymachus as similar in certain respects to philosophers and Socrates as similar in certain respects to sophists. Second, I trace the dialectical development of the philosopher and sophist

---

[1] As David Roochnik argues, many ideas unfold dialectically over the course of the dialogue. See Roochnik, *Beautiful City: The Dialectical Character of Plato's Republic* (Ithaca and London: Cornell University Press, 2003).

from the *Republic* Books Two through Seven. I argue that the distinction between the philosopher and the sophist only makes sense from the point of view of the philosopher. Third, I briefly look at Socrates' rhetoric, which is characterized by the philosopher's love of the forms and his desire to lead others to them.

II.

Thrasymachus is a figure of interest for understanding the sophist in part because he presents a genuinely intellectual position about the nature of justice.[2] Thrasymachus is neither a sloppy thinker nor one concerned only with winning the argument. Instead, he sets out a position that might reasonably be called philosophical in our contemporary sense of the term (although not in what will be Socrates' much more restrictive sense). Thrasymachus' position is a point of contention in the literature on the subject, particularly because he restates his position throughout the discussion with Socrates.[3] The dispute revolves around whether his real definition of justice is the "advantage of the stronger" (337c1); the advantage of the ruling body (337a); obeying the laws (339b9–10); or another's good (where injustice benefits the moral actor; 343d–344c).[4] The key interpretive question is whether Thrasymachus thinks that justice is conformity to whatever laws are put in place by the strong, or an objective sense of justice and injustice, where injustice turns out to be more advantageous. In other words, is Thrasymachus a conventionalist or an immoralist?[5]

---

[2] Portions of this chapter are reprinted here with permission from *Polis*. See Marina Berzins McCoy, "Sophistry and Philosophy in Plato's *Republic*," *Polis* 22 (2) (2005): 265–286.

[3] See John Beverslius, *Cross-Examining Socrates* (Cambridge: Cambridge University Press, 2000), 221–244.

[4] I use Bloom's translations throughout. See Bloom, *The Republic of Plato*, 2nd ed.

[5] Julia Annas helpfully lays out the terms *conventionalism* and *immoralism* here and argues that Thrasymachus is an immoralist. See Annas, *An Introduction to Plato's* Republic (Oxford: Clarendon Press, 1981). In contrast, Bloom sees Thrasymachus as a conventionalist (326). Taylor, *The Man and His Work*, argues that Thrasymachus is an ethical nihilist. For other views, see T. J. Henderson, "In Defense of Thrasymachus," *American Philosophical Quarterly* 7 (1970): 218–228, who argues that the "advantage of the stronger" means that in any interaction, if one party acts justly, he is left vulnerable to the actions of the other party. G. B. Kerferd, "The Doctrine of Thrasymachus in Plato's 'Republic'," *Durham University Journal* 9 (1947): 19–27, suggests that justice always means "another's good" for both ruled and ruler, and that the initial definition Thrasymachus proposes is a "deliberate paradox" (26). Robert Cross and Anthony Woozley, *Plato's Republic: A Philosophical Commentary* (New York: 1964), 38–41, argue that Thrasymachus is simply inconsistent. See also Theodore L. Putterman, "Socrates/Thrasymachus: The Extent of

I suggest that Thrasymachus does not consider justice in a conventional sense to be at odds with immoralism because he looks at two different aspects of justice with Socrates. Thrasymachus begins with the perspective of those who rule (how they define what justice is for a society) but later looks at those who are ruled (and whether or not they ought to obey these rules, if they are rational). He explains that justice has no objective meaning other than naming the advantage of a particular group, the fulfillment of a particular group's desires. The many have a variety of opinions as to what is "just," and whoever is strongest dominates in the public battle to define what the term *justice* means. The term *justice*, as it is commonly used, reflects whatever group or groups are strongest in a particular society. However, knowing that the term *justice* is used conventionally also gives an advantage to those who know this – for example, Thrasymachus and his students. A person who realizes that justice is applied merely to whatever opinion is strongest should also see that justice in its usual sense is not worth having, as it looks to someone else's good. Justice is a convention, but unless one is lucky or able enough to be the ruler, one is better off pursuing what is typically named as injustice.[6] Those who know that justice names the advantage of those who dominate politically can see that the unjust man gets more than the just one.

Thrasymachus begins with the definition that justice is the "advantage of the stronger" (338c1–2). When Socrates asks him to clarify his meaning, he replies in terms of different sorts of governments: in each society, the ruling group sets down laws for its own advantage and calls these laws just, expecting others to obey them. In a democracy, the laws benefit a larger group of people, while in a tyranny, they benefit the tyrant. Thrasymachus gives the name of justice to whatever the rulers say is just, but his position is still indeterminate with respect to what the rulers know or do not know. Socrates then asks whether or not rulers make mistakes in seeking their own advantage (339c–d). Thrasymachus means that the rulers in the precise sense know what is their own advantage rather than just believing what is to their own advantage (341a2–3). Knowledge defines being a ruler. However, at this point, it is still unclear what Thrasymachus

---

their Agreement," *Polis* 17 (2000): 79–90, who argues that Thrasymachus is initially a conventionalist but later amoral.

[6] Robert Arp argues that the alleged inconsistencies in Thrasymachus' position can be resolved by introducing a third category, the "stronger," who desires to rule but may be an unjust man who takes on the appearance of justice in order to better pursue his own ends. See Arp, "The Double Life of Justice and Injustice," *Polis* 16 (1999): 17–29.

means when he says that knowledge is what allows rulers to gain power in the first place.

Socrates attempts to argue against the claim that a precise ruler will seek his own advantage by using analogies from other ruling arts.[7] If doctors seek the advantage of their patients, and pilots the advantage of their sailors, then no sort of knowledge considers the advantage of the stronger but rather the weaker – that is, what is ruled by that body of knowledge (341c3–342e1). He claims that the particular arts that Socrates has looked to are not analogous to the art of ruling. There are other examples of ruling (e.g., shepherding or cow herding) where the aim is to care for the ruled but ultimately to one's own advantage (e.g., one cares for the sheep ultimately in order to eat them). Thrasymachus wants to look at whether justice or injustice is advantageous. To look at how people actually act with respect to justice and injustice, Thrasymachus rejects the abstract use of analogies to characterize the arts. That is, he rejects the very idea of using a universal definition of knowledge that must hold true for all cases, in favor of an empirical look at human motivation and human desire. Perhaps some arts look only to the advantage of what they rule (e.g., good doctors care primarily about their patients' health), while others do not (e.g., shepherds care for their sheep only as a means to the slaughter). Knowledge need not play the same role in all enterprises. Thrasymachus suggests a better approach is to look at what the rulers and the ruled actually do and what motivates them.

In the passage where Thrasymachus claims that the unjust man has more than the just one (343d–344c), Thrasymachus shifts away from the discussion of the just ruler to the discussion of human beings in general, giving both examples of rulers and non-rulers. There, he argues that justice is someone else's good – that is, "the advantage of the man who is stronger and rules, and a personal harm to the man who obeys and serves" (343c2–4). This is not a change in definition or an inconsistency on Thrasymachus' part but instead a change in perspective: from the point of view of the ruled, justice is the name given to what is to the advantage of the ruler (and not their own good). Socrates has tried to claim that justice looks to the good of the ruled if it is analogous to other crafts. But Thrasymachus suggests there is empirical evidence for his case that justice is the advantage of the stronger: if we look at how

---

[7] Although the term *technê* is not used here but rather *epistêmê*, Socrates' own examples all reasonably would be considered *technai*.

people regard the relative happiness of the just and the unjust, justice is surely not the good of those who obey.[8]

The unjust has the advantage in contracts, in taxes, in all dealings with those who are just because he can make more money, or pay out less, or gain more power or goods than the just person, who is considering someone else's good.[9] Thrasymachus again looks at the perspective of the ruled rather than the ruler. Some of those who are ruled do not obey the ruler and his laws; they gain more by being unjust than by being just, even if they do not have the ruler's power. This implies that there is a set of people who have the knowledge that justice is conventional and who are happy – or at least happier than the just – but who are not themselves rulers in an overt political sense.[10] These individuals who are unjust "rule" in an analogous and covert way, by virtue of their injustice (not their office): "Injustice . . . rules the truly simple and just (*euêthikon kai dikaion*)" (343c).[11] Moreover, although a few rulers naively do not pursue their own interests (343e–344a), Thrasymachus suggests that most citizens see that injustice is advantageous; they only blame injustice because they fear suffering its consequences (344b–c).

Thrasymachus, therefore, suggests that there are a variety of different relationships between ruling and knowledge. Among rulers, there are precise rulers who look to their own advantage and those who do not (who are not rulers in a precise sense). Among the ruled, there are those who naively obey and those who disobey for their own advantage. Ultimately, it is not that knowledge of the true nature of justice distinguishes the class of rulers from the class of ruled (for some among both the rulers and the ruled lack knowledge of justice's true nature). Rather, knowledge of the true nature of justice and injustice distinguishes the happy from the unhappy. Rulers who know how to seek their own advantage are happy when they lay down laws that help themselves (which are called just laws); but those who are being ruled are better off disobeying these rules

---

[8] Kerferd, in "The Doctrine of Thrasymachus," 19–27, suggests that this sort of position is internally consistent but implausible as it involves Thrasymachus changing his use of the term *justice* midstream. However, it seems to me entirely reasonable that Thrasymachus should want to explore how non-rulers are affected by the justice established by rulers, especially after Socrates has insisted that the precise ruler enacts laws for the good of the people.

[9] His term here is *pleonektein*. As Jacob Howland, *The Republic: The Odyssey of Philosophy* (New York: Twayne Publishers, 1993), 71, points out, Thrasymachus assumes that *pleonexia*, the unlimited desire always to have more, characterizes all human beings.

[10] See Arp, "Double Life," 16–23.

[11] See Arp, "Double Life," 17–29.

(i.e., being unjust). Thrasymachus' position here is entirely consistent, but the operative category of distinction for him is happiness rather than justice.

Thrasymachus gives an internally consistent picture of the human being: we all desire power, honor, and material gain. Just laws and the consequences of disobeying them are obstacles to this for everyone who is not a ruler. In addition, among both ruler and ruled, the belief that a just life is a better way to live is a flawed one that makes any person less happy than he would be if he knew the truth. Thrasymachus' account explaining why the unjust life is better is not addressed fully in Book One.[12] Moreover, as Beverslius has argued, Socrates' arguments in Book One do not fully address Thrasymachus' position.[13] To begin, Thrasymachus' contention that Socrates only questions others without offering explanations of his own might very well resonate with the Athenians, who are accustomed to seeing Socrates question others while claiming ignorance. His claim that Socrates seems more interested in cutting down others' ideas than building up his own theory anticipates the later claim in Book Six that the philosopher is either vicious or useless. It is only in Book Six that this objection to the philosopher is fully addressed. Book One has Thrasymachus present a relatively sophisticated theory, while Socrates initially seems interested only in refutation.

In addition, at least one of Socrates' arguments against Thrasymachus' ideas uses faulty argumentation. Socrates' comparison of the just man and unjust man to the wise and the foolish is fallacious (349d–350c). There, Socrates asserts that in every craft, knowers wish to "outdo" non-knowers but not other knowers like themselves. Those who do not know, the foolish, wish to outdo both those like and unlike themselves – that is, both non-knowers and knowers. Those who are knowers are good and wise, so the good and wise wish to outdo only those unlike themselves. In contrast, the ignorant and bad person wants to outdo those both like and unlike himself. Socrates concludes that the unjust man wants to outdo those like and unlike himself and so is ignorant and bad. However, Socrates' logic is faulty. To claim that the unjust are in the same logical relation to the just as the ignorant are to the knowledgeable is not a proof that the class

---

[12] Quite differently, Basil O'Neil offers an interesting argument that Socrates moves Thrasymachus from being unconcerned with *logos* to becoming at least half-heartedly friendly to Socratic *logos* by the end of Book One. See O'Neil, "The Struggle for the Soul of Thrasymachus," *Ancient Philosophy* 8 (1988): 167–185. I think this unlikely, given his near silence for the rest of the dialogue.

[13] See Beverslius, *Cross-Examining*, 221–244.

of unjust people is *identical* to the class of the ignorant. That is, unless one grants that justice is a craft that requires knowledge (the very point under dispute), Socrates' argument is not valid.[14]

Thrasymachus' position remains a coherent, if immoral, alternative to the Socratic position that it is better to be just than unjust because his main claim that the unjust person is happier than the just person still has not been addressed. Even if Socrates is correct that the just person is more knowledgeable than the unjust person in certain ways, Socrates has not yet addressed Thrasymachus' more basic claim that the unjust "have more" and are happier than the just.[15] Glaucon and Adeimantus recognize the inadequacy of Socrates' arguments on this point when they raise the issue of the relative happiness of the just and unjust, as well as the question as to whether justice is only assented to as a way of avoiding harm in Book Two. Book Two follows naturally from Book One insofar as the fundamental issues that divide Socrates and Thrasymachus go far deeper than whether or not rulers possess knowledge.[16] Socrates must defend a wholly different conception of the human soul in which a just soul is happier than an unjust one. Moreover, he needs to show that it is possible to conceive of a regime that looks to the happiness of the whole and not only a part. Thrasymachus clearly puts certain goods – money, profit, the goodwill of relatives, power, freedom from external control – at the center of human happiness (343d3–344d1). Socrates must show that there are other sorts of desires, such as the desire to know the forms, the pursuit of which leads to a deeper, more lasting happiness. Thrasymachus' theoretical stance about the good life drives much of the discourse of the remainder of the *Republic*. He is not merely a rhetorician set on winning an argument but rather a person with a vision of the good life that is deeply at odds with Socrates' own vision.

III.

Socrates develops his picture of the philosopher dialectically in the *Republic*. As the city in speech grows and becomes more elaborate, Socrates

---

[14] See Beverslius, *Cross-Examining*, especially 237–238.
[15] See Sallis, *Being and Logos*, 345.
[16] Whether there is a clear connection is sometimes disputed; see, e.g., Cross and Woozley, *Plato's Republic* (chapter 2), who argue that the argument about justice is entirely restated in Book Two by Glaucon and Adeimantus, and who take the view that Book One was once a separate dialogue. Annas, in *Plato's Republic*, argues for a closer connection.

gradually unfolds a more complex and nuanced version of the human soul. It is within the context of examining the philosopher – his identity and especially his desires – that the ontology of the forms is also developed. My presentation here of the philosopher is necessarily broad. My point is to show that the philosopher is defined primarily by his orientation toward and love of the forms. In this sense, the philosopher has a theoretical stance that is different from that of the sophist. Socrates has a vision of the world in which he is turned toward the forms. However, this theoretical stance is grounded upon the philosopher's desire. That is, Plato does not suggest that the philosopher knows the forms while the sophist lacks knowledge. Socrates expresses a considerable amount of skepticism as to whether *anyone* can know the good adequately. The good is described as beyond being and beyond our perfect knowledge of it, although Socrates also suggests that we can grow in our understanding of it. Instead, the philosopher is defined by his love of the forms, which then spurs him on to seek and to know them. Plato's emphasis in the *Republic* is upon desire rather than knowledge as the distinguishing mark of the philosopher.[17]

Perhaps the first point to note is that in the simplest city of all, there is no philosopher. The development of the philosopher begins in Book Two, in the "feverish" city that Socrates and Glaucon build up when it is determined that a simple city composed only of craftsmen is insufficient and fit only for pigs. The philosopher arises only as the desires of the city are expanded beyond the most basic needs of food, shelter, and clothing. Because Glaucon thinks that a good city must have some luxuries, the class of guardians arises. The feverish city will need more land and will also have to defend itself against enemies who attack it for its goods, and so requires soldiers who are trained to protect the city and its interests (372e–374e). The development of a guardian class in the city arises specifically from the presence of desire for "more" among the citizens. The idea of the "philosopher" first arises in the city in relation to the need for the guardians to be both spirited and gentle. The model for such a personality turns out to be the "dog," which is said to be like the philosopher: a good dog is fierce with enemies and friendly with those familiar to him, and so this requires knowledge of who is a friend and who is an enemy (375b–376b).

---

[17] David Roochnik makes a similar argument with respect to the *Symposium* that the existence of the forms is inferred from human desire. See Roochnik, "The Erotics of Philosophical Discourse," *History of Philosophy Quarterly* 4 (1987): 117–129.

While the comparison of a philosopher to a dog is no doubt intended to be humorous, Socrates is also pointing out a kind of limited truth in the comparison that helps us to understand something about the philosopher and his relation to the city. First, the image establishes a clear link between the good of the city and the need for knowledge. Even a very simple city that has nothing more than two classes, craftsmen and soldiers, requires knowledge in order to sustain and to protect itself. While the knowledge of the craftsmen is technical, the kind of knowledge that these "philosopher dogs" need is different: their knowledge concerns friendship – that is, determining who is inside or outside the city on the basis of familiarity. Socrates is careful to specify that dogs do not make judgments of a potential friend or enemy on the basis of their past actions but rather only according to whether or not they "recognize" the other. Friends are those who go recognized and enemies are those who are unfamiliar. These guardians, in other words, are loyal to the city and have a commitment to the city simply because it is their own. They do not need to possess a complex understanding of good and evil in order to protect their city but rather only a love of their fellow citizens as citizens.

However, Socrates' argument against Polemarchus in Book One renders this understanding as philosophically inadequate. There, he showed that helping one's friends and harming one's enemies does not take into account whether the friend is really good or the enemy is really evil (332d–334d). This initial picture of the guardians will prove to be incomplete, once it is recognized that the city needs knowledge of justice itself, and not only familiarity with friend and enemy in order to flourish. At the same time, Socrates here seems to recognize that there is a limited value in *loving* one's city and not only in *understanding* it. If, as Socrates will later say, we only can care for what we love, then a good guardian must love his city and not only make a detached, rational evaluation that it is just. Socrates himself embodies this love of his city in the drama of the dialogue. Although we find in Books Two and Three that Socrates shares little in common with the traditional Greek view of the gods, he nonetheless goes down to Piraeus to participate in a new civic festival. Socrates spends his time in the dialogue speaking with non-philosophers, even those opposed to or offended by his philosophy, and he fights in wars and fulfills his obligations to the city, despite its shortcomings. Even in this primitive conception of the philosopher as a "dog" who loves friends and hates enemies, the philosopher is a lover of the concrete city, of other people in the city; he is protective of its good. He is not an intellectual concerned with the discovery of unchanging truths. At this stage, the philosopher–guardian is more political than contemplative.

Books Three and Four further develop the picture of the philosopher through offering a more complicated picture of the soul.[18] The guardians proper, as distinct from the auxiliaries, arise in the city as a result of the need for educators who can be in charge of the formation of all the souls in the city, including those in their own class. To be adequate educators, they must know both what is good and bad for the city, as well as how to educate the souls of the other human beings in their city. It is in this context that the tripartite nature of the soul – composed of reason, spirit, and the appetites – is developed. The reasoning part of the soul is a calculator of what is good but also in charge of keeping the rest of the soul in order by determining what is due to each of the other parts and enforcing their obedience (441d–442b). Knowledge – not only of friend and enemy but also of what is objectively good and bad for the soul – turns out to be central to the philosophical soul.

This tripartite soul is a great improvement over the picture of the "philosopher dog," for the just soul must know what really is good for the soul rather than resting comfortably with the familiar and recognizable. However, one limitation of Book Four's description of the soul is that it says virtually nothing about knowledge outside of itself, which proves to be central to understanding reasoning in relation to the forms by the middle parts of the book. In Book Four, Socrates primarily presents the soul as a calculator of what the other parts of the soul desire and how these desires are to be balanced. But nothing is said about what reason's distinct needs are for itself – that is, its own desired objects, apart from its role in ruling this "city" of a soul. As Roochnik has argued, the picture of the soul presented in Book Four is not Plato's final understanding of what the soul is; rather, it is one stage in a longer process in the dialogue of developing a picture of the soul, a picture that grows to include elements of desire.[19] While in Book Four reason seems to be more about calculation about the soul's other desires, the middle books of the *Republic* go on to argue that *eros* is an important aspect of the reasoning part of the soul.

The middle books' description of the philosopher is offered in response to the opponents of philosopher–kings – that is, to those like Glaucon who do not think that the philosopher ought to rule the city.

---

[18] See Roochnik, *Beautiful City*, 10–40, for a discussion of the arithmetical character of the tripartite soul.

[19] See Roochnik, *Beautiful City*, 51–77.

Socrates responds that the philosopher is the lover of all, not just one part, of wisdom. He compares the philosopher to those who love boys or wine. The erotic lover loves and appreciates a wide variety of characteristics in his beloveds and not only one type or look of a person; this, Glaucon admits with a little embarrassment, obviously is meant for him, since he loves boys with many different appearances (474d–475a). Lovers of honor will not settle for just one kind of honor but will satisfy their desire for honor wherever they can find it, even among lower men whose praise is less worthy than the praise of better men. Similarly, Socrates says, the philosopher will love all of wisdom (474a–475c). While the soul in Book Four is described as "moderate," the philosopher that Socrates has described here is not moderate at all. He is not someone who loves knowing about just one thing – for example, how to rule the city – but instead loves knowledge in general. The philosopher is immoderate not only in the number of objects that he might love but also in the intensity of his desire to know the good. The philosopher's desire for wisdom is to know for its own sake. His desire to know never seems to end: learning about one thing only makes him want to go off and learn still more. There is something about the desire for philosophical knowledge that increases as it is satisfied; its satisfaction does not lead to tranquility or the diminishment of desire, as happens when we drink water when we are thirsty. As Socrates presents the philosopher, his desire for knowledge seems only to increase when he has a little taste of learning. He is, in short, "insatiable" (475c).

In describing *eros* here, Socrates honestly acknowledges this aspect of love or desire: our desires seem to be endless. We are the kinds of beings who are fundamentally incomplete by our very nature. It is not that we are not easily satisfied; we are *never* satisfied completely. In this respect, Socrates is similar to Thrasymachus who also claims that human beings always desire "more." It turns out that the philosopher is not free of this desire for "more" identified by the sophist. Instead, the philosopher exhibits his erotic desire in his own peculiar way, in his thirst for knowledge. Socrates gives *eros* its proper place in the city, in the souls of the philosopher–kings and their desire for knowledge.

When Socrates tells us that this philosopher approaches every type of learning with delight and is "insatiable," Glaucon objects. If the philosopher loves all kinds of knowledge, will we not have to include the lovers of sights and sounds – for example, those who love to hear choral performances or see paintings – among the philosophers? Socrates responds that there is a certain sort of truth in the comparison to sights and sounds:

philosophers are lovers of the sight of truth. However, Socrates says that there is an important contrast as well: the lovers of sights and sounds delight in fair colors, and shapes, and sounds, and the products of the craftsmen but not in the "beautiful itself." The lovers of sight and sounds, if asked what the beautiful is, will say, this piece of music is beautiful, that sunset, this flower, or that beautiful boy. The philosopher is different: he relates all of these beautiful things back to the beautiful itself. The man who thinks that there are only beautiful things – but not beauty itself – is like a man in a dream who does not realize that he is only dreaming about things that are likenesses of reality. But the man who can somehow "catch sight" of the beautiful itself and also enjoys the instances of what participates in it is fully "awake."

Socrates' point here about the "awake" quality of the philosopher is significant, for as we shall see in the cave image, the sophist is one who is unaware of or not yet awake to the forms. He denies their very existence. While Socrates has not yet formally distinguished between the philosopher and the sophist, we can see that the philosopher's orientation to the forms sets him apart from the non-philosopher, but in a way that would be difficult to explain to the non-philosopher.

On Socrates' account of the philosopher, someone who places all value in things (e.g., sights and sounds) rather than in forms is not a philosopher. Here, Socrates offers an incredibly restrictive definition of the philosopher. He does not merely say that if one is a philosopher for long enough, one will realize that the forms exist and will love them. Rather, he seems to be suggesting that unless one loves the forms and understands them as the ultimate reality, then one is not really a philosopher. This would, of course, exclude from the category of philosophers many prominent figures in the later history of philosophy, such as empirical or naturalistic philosophers along the lines of Mill, Hume, Hobbes, and the pragmatists. Philosophy is defined as a love of "what is," in a strong, metaphysical sense. However, the *Republic* goes on to show that the philosopher does not possess full knowledge of what is; the form of the good is beyond the capacity of the human soul to know completely. Socrates can offer Glaucon only opinions about what the forms might be like. In this way, the philosopher's theoretical stance is not about having the right metaphysical theory in detail but rather about understanding his own deepest desires as a person. The philosopher loves the forms more than he loves anything else and wishes to understand them more and bring others to love them as well.

Accordingly, Book Six emphasizes not knowledge but love as central to the philosopher's identity. The philosopher is in love with "that which is," with what does not wander about and either generate or decay. He loves all of knowledge, both what is honorable and even what is contemptible in knowledge. The philosopher hates a lie and cherishes the truth. He must love learning so much that he forsakes other pleasures, such as the pleasures of the body or money, since his desire is oriented toward the truth. The philosopher will not engage in "petty speech." He will not fear death or think that human life is great, and so he will not be a coward. He learns easily, does not seem to suffer and toil much in his pursuit of truth, has a great memory, and is measured and "charming" in his soul (485a–487a).

While Socrates' description of the qualities of the philosopher can read a bit like a laundry list at times, there is a central and unifying theme to them all: the philosopher is so possessed by his love of the forms that everything else in his life becomes secondary to the quest for coming to know them. Socrates' discussion here is overwhelmingly psychological. He focuses on the state of the philosopher's soul rather than his method, his precise metaphysics, or his knowledge. While ideally a philosopher will come to know the good, what defines him is not his *knowledge* of it but rather his *desire* for it. Here, Socrates does not describe the philosopher as a person who uses a particular method. If dialectic characterizes the highest way of coming to know things, its nature is never explained very clearly in the *Republic*, while the psychology of the philosopher is described in great detail. In place of a careful description of philosophical methodology, we find a praise of the philosopher, seemingly designed to awaken Socrates' interlocutors to discover their own desire as well. Socrates' adulatory remarks about the philosopher's courage, intellectual prowess, and devotion are more than a description; they are an encomium. They are a praise of his nature to Glaucon and Adeimantus, perhaps intended to arouse a similar kind of passion for the forms in them.

Adeimantus objects to this high-minded portrayal of the philosopher. He claims that most people will see the philosopher as either "vicious" or "useless." According to Adeimantus, the popular perception of the philosopher is diametrically opposed to the noble picture that Glaucon and Socrates have just developed. The philosopher in the popular imagination cares not about the truth or contemplation but rather about duping his opponents by leading them just a little at each argument, step by step, until they have been trapped, as in a game of checkers (487b). Those who dwell in philosophy too long become vicious. Those who somehow manage to remain decent are useless to the city.

Somewhat surprisingly, Socrates admits that those who bring these charges against philosophers speak the truth. But, to address these charges fully, Socrates uses the image of the pilot of a ship. Socrates asks us to imagine a ship, where the ship owner and sailors alike know relatively little about how to pilot a ship. The sailors argue among themselves as to who ought to rule. Each of them attempts to persuade the ship owner to turn over the rule of the ship to himself, either by persuading through drink, food, speech, or, failing this, force. These sailors do not even know that there is such a thing as a need for knowledge of the art of piloting a ship, and they do not think that it is possible both to get hold of the knowledge of how to persuade and the knowledge of how to pilot a ship at the same time. Meanwhile, the true pilot will be called a "stargazer" and be regarded as useless to the city (488a–489c).

Socrates next addresses the apparent viciousness of the philosopher. He says that this accusation is the result of slander and is due to the practice of those who claim to be philosophers but really are not (i.e., the sophists). Both the philosopher and the sophist come from the same nature, but the sophist is a corruption of the philosopher. Socrates' claim as to the identity of their nature is perhaps a bit surprising in light of the extreme opposition of the views of Thrasymachus and Socrates in Book One. Even more surprising, it is not a *lack* of virtue but rather a natural *disposition* toward virtue in those with this nature that leads some of them to become sophists. The same courage and moderation needed to pursue philosophy can also tear away a person from philosophy and toward the corrupt world of politics and power.

The young proto-philosopher is not indifferent to honor and acclaim. He is courageous and wants to fight to defend his city in a time of war. He is still interested in appropriate honor, in spirit getting its due. His desire for contemplation, however, does not yet so completely overwhelm his soul that he possesses no care for what others think of him. In particular, Socrates focuses on the role of the praise and blame of the Assembly. The uproar, shouts, applause, and, in general, the reactions of the crowd cannot help but affect the soul of the potential philosopher. He will end up praising and blaming whatever the many do. Those who continue to dissent will be punished with dishonor, fines, and even death. The many of the Assembly are the greatest sophists of all (492a1–492b2). No private education, good or bad, has the power to overcome these powerful psychological forces found in the larger political world. Again, the key difference between the philosopher and sophist is found in what each one loves, those goods to which he is most deeply committed.

As a result of passages such as these, some commentators have suggested that the sophists were not really attempting to harm anyone but rather only teaching the values of their own time and place.[20] On this view, the sophist offers the youth something pretty innocuous, which is to teach a young person how to succeed according to his own society's standards of success. The sophist on this view is not particularly threatening since he only teaches what is culturally condoned as good, but Plato objects to sophistry because it never rises to the level of philosophy. The sophist never asks fundamental questions about what is good, or why, or what human nature is really like. Sophistry is not an intellectual enterprise but rather more of a business designed to elevate the sophist to a better economic and social standing.

However, this view of the sophists as the harmless followers of the many is not well supported by the passages that follow a bit later. There, Socrates suggests that the sophists are different from ordinary members of the public, insofar as the former are quite self-conscious of what they are doing in feeding back to the many their own views. Socrates says that each of these private, wage-earning sophists educates "in nothing other than these convictions of the many, which they opine when they are gathered together, and he calls this wisdom" (493a8–9). Like a trainer who learns how to approach a strong beast and how to anger or to tame it, the sophist learns what sounds to utter in order to manipulate the public. Socrates elaborates:

When he has learned all this from associating and spending time with the beast, he calls it wisdom (*sophian*) and, organizing it as an art (*technên*), turns to teaching. Knowing nothing (*mêden eidôs*) in truth about which of these convictions and desires is noble, or base, or good, or evil, or just, or unjust, he applies all those names following the great animal's opinions – calling what delights it good and what vexes it bad. He has no other argument about them but calls the necessary (*tanaykaia*) just and noble, neither having seen nor being able to show someone else how much the nature of the necessary and the good (*kala*) really differ (493b–c).

Socrates concludes that the sophist is out of place as an educator because he does not see the difference between knowledge and opinion.

---

[20] See, e.g., George Grote, *History of Greece, Selections*, eds. J. M. Mitchell and M. O. B. Caspari (New York: Routledge, 2001). See also Taylor, *The Man and His Work*, 237–238; and Guthrie, *History*, 502.

Socrates places the sophist at an intermediate position between the many and the philosopher. On the one hand, the sophist shares some characteristics with the many: he equates the necessary with the good, and he does not know the truth about justice. On the other hand, the sophist is different from the many since he is deliberate in his management of public opinion and self-aware in a way the many are not. While the sophist does not see opinions as objectively good or bad, he can potentially change others' opinions if he learns how to work with the forces of public approval. If the analogy of the trainer is to be taken seriously, he sees the public as beneath him, a beast to be manipulated. He has taken his wisdom and converted it into an art (*technê*). And, if the sophist really possesses an ability to work with the public "beast," he is likely to have some influence in an imperfect regime that the philosopher lacks. The sophist, then, is not powerless; his power is to manipulate the public for his own apparent benefit. The sophist is a statesman of a peculiar sort, interested in his own rather than in the city's welfare, and yet still dependent upon the city for the achievement of his own ends.

This passage suggests that Plato condemns the sophists partly for their interest in money, honor, and power. Yet, Socrates' main focus is upon what the sophist *sees* as good and how he regards his own knowledge, not upon his interest in wage earning or honor (493b–c). Socrates emphasizes that the sophists lack knowledge of the difference between the necessary things (*tanaykaia*) and good things (*kala*) (493c). Socrates uses the term *anaykaios* elsewhere in the *Republic* when he explains that some desires are necessary, while others are unnecessary: the "necessary" desires are those which we cannot justly turn aside, as well as those whose satisfaction benefits us (559a). On this account, "necessities" seems to refer to those things that fulfill our most basic physical desires such as food, sex, the need for water, sleep, and other human needs. Socrates also uses the term *the city of utmost necessity* (*anaykaiotatê polis*) to describe the very simple city consisting of only four or five men with which he begins in Book Two (369d); that city only contains individuals who can provide for the city's food, clothing, and housing. But this is the same city that Glaucon later objects to as overly simple and incomplete (372c–d). Given the prominence of the city–soul analogy throughout the *Republic*, Socrates seems to be hinting at 493b that the sophist's ideal soul is like an incomplete city: he only considers a limited portion of human desires and overlooks others. The sophist's characterization of the good as what is necessary is incomplete.

Nonetheless, the sophist has a theoretical position about the nature of the good for human beings. For while Socrates emphasizes the ignorance of the sophists – they "have not seen (*mêden eidôs*)" the distinction between the good and the necessary – he also gives a great deal of weight to their perception of themselves as possessing an art (*technê*) grounded upon what they believe to be wisdom (*sophia*). Socrates probably means by a *technê* the art of rhetoric that the sophist thinks he has and uses to manipulate the public. However, this *technê* is grounded upon *sophia*. The fact that Socrates says that one type of knowledge stems from another suggests that the sophist sees his art as based upon some other sort of knowledge separate from rhetoric itself. It seems reasonable to consider that this wisdom is a speculative or intellectual position that the sophist holds about the good.

The presentation of Thrasymachus in Book One is consistent with this understanding of the sophist. Thrasymachus has a theory as to why one sort of life is the best and gives an account of it.[21] He has a different theoretical stance toward the world, a set of moral commitments centered on the use of power to secure material advantages and honor for himself. His intellectual position might be an example of the *sophia* the sophist thinks he has, but his rhetoric is the *technê* that allows him to use this *sophia* and manipulate the "beast" of society. Like the sophist in Book Six, Thrasymachus seems to think that material desires define what is desirable.

From the point of view of the philosopher, then, the sophist is ignorant of the good itself or of an ethical distinction between what is truly desirable and what is necessary. But, from the point of view of the sophist, the sophist knows something that the many do not know. He "knows" that what the many call "just" or "unjust," "good" or "bad," are nothing more than fancy names for a certain set of desires. Understanding this about the "beast," the sophist, as he sees himself, has an advantage over the many; he can use it to his own advantage and teach others to have such an advantage.

To take a concrete example, the many might believe that the disfranchisement of those who fail to pay their debts is the just thing to do (a common punishment in Athens).[22] The many may see this loss of privileges

---

[21] As Beverslius points out, Thrasymachus "is credited with understanding both that definitions are important, and why." See Beversluis, *Cross-Examining*, 225.

[22] See Douglas MacDowell, *The Law in Classical Athens* (Ithaca, NY: Cornell University Press, 1986), 164–167.

as "just," perhaps believing only broadly that it is a fair punishment, but nonetheless believing that their claim has moral content. Perhaps at an earlier point in history the many agreed that disfranchisement was a threat to democracy – for example, if wealth were controlled by only a few. But the sophist "knows" as the many do not that this new belief about justice is only an expression of the natural human desire for wealth and power rather than any high-minded sense of justice. The sophist sees himself as possessing an advantage over the many in knowing this. He might feel free to use a variety of arguments to speak in favor of disfranchisement, reshaping whichever of the public's desires is most effective for his purposes – including those that appeal to abstract notions of justice – and letting go of an argument if it is ineffective or if public opinion changes. Furthermore, the sophist can take pride in his knowing that any controversy over "just" penalty for failure to pay debt is nothing more than a quarrel over different desires; he sees himself as in a privileged position compared with the "beast" who does not know better.

The sophist does not simply believe whatever the many believe, and he does not simply manipulate the many without ever considering whether there is a distinction between the necessary and the good. Rather, the sophist as Socrates presents him here seems to take the intellectual position that there is no such distinction; instead, what we call "good" is a reflection of a few necessary desires. The sophist sees himself as above the many, as possessing a body of knowledge, a *technê* that the many lack – that is, the ability to respond to and in turn shape the direction of others' desires. They think themselves far better than the many because they possess both the skills to do so and knowledge about the true nature of our desires. The main source of contention between the philosopher and sophist, then, becomes a dispute about the nature of desire itself. To be a philosopher for Plato implies a commitment to the claim that the soul (like the city) has other desires aside from the necessities of living – specifically, that there is a part of the soul that wants to know the forms.

In other words, what makes a philosopher different from the non-philosopher is that the philosopher loves and wants to know the forms. But nowhere in the *Republic* does Socrates prove the forms' existence; he only describes what they are like through a series of images (i.e., the sun, the divided line, and the cave). These images assert the existence of forms but do not provide details as to their nature as, for example, Aristotle does in his *Metaphysics*. Neither does Socrates imply that he has seen them; in fact, he cautions Glaucon that his opinions about the good might be wrong. Implying that he himself has not yet seen the forms,

Socrates describes what he is about to say as potentially "ugly," "blind," and "crooked" on account of its being a mere opinion rather than knowledge (506c–d). While Socrates might have caught a glimpse of the forms (and Plato does delve into more detailed issues of metaphysics in other dialogues such as the *Parmenides*), here Socrates explicitly denies the completeness to his knowledge. More significant than the philosopher's epistemological state about the forms is his self-awareness of his need for them, his being "turned toward" them, like the freed prisoner in the image of the cave.

One last place to look for the difference between the philosopher and the sophist in the *Republic* is in this image of the cave in Book Seven. The cave image is designed for the purpose of describing education, or the path of the prisoner from his complete ignorance to his emergence from the cave. Philosophical education is primarily about being reoriented away from the world of shadows and ordinary things to the world of the forms. Here, the philosopher is described as one who is freed from a kind of enslavement. (Presumably in the perfect city, philosopher–kings will not be enslaved since their educations will guide them toward the truth, while in the ordinary and imperfect world, even the potential philosopher is at first enslaved.) Knowledge is described as a kind of liberation, although the process of becoming free involved confusion, disorientation, and suffering before it ends in happiness. The prisoner's freedom arrives when someone else sets him free; another human being must release him from his chains and drag him up the rough and steep path out of the cave. While the philosopher is not dependent on the community as a whole – who are, for the most part, also enslaved – he is still dependent on whoever helps to free him from false goods. The experience of seeing the world outside of the cave is intensely personal, but his freedom still comes through another person (presumably, one who was previously freed). His education is not a "pouring in" of knowledge into an empty vessel but rather a "turning around" of the soul to reality.

The sophist is not mentioned by name in the cave image. However, there is a third group of people in the cave aside from the freed man and the shackled prisoners: those who are puppet-handlers who cast the shadows on the walls of the cave. No elaborate description is given of them other than that they are on a road, behind a low wall, and in front of the fire that allows them to cast shadows. The shadows on the cave wall come from "all kinds of artifacts" including "statues of men and other animals wrought from stone, wood, and every kind of material" (514b9–515a3). Some of the carriers make sounds while others do not.

Given the relative brevity of the description, many commentators reasonably choose to say little about the puppeteers. However, their presence
is quite strange for a couple of reasons. First, they raise the question as
to why there is a group of people who remain in the cave if they are
not imprisoned. Who are they? Do they not know of the existence of
the outside world? If they do, have they been outside? Second, where do
they get the images for making their artifacts: from the outside world or
elsewhere? And why do they actively manipulate the prisoners? Socrates
does not answer these questions directly, but his image gives some clues
as to an answer. Regardless, the presence of these puppeteers is significant since Plato need not have had a third group mediate between the
prisoners and the outside world. He easily could have made prisoners
another setting in which only see the shadows of reality, ignorant of what
casts these shadows. It is unnecessary for the epistemological point about
the forms to introduce individuals who manipulate the prisoners. Their
presence, therefore, seems important.

It is reasonable to consider that the sophist would be found among the
puppeteers, for the sophist has already been presented in Book Six as the
manipulator of public opinion. Others have argued that the puppeteers
are the poets,[23] in part because the term *thaumatopoios* here recalls the
term *thaumatos*, or poet. But Socrates does not use the more restrictive
term *poiêtês*, which would have suggested that he had only poets in mind.
The term *thaumatopoieô* more broadly refers to the idea "to work wonders" and has been used in reference to jugglers and acrobats as well as
orators. What is crucial in the use of the term here is that the speakers
are performers, those who *deliberately* cast shadows on the walls: if the
sophists are to be found anywhere in the cave, it must be among those
who manipulate others rather than among the freed men or the enslaved
audience. Socrates notes that they not only carry imitations of real things
but also provide the right sound effects for their audience, perhaps indicating those who practice public rhetoric. The many believe much of
what they do because of the sounds and images that the puppeteers provide for them. The prisoners are said to discuss the shadows they see,

[23] C. D. C. Reeve takes them to be moneymakers. See Reeve, *Philosopher-Kings: The Argument
of Plato's* Republic (Princeton, NJ: Princeton University Press, 1988). Howland and Bloom
take them to be poets. While the distinction between poet and sophist might seem to be
crucial in other contexts, it need not be for the more limited purpose of the cave analogy.
In terms of their commitments to knowledge, there are those who think of knowledge as
being oriented toward something outside of themselves, those who think of knowledge
as a human construction, and those who uncritically follow opinion.

so the puppets and statues might be the constructions in speech of the sophists, their *logoi*. The question as to what motivates the puppeteers is more difficult. Do the puppeteers know that there is an outside world and deliberately hide it from the imprisoned, or are they ignorant of the outside world as well?

I suggest that the puppeteers are ignorant of the outside world. Although it may seem difficult to believe that they could not know of its presence, Socrates does say that the path out of the cave is incredibly rough and steep and that the released prisoner must be dragged up it. (Even the released prisoner's curiosity about the artifacts he sees is insufficient to motivate further exploration (515d–e).) Socrates also claims that anyone who has seen the outside world will not want to return (516d–e); it would be difficult to explain why anyone who has seen the truth would return to casting images for others. In addition, all of the statues seem to have been created by human beings. Nothing entirely natural (e.g., from the world outside of the cave) is carried along the path in these descriptions; nor are the statues said to be of things that could only exist outside of the cave itself.[24] The specific examples given are of humans (who, of course, exist inside the cave) and of animals (who might reasonably be found in it). If this is true, then the sophists know that the prisoners are imprisoned but are still ignorant of the highest reality. Consistent with the description of the sophist discussed previously, the sophist is above the many since he possesses knowledge of how to manipulate the many, but he is ignorant of what is really good. The sophists live in a world that is entirely determined by the human being; to this extent, their understanding of the world is akin to that of Thrasymachus.

Again, the sophist holds an intermediate position between the philosopher, or the prisoner who escapes from the cave, and the many who never do so. The sophist understands that people believe in things that are changeable and reflective only of their own opinions. The ordinary person lacks an understanding of his own situation, while the sophist can see himself as superior to the prisoners because he does think that he knows (although he turns out to be woefully ignorant). The sophist believes that our desires are ultimately human-centered; he possesses freedom insofar as he manipulates rather than being manipulated. However, for Plato, the ultimate object of human desire is not ourselves but something external to us (i.e., the forms). The sophist does not possess true freedom precisely because his soul is not oriented toward an external truth apart

---

[24] See Howland, *Odyssey*, 139, who makes a similar point.

from his own desires. In fact, the sophist might be worse off than the newly released prisoner as the sophist is confident of his understanding of reality as human-centered, while the newly freed prisoner at least has realized his own ignorance. We see here again Plato's concern with the power of *logos*, which can both manipulate the crowd into believing in mere shadows and also help to turn around the soul to the forms. Plato's use of the cave image is a positive use of language to endorse the need for the human being to seek the forms, but the images cast on the cave wall *within* the *Republic*'s cave image remind us of the dangers of arguments that can just as easily lead us to untruth.

The *Republic* contributes to a separation of the philosopher and the sophist in three ways. First, the sophist equates the necessary and the good, or what Socrates considers "lower" desires. He does so because he thinks it is true; his evidence is that we can see from experience that individuals who successfully pursue their own desires are happier than those who do not. In contrast, the philosopher believes that there is often a distinction between what people think makes them happy and what really does. The philosopher understands his own desires more deeply than the sophist or the many, regardless of how much he knows about the forms. Although much of the *Republic* addresses this issue, Book Nine sums up the counterargument: different parts of the soul have different pleasures, but only the lover of wisdom has experienced all of the different types of pleasures and can see that the highest pleasure of all is seeing "what is" (582c–d). Socrates admits that not all people are aware of the pleasure of philosophical knowledge; there is no proof apart from actually taking part in philosophy to show that such activity is pleasurable.

Second, both the sophist and the philosopher pursue what they understand to be objects of wisdom. I suggested that the sophist's body of "knowledge" might include two things: first, the wisdom that there is no distinction between the desired and the desirable; and second, the means by which one can pursue one's desires effectively (e.g., rhetoric). Socrates, in contrast, states that the philosopher is specifically the person who loves "what is" and is unchanging. The philosopher by definition loves the forms, while the non-philosopher wanders among what is many and varies (485b1–3). The philosopher's and the sophist's understandings of human desire inform how each constructs a theoretical vision of the value of different objects in the world.

Third, certain key personality differences between the sophist and the philosopher reflect their different theoretical stances. The philosopher, in being oriented toward something outside of himself, is by definition always also committed to being in a state of becoming himself. That is, he is open in his soul to being changed and transformed by something utterly other than himself.[25] Again, Plato emphasizes the moral dimensions of the philosopher's theoretical commitment. Loving the forms is transformative even before the philosopher knows them, for his love of them leads him to be willing to be changed. There is always for the philosopher the possibility that not only his own opinions but also his soul, out of which these opinions arise, are in need of transformation. The sophist wishes to exert control over the changing world of politics but is not himself open to being changed by the forms or by other people with whom he is in conversation. While any given philosopher does not possess perfect knowledge, the sophist lacks self-knowledge and is not even oriented toward what could complete him.[26]

It is interesting that this distinction between the philosopher and the sophist only makes sense from the point of view of the philosopher. That is, to the philosopher, the sophist is something like an incomplete philosopher. But only the philosopher can know this because only the philosopher has the greater context of the whole for understanding what the human being really desires. From the point of view of the sophist, however, the philosopher might only appear to be a bad sophist. A sophist, lacking the commitment to forms or any other sort of knowledge to be sought apart from the human realm, will not define his activity as being distinct from philosophical activity because, on his view, philosophy is not a real possibility. At most, he might define the philosopher as someone unable to persuade, foolish in his metaphysical assumptions, or unskilled in practical argument. A sophist such as Thrasymachus, who contends that those who believe that a just life is good are naive fools, might even consider Socrates to be down among the "many" who are manipulated by the rhetorician. So, as Plato presents the problem, the distinction between the philosopher and the sophist is not merely reducible to two different competing intellectual positions about the "good." Instead, the way in which the distinction between philosophy and sophistry is understood depends upon one's prior theoretical stance – a theoretical vision defined less in terms of precise characterizations of the forms and more by understanding one's own deepest desires as a human being.

[25] At the same time, myths in the dialogues about recollection (e.g., in the *Meno* and *Phaedrus*) suggest that a turn into deeper aspects of oneself is also simultaneously a turn to the forms.

[26] See J. R. Peters, "Reason and Passion in Plato's *Republic*," *Ancient Philosophy* 9 (1989): 173–187, for an interesting look at Plato's concepts of reason and passion here.

As a result, the philosopher cannot teach in a direct way; the cave analogy suggests that the person who is to see the truth must be brought to see it for himself. Certain educational programs might prepare the student for a dialectical ascent (e.g., mathematics), but there is no substitute for "seeing" the good for oneself. One might, therefore, be tempted to say the following. The philosopher can make a clear distinction between what it means to be a sophist and what it means to be a philosopher, while the sophist cannot, insofar as he lacks knowledge of the forms. This might seem to "save" the possibility of a clear definition of the philosopher and of the sophist.

Recall, however, that Socrates claims that with respect to the forms, he must not speak of things that he does not know as if he did know them (506c). In some way or another, Socrates' knowledge of the forms is either absent or incomplete. So, there is no standpoint of absolute knowledge from which to separate the sophist from the philosopher. The philosopher who separates himself from the sophist is always doing so from a position of incompleteness himself. Still, Socrates tries to draw others in the dialogue to a life of justice and philosophical reflection. His rhetoric is grounded in his love of the forms but also relies upon finding ways of taking the desires of his audience and transforming those desires so that they might be redirected toward the forms. Through the images of the cave, the pilot of the ship, the philosopher dog, the sun, the divided line, and others, Socrates attempts to draw others to the life of philosophy by appealing to the goods that his audience already desires. In particular, we can see that Glaucon already desires certain goods that Socrates then connects to the philosophical life, which he presents as already embodying many of these same ideals.

As we saw previously, Socrates characterizes the ideal philosopher as an "insatiable" lover of learning who is courageous in war, loves honor, has a good memory, and learns easily. All these qualities are an excellent description of Glaucon as well.[27] Both Glaucon and Adeimantus were distinguished for their courage at the battle of Megara.[28] Glaucon

---

[27] See Robert Gallagher, "Protreptic Aims of Plato's *Republic*," *Ancient Philosophy* 24 (2004): 295–302, for an excellent account of how Socrates' rhetoric is oriented toward the soul of Glaucon. Also helpful is Mitchell Miller's discussion of mimetic irony in Miller, *Plato's Parmenides: The Conversion of the Soul* (University Park, PA: Pennsylvania State University Press, [1986] 1991), 4–5. Socrates often takes on the views of his interlocutors and tests them so that his interlocutors might see the consequences of their views.

[28] See Debra Nails, *The People of Plato* (Indianapolis and Cambridge: Hackett Publishing Company, 2002), 154–156.

especially seems to have enjoyed the praise that he received as a result. Socrates mentions that his lovers have written him poetry to praise him (368a), and Adeimantus tells us that Glaucon is a lover of victory (548d). Socrates also calls Glaucon an "erotic man" (474d), and even Glaucon realizes that Socrates is talking about him when Socrates uses the example of the man who loves boys of every type in order to explain the philosopher's love all of wisdom (474d–475a). Earlier, Glaucon suggested that the most successful military men should be allowed to kiss whomever they please (468b), further suggesting that Glaucon is an erotic soul. Glaucon was also known to be talented as a student of mathematics.[29]

Socrates' images of the sun, the cave, and the divided line can all be understood as working with desires in Glaucon's soul and refocusing those desires on the forms rather than on lower goods. For example, Socrates describes the sun as the most honorable (*timiôteron*) of all the things that "yoke" together powers and their objects (508a).[30] The form of the good has tremendous "dignity" and "power," a statement that has persuasive effect on Glaucon. In response to Socrates' remarks about the form of the good, Glaucon says that Socrates has spoken with "demonic excess" but soon after insists that Socrates not stop speaking about the good (509b–d). Glaucon is himself an excessive sort of person and so finds Socrates' high-minded remarks about the form of the good as akin to the sun appealing.

The divided-line image, of course, uses the mathematical imagery of a divided line segment in order to describe the forms, and mathematicals are the class of objects just shy of the best objects of knowledge on the line – that is, the forms. Geometrical objects are described as being given "honor" here as well (511a). Socrates hints at the way in which philosophical dialectic is even better than the noble enterprise of mathematics, insofar as it acts as a springboard to reach what is entirely free of hypothesis, while mathematics remains reliant upon hypotheses (511b–d). Glaucon is actively engaged and interested throughout Socrates' discussion of the forms in Book Six. Again, Socrates seems to use what Glaucon already cares about – mathematical objects – and then uses this imagery to draw him even closer to the forms; in effect, to go one step beyond the math that he already loves to the next higher stage.

Moreover, in the cave image, Socrates presents the freed philosopher as someone who possesses many of the traits that Glaucon values. Socrates

---

[29] See Gallagher, "Protreptic Aims," 304–306.
[30] See Gallagher, "Protreptic Aims," 307.

compares the philosopher to the Athenian ideal of a free man, while the non-philosopher is put in the class of a passive prisoner. Whereas in the *Apology* Socrates suggests that all human beings are similarly ignorant in a more democratic fashion, here Socrates emphasizes how very different the freed prisoner is from those who remain in chains. The freed prisoner or philosopher is literally elevated above the poor prisoners who remain shackled in chains, as he ascends from the cave into the outside world. Again, one easily could imagine Glaucon's interest in this revised version of aristocracy, in which the "best" are defined by what they know rather than by their social class, rank, or political power. While the newly freed philosopher is initially in pain and distress, his struggle might very well have a strong appeal to Glaucon, who seems to enjoy the challenges of both military battle and the pursuit of lovers. Socrates' emphasis on the difficulty posed to the person who is to be freed from his enslavement to ordinary desires is less likely to be a deterrent than an appeal to someone of Glaucon's temperament. By the end of the presentation of the cave image, Glaucon is in agreement with Socrates that the prudent man must see the idea of the good in order to act well (517c). Socrates seems to have awakened in Glaucon a desire to know the forms.

Through these images, Socrates uses a rhetoric that is attentive to his audience's current desires to inspire them to take up philosophy. Like the sophist, Socrates uses the opinions and commitments of his audience in order to attempt to persuade them. However, Socrates does so not to elevate his own status, to achieve political power, to earn money, or to be in a position to fulfill his own appetites. Instead, Socrates himself is like the freed person who descends back into the cave in order to free others: his descent into the Piraeus from Athens and entry into the house of Cephalus are akin to that freed prisoner's return to the cave. Like the philosopher–king who paints what he knows of justice onto the souls of his city (501a), Socrates artfully attends to the souls of his audience – not by wiping them clean of all of their desires but by reorienting those desires to the forms through helping his interlocutors to attend to their own desires more carefully. While the philosopher's ability to persuade relies on his audience's desires as much as the rhetorician's, he seeks to connect those current desires with the person's still hidden desires for the forms. The philosopher's goal is not to lift up himself over others but rather to bring others to his own level as a seeker of the forms.

In this way, not only the sophist but also the philosopher value rhetoric. Socrates uses a variety of images to describe the ultimate nature of reality as the philosopher sees it. Socrates' images are almost all universally concerned with the importance of the soul's connection to what is out-side of it – that is, with a commitment to the unchanging truth of the forms as opposed to the self-interested desires of the sophist. Even so, his rhetoric is not clearly based upon secure and complete knowledge of the forms, for Socrates himself lacks this. It differs from sophistic rhetoric in the philosopher's *love* of the forms as the true objects of desire and in the philosopher's understanding of his own desires. In other words, the philosopher's differentiation of the sophist from himself begins with love and the soul's longing for the forms. Love, more than knowledge, defines the soul of the philosopher in the *Republic*.

6

Philosophers, Sophists, and Strangers in the *Sophist*

I.

If one were to seek a definitive answer to the contrast between the sophist and the philosopher, one might naturally turn to Plato's *Sophist*. The dialogue enumerates a number of collections and divisions, ending with a specific definition of the sophist. The dialogue's final definition of the sophist has the Stranger declaring that they have reached the truth about his nature:

> The man, then, who has arisen from the contradiction-making art of the dissembling part of the opining art – the imitative man – who himself has sprung from the apparition-making kind descended from the image-making art and has marked off for himself the portion of making, not divine but human, that makes wonders in speeches – whoever claims that the sophist in his very being is of this "breed and blood" will, it seems, speak the utter truth (*talêthestata*) (268c–d).[1]

However, despite the Stranger's own sense of clarity about his definition of the sophist, Plato's own voice in the dialogue is more difficult to discern. Unlike most Platonic dialogues, in which Socrates is a major speaker, here Socrates sits silently at the feet of the Eleatic Stranger as he performs diaresis and explores metaphysics. The identity of this stranger is mysterious. While other dialogues such as the *Theaetetus* often give us detailed accounts of their character's personalities or biographies, the Stranger is never full explained. We know little about him, other than that he is from

---

[1] Translations are from *Plato's Sophist: The Professor of Wisdom*, translated by Eva Brann, Peter Kalvakage, and Eric Salem (Newburyport, MA: Focus Publishing, 1996).

Elea. In addition, the drama of the *Sophist* is part of a longer sequence of dialogues. This conversation between the Stranger and Theaetetus takes place one day after the *Theaetetus'* conversation between Socrates and Theaetetus. The *Statesman* takes place one day after that of the *Sophist*. Socrates sits at the feet of the Stranger, silent, for all but the first few pages of the *Sophist*. His dramatic presence and particularly his uncharacteristic silence ought to be puzzling to readers of the dialogue. The dialogue especially invites us to compare the way in which the Stranger speaks to Theaetetus with Socrates' own conversation with Theaetetus the day before.[2]

In this chapter, I argue that part of Plato's purpose in the *Sophist* and *Theaetetus* is to offer two different accounts of the nature of philosophy. Plato engages his audience in a reflection upon the nature of philosophy through the contrast between Socrates' and the Stranger's ways of speaking. I focus on two main questions about the *Sophist*. First, how is the Stranger's character and way of speaking distinct from Socrates' character and speech in the *Theaetetus*? Second, how do the divisions and collections of the *Sophist* illuminate some of the differences between Socrates and the Stranger? I argue that the Eleatic Stranger is deliberately presented as an enigmatic figure who may alternately be identified as either a sophist or a philosopher. While the Stranger defines sophistry in such a way that he would separate his own activity from that of the sophists, the drama of the dialogue suggests that Socrates would *not* consider the Stranger to be a philosopher. That is, the dialogues function to draw us into the philosophical question of what philosophy is. The *Sophist* and *Theaetetus* as a pair demonstrate that the philosopher–sophist contrast is relative to the way in which one constructs a positive understanding of philosophy.[3] I argue that the Stranger's understanding of himself as a philosopher is inadequate from Socrates' standpoint, although the Stranger seems to identify himself as a philosopher. While the Stranger identifies philosophy with a method of division and collection, and especially with applying that method to metaphysical questions, Socrates emphasizes self-knowledge and knowledge of the human soul and its moral good as

---

[2] For a different take on the links between these dialogues, see Blondell, *Play of Character*, which argues that Plato uses the Eleatic Stranger in the *Sophist* to go beyond his philosophical "father," Socrates to a more mature vision of philosophy (386).

[3] Here, I set aside the *Statesman* to keep my focus on the philosopher–sophist contrast; however, Plato is as interested in the philosopher–statesman and the sophist–statesman contrasts as the ones that I explore herein.

central to philosophical practice.[4] Both Socrates and the Stranger are interested in persuasion, but Socrates' rhetoric is to be found in the role of a midwife who is helping others to give birth to ideas and to grow in self-knowledge, while the Stranger's rhetoric is oriented toward making his interlocutor more compliant and dispassionate.

II.

The most striking feature of the Stranger is how very little information about him we receive in the course of the *Sophist*. He truly remains a stranger to us as well as to his audience within the dialogue. We know that the Stranger comes from Elea and associates with Parmenides' and Zeno's circle, but these social and geographic ties do not automatically identify him as a philosopher. Aristotle certainly treats Parmenides and Zeno as philosophers, particularly insofar as their thinking helps to illuminate our understanding of the nature of being. However, we should hesitate immediately to classify the Stranger as a philosopher simply because he associates with those whom Aristotle views as philosophical. Plato emphasizes not only the metaphysical questions of the Eleatics but also their refutational style with Socrates' remark that the Stranger may be a "refuting god" (216b). He links such refutative practice to the divine, suggesting that the Stranger might be a god in disguise, like the gods in Homer who come down in order to refute human beings "since we are feeble at giving accounts" (216b). Socrates alludes to the Homeric idea of Zeus as protector of strangers who "looks down on both outrages and lawful conduct" (216b). A god might appear as a human being in disguise with a view to examining whether others are being just to others or not. Socrates suggests that it is unclear whether the Stranger should properly be understood as a mortal or a god, as a stranger or as a divine protector of strangers.

Plato does not clarify the problem but rather only muddies the waters when Theodorus suggests that the Stranger is "not a god, though certainly

---

[4] Catherine Zuckert also addresses this question of the differences between the philosopher and the sophist in Plato's *Sophist*. She argues that if philosophy is knowledge, then neither Socrates nor the Stranger is a philosopher, but together they can be viewed as two different ways of being able to offer accounts of the world, without either one being capable of accounting for everything. I am indebted to her insights here. However, Zuckert remains with the *Sophist* for her analysis, while I examine the *Sophist*'s methodology in contrast to that of the *Theaetetus*. See Zuckert, "Who's a Philosopher? Who's a Sophist? The Stranger vs. Socrates," *The Review of Metaphysics* 54 (September 2000): 65–97.

godlike" and then calls him a philosopher. Theodorus specifically links the philosopher to those who are moderate and who avoid polemics (*tas eridas*; 216b). But Socrates responds that identifying the philosopher is as difficult as identifying a god in disguise. Philosophers seem to be of different worth to different people and appear sometimes as statesmen, sometimes as sophists, and sometimes as mad (216d). Socrates then asks this Stranger to identify the sophist, statesman, and philosopher. Socrates here raises questions not only about whether Theodorus is right that the Stranger is a philosopher but also whether there is any clear rule for identifying the philosopher. The problem is not only how to discern the philosopher's nature but also the deeper problem as to what the right questions are to ask about the philosopher's identity. Is he to be identified by his knowledge, his way of speaking, the moderation or madness of his soul, or the subject matter that he studies? The dialogue does not provide an immediate and clear answer to this question. By promoting rather than resolving confusion, Plato draws his own reader into the process of asking who the philosopher is – in particular, whether the Stranger is a sophist, philosopher, a statesman, or even a madman.

Neither does Plato give us a clear portrait of the Stranger as a character. Plato does not offer any stories of courage in battle, past successes or failures of the Stranger, or any sort of history. The Stranger does not get angry, blush, or otherwise reveal his emotions, as so many Platonic characters do. He remains difficult to see. I suggest that one reason that Plato keeps us in the dark about the Stranger is that this very fact – the absence of any clear relevance of the Stranger's "person" or "character" in his discourse – is what Plato wants us to notice about him. While Socrates' discourse is informed by his character, the Stranger is peculiarly absent from his own discourse. He does not bring himself to his speech but rather abstracts the problem of philosophy, sophistry, and statesmanship from himself as an individual.

We learn considerably more about the Stranger's understanding of good speech than we learn of his character, however. When Socrates asks the Stranger whether he prefers to give a long account, like Parmenides, or to ask short questions, he replies: "When the person to whom the conversation is directed is unirritating and compliant, Socrates, the easier way to go through it is with another. If not, by oneself is easier" (217c–d). Socrates suggests that a suitable partner in conversation might be Theaetetus – an interlocutor who showed himself just the day before to be an acute thinker, capable of modifying his definitions of knowledge in response to Socrates. The Stranger thinks that a longer account is more appropriate to answer this sort of question, but that he would be ashamed to give a long display when they have just now met (217d). That is, he sees the deficiency of a long speech as a matter of good manners. The Stranger agrees to engage in question and answer with Theaetetus but says that if the work ends up being too difficult for the youth, then Theaetetus will be to blame, not the Stranger (217d–218a). The Stranger's preference for a complaint interlocutor suggests that his aim is to present his own position to others and to persuade them rather than to test or to refute his own or others' ideas.[5]

We can contrast the Stranger's preference for a compliant interlocutor to Socrates' requests to Theaetetus the previous day. To begin, Socrates is interested in Theaetetus' character. Socrates tells Theodorus that he wishes to know whether there are any promising young men in Athens. Theodorus thinks that Theaetetus is a talented young man; in describing him to Socrates, Theodorus gives a long explanation of both his moral and intellectual virtues. Socrates follows up by asking whose son Theaetetus is, remarking upon the young man's good family (144b). Plato, too, emphasizes Theaetetus' courage in battle at the end of his life, by giving a dramatic frame to the dialogue that has Theaetetus' contemporaries witness to his courage and civic devotion. Later, in their discussion of knowledge, Socrates frequently encourages Theaetetus to bring himself to the conversation. Rather than offering his own ways of dividing up knowledge, Socrates asks Theaetetus to answer the question, "What is knowledge?" (146c).

Certainly, Socrates guides Theaetetus and is active in directing the line of questioning. When Theaetetus later defines knowledge as perception, it is Socrates and not Theaetetus who associates this definition with the theories of Protagoras, Heraclitus, and others. Socrates clearly brings his own thoughts to their discussion. However, Socrates does not initially offer the framework of categories by which a definition of knowledge is to be given. He does not, for example, divide up knowledge into two or three classes and then ask Theaetetus to classify mathematical knowledge into those preformulated categories. Instead, Theaetetus must at least make the beginnings of how to conceive of the project as a whole.

Socrates insists that Theaetetus look into himself in order to offer answers to these questions. When Theaetetus thinks that he cannot offer a good answer to the question, Socrates encourages him: "You must put your whole heart into what we are doing – in particular into this matter

---

5 See Zuckert, "Who's a Philosopher?," 70, who makes a similar point.

of getting a statement of what knowledge really is" (148d). Socrates responds to Theaetetus' initial frustration with the description of himself as a midwife who will help Theaetetus to give birth; Theaetetus is pregnant with an idea and has something of his own to offer to the conversation. Later, when Theaetetus revises his definition of knowledge as true judgment, Socrates praises him for his goodwill and willingness to answer (187b–c). Socrates continually encourages and praises Theaetetus for his willingness to search out his own soul for ideas about knowledge. Socrates encourages Theaetetus to bring curiosity, passion, and courage to inquiry. Although Theaetetus is a mathematician who values abstract inquiry, Socrates pushes Theaetetus to use these other personal qualities in his philosophical inquiry. Socrates guides Theaetetus into learning more than a definition of knowledge; he also helps him to understand further what qualities are required for the process of seeking knowledge.

Socrates also brings his love of virtue and of his own city to the conversation. While the opening frame of the *Theaetetus* tells of Theaetetus' virtues, the first words between Socrates and Theodorus reveal much about Socrates. He begins, "If Cyrene were first in my affections, Theodorus, I should be asking you how things are there, and whether any of your young people are taking up geometry or any branch of philosophy. But, as it is, I love Athens better than Cyrene, and so I'm more anxious to know which of our young men shows signs of turning out well" (143d). Socrates shows himself to be different from the Stranger in his loyalty to and love of Athens. Socrates remains at home in Athens and does not venture abroad to speak, while the Stranger is a *xenos*, a foreigner, who seems to have little interest in Athens. In fact, when Theodorus introduces the Stranger, he states not that he is from Elea but that his "kin" are from Elea (216a). While the Stranger spends time with those in the Eleatic circle, Theodorus emphasizes that he is more moderate in refutation than the others; he is not especially committed to the Eleatics' way of speaking either. The Stranger stands alone as an unnamed person from an unnamed place.

Socrates, however, is both an insider and an outsider in Athens. On the one hand, Socrates is the biting gadfly who seeks to rouse the city from its slumber; to this extent, he stands outside or above the city and criticizes it. On the other hand, Socrates is deeply committed to Athens; his role as outsider stems from his great love of his city and from his desire that his fellow citizens become more virtuous. This love of his fellow citizens motivates Socrates to ask whether there are any promising young Athenians. Socrates listens attentively to Theodorus' description of Theaetetus as mentally quick, gentle, and courageous (144a–144b). These qualities make Theaetetus an excellent interlocutor. Unlike Charmides, Critias, Laches, Meno, and most other interlocutors, Theaetetus shows a remarkable resourcefulness in his answers and displays a combination of moderation and courage that, as Theodorus says, is so difficult to find. Theaetetus is moderate enough to know that he probably does not have an adequate definition of knowledge but courageous enough to offer up new definitions repeatedly anyway, with Socrates' encouragement. Theaetetus displays neither the self-assured arrogance of Meno nor the intellectual timidity of Charmides. Socrates' concern to know something about the nature of his different interlocutors sets him apart from the Stranger. The Stranger speaks to Theaetetus because he needs an interlocutor – anyone would seem to do – while Socrates speaks to Theaetetus because of his promise as a courageous, moderate, and intelligent person. That is, Socrates exhibits a kind of love and care for Theaetetus as an individual with attention to his specific character traits; this concern is absent from the Stranger's attitude toward Theaetetus.

This care of his interlocutor and desire to make him into a better person distinguishes Socrates' rhetoric from that of the Stranger.[6] While both the Stranger and Socrates use question and answer, their aims with their interlocutors are entirely different. Socrates' description of himself as a midwife is particularly revealing of how he sees his own role as questioner. Three qualities especially stand out in Socrates' image of the midwife. First, he says that, like a midwife, his method here is only for those who are "pregnant" with an idea. Not all interlocutors are equally able; not all will benefit from the same sorts of questions. Socrates chooses his interlocutors carefully and suggests that his method with the "pregnant" Theaetetus might not be appropriate for a different kind of interlocutor. For example, if Socrates' wish were to diminish hubris in an arrogant interlocutor, he might not act as encouragingly as he does with Theaetetus. As we have seen, Socrates refutes people such as Callias or Thrasymachus partly in order to moderate their excessive senses of self-worth. Here, Socrates spends a good deal of time encouraging a bright and intellectually curious – but not always self-assured – Theaetetus. The Stranger seems entirely indifferent to the development of Theaetetus' character or the young man's views in relation to his character.

---

[6] See Stanley Rosen, *Plato's Sophist: The Drama of Original and Image* (New Haven and London: Yale University Press, 1983), 20, which also notes the difference between Socrates' attentiveness to the souls of his interlocutors and the Stranger's relative indifference.

Second, Socrates uses the image of the midwife in order to assert his understanding of himself as ignorant. He reminds Theaetetus that the best midwives are barren and no longer give birth themselves; instead, they aid others in giving birth to ideas. Socrates does not use question and answer as a way to simply present his own ideas to Theaetetus but rather asks questions in order to get Theaetetus to see whether he has a true child or a "phantom" (*Theaetetus* 150b). This language of mistaken identity, of phantoms, to describe the state of human knowledge is reminiscent of the *Sophist*'s claim that the sophist, philosopher, and statesman appear to be like one another. But Socrates identifies the root of the problem in the limits of human knowledge itself. His admission of his own ignorance is an acknowledgment of a truth about the limits of humanity. Socrates states that God "has forbidden me to procreate. So that I am not in any sense a wise man; I cannot claim as the child of my own soul any discovery worth the name of wisdom" (150c–d). Theaetetus also discovers through the course of the dialogue that he does not perfectly grasp the nature of knowledge. The Stranger, however, never admits to any shortcomings in himself during his inquiry. He is confident that he can solve the difficult problem of distinguishing the philosopher and the sophist. He tackles difficult metaphysical questions with apparent ease. The *Sophist* ends with a final definition of the sophist, while many Socratic inquiries end aporetically (e.g., the *Laches, Charmides, Euthyphro, Meno, Protagoras,* and *Theaetetus* itself). But Socrates' aim is not only to find a good definition of knowledge. Instead, his care is for his interlocutor, whom he hopes will recognize the value or the shortcomings of himself and his ideas. Socrates promotes the self-knowledge of his interlocutors along with encouraging better understanding of the topic at hand. He encourages in Theaetetus genuine humility – that is, telling the truth about one's self to one's self and to others. Socrates' open admission of his own ignorance makes him an exemplar of philosophical humility.

Third, Socrates suggests that he, like other midwives, takes on the role of a "matchmaker" who can see how to "sow" the right crops or prepare the soil for planting (149e).[7] Socrates acts like a matchmaker insofar as he chooses lines of questioning that help to illuminate something about his interlocutor's ideas. For example, when Theaetetus proposes that knowledge is perception, Socrates introduces the ideas of Protagorean

---

[7] See Scott Hemmenway, "Philosophical Apology in the *Theaetetus,*" *Interpretation* 17 (3) (1990): 323–346, for an excellent discussion of midwifery in the dialogue.

relativism. While Theaetetus may not have had Protagoras in mind when he offered his definition, Protagoras' theory helps to develop Theaetetus' ideas in more detail. Socrates does not act as a proponent of the theory but rather uses Protagorean ideas in order to get Theaetetus to learn more about the philosophical problems associated with treating knowledge as perception – for example, the difficulty of making universal judgments in such a theory.[8] Again, the Stranger seems more interested in the interlocutor's answers as support for his own ideas, while Socrates offers the thought of Protagoras, Heraclitus, and others as ways to explore and to develop his interlocutor's ideas.

Matchmaking might also include finding the right partners in conversation for one another.[9] For example, Socrates and Theaetetus make better partners than do Theodorus and Theaetetus. One reason given that Theodorus is not a good interlocutor is that he is not willing to strip down naked and make himself vulnerable in order to wrestle; he prefers to keep his cloak on, he says (169b–c). In other words, he does not wish to be self-revealing. Again, we can see how personally Socrates treats philosophical conversation in Socrates' use of the erotic images of childbirth and naked wrestling; in both images, the interlocutor shows himself in ways that might make him vulnerable, in fact, most likely *will* make him vulnerable to criticism. The Stranger, in contrast, remains dispassionate in how he speaks to Theaetetus, who is not asked to reveal much of himself.

We see, then, in the dramatic characterizations of Socrates and the Stranger several important differences in how they each understand their own practice. Socrates presents himself not primarily as the possessor of positive ideas about the nature of knowledge but as a midwife who exhibits care for the development of his interlocutor's ideas and character. Socrates regards himself as an educator more than as a metaphysician. The Stranger treats interlocutors as compliant partners who will assist him in his search for the sophist. He strongly identifies the ability to reach a final answer to a question as a mark of success. Socrates identifies philosophy closely with self-knowledge and humility. In general, the Stranger's idea of success is strongly oriented toward the content of the answers given. Socrates' questions to Theaetetus are always simultaneously about

---

[8] See Marina Berzins McCoy, "Reason and Dialectic in the Argument against Protagoras in the *Theaetetus*," *International Philosophical Quarterly* 45 (1) (March 2005): 21–39.

[9] This theme of finding a good guide is also raised in the *Myth of Er* in the *Republic* and in *Alcibiades I*.

the content of Theaetetus' ideas and Theaetetus' self-understanding as one who searches for but has not fully arrived at the truth.[10]

III.

The Stranger's and Socrates' verbal descriptions of their methods and of philosophy also reveal significant differences in their approaches. The Stranger indicates his understanding of the interplay between himself and Theaetetus as follows:

> But in common (*koinêi*) with me you're now to join the investigation, starting first, as it appears to me, from the sophist; and you're to search for and make apparent in speech whatever he is. For right now you and I have only the name in common about this fellow; but each of us may have, for ourselves, his own private notion of the job (*pragma*) we call by that name. But we must always and about everything be in agreement with each other (*sunômologêsthai*) about the thing itself through accounts rather than about the name alone apart from an account (218c–d).

Here, the Stranger reveals at least three of his assumptions about the nature of good inquiry. First, the Stranger emphasizes the need to find what is in common (*koinos*) between Theaetetus and himself. He is interested in agreement and harmony in their discourse. Second, the Stranger identifies the main obstacle to finding a common definition as two competing private notions that each of them might hold. That is, the Stranger assumes that Theaetetus has a clear idea of the sophist's activity; the key problem is whether the two of them are using the same name for the same thing. Philosophy is about finding the right correspondence between a name and an idea; this is what it means to give a good account. Third, as he makes divisions, the Stranger will assume without question that the "thing" (*pragma*) that defines the sophist is his activity rather than his character, theoretical commitments, or method, for example. All of the Stranger's divisions in the dialogue are guided by these three assumptions.

However, each of these three assumptions about the nature of good inquiry is called into question in the *Theaetetus*. To begin, Socrates is not interested in getting Theaetetus to agree with him. His goal in the dialogue is expressly to test Theaetetus' ideas. Socrates is insistent that he

---

[10] Perhaps this is also why Socrates is so much more playful with his interlocutors than the Stranger is with his, as authors such as Rosen have noted (see Rosen, *Plato's Sophist*, 22). Socrates jokes around with his companions, enjoying their presence as persons as well as others looking for the truth.

does not simply present his own views in the dialogue; he does present ideas, however, that are helpful in fleshing out or testing Theaetetus' ideas (157c). As in the *Protagoras,* both Socrates and his interlocutor contribute to the development of the ideas. But the way in which Socrates tests Theaetetus' ideas is through opposition, not harmony. Socrates deliberately poses counterexamples to Theaetetus' definitions, and even counterexamples to his counterexamples. For instance, Socrates opposes the ideas of Protagorean relativism by countering that the authority of good judgment seems impossible if we grant the idea that all knowledge is relative (161c–162a). Then, although Socrates clearly sees deficiencies in the Protagorean view, he goes on to "rescue" Protagoras' "orphaned" argument. If Protagoras were present, Socrates says, he would argue that wisdom is still possible but ought to be understood as the ability to change a worse perception to a better one rather than as knowledge of the truth (166d–167e). Later, Socrates continues to provide counterarguments to Theaetetus' other definitions, with the result that Theaetetus develops new and better (if still incomplete) accounts of the nature of knowledge. These oppositions aid Theaetetus in developing his own ideas about knowledge. While the dialogue ends aporetically, it is clear that Theaetetus progresses in his understanding of knowledge. For example, his definition of knowledge as perception does not address the issue of whether judgment is a part of knowledge, whereas his later definitions do. Earlier definitions exclude the question of interpersonal communication, while his last definition requires that those who know can give an account of their ideas to others. Much of the forward movement of each subsequent definition arises from Socrates' positing ideas in opposition to the ones currently on the table.

Socrates suggests that there is one kind of agreement for which Theaetetus ought to be looking: the internal agreement of his ideas with one another. Whereas if the two of them were wise, they could engage in sophistical arguments, because they are only ordinary men, they will instead have to examine their "thoughts themselves in relation to themselves, and see what they are – whether, in our opinion, they agree with one another or are entirely at variance" (154e). Socrates emphasizes that Theaetetus must care for whether or not his own ideas are consistent more than concerning himself with whether his ideas harmonize with others' ideas.[11] At the same time, Socrates' use of opposition in argument helps

---

[11] As Rosen points out, consistency is important for Socrates and Theaetetus here but might be only of secondary importance for a sophist, who might value the efficacy of persuasion over logical consistency. See Rosen, *Plato's Sophist,* 139.

him to see the limitations in his understanding and to grow in his knowledge of his limits as well as his abilities. The Stranger sees the agreement of ideas as relatively easy because he assumes that each person has a clear internal idea of the question at hand.

Thus, when the Stranger begins the division into kinds, he places the sophist into the category of "hunters." From the beginning of his series of divisions, the Stranger assumes that the sophist is a person who seeks out young men in some way that is analogous to those who hunt animals. While what it means to "hunt" is not yet been made clear and must be clarified through further divisions, we might also wonder whether this categorization of the sophist as a hunter is adequate to describe Theaetetus' understanding of the sophists after the discussion of the previous day. For example, the *Theaetetus* presents Protagoras as an intellectual who proposes an innovative understanding of concepts such as truth and goodness. Nowhere in the *Theaetetus* do we see Protagoras as primarily concerned with hunting down young men for financial gain. Still, other dialogues such as the *Protagoras* or the *Gorgias* emphasize how the sophists attract and compete for students – Protagoras' claim that he will not teach his students arithmetic, astronomy, literature, and other superfluous studies as other sophists do is clearly a pitch to attract new students (*Protagoras* 318e). Theaetetus' understanding of the sophists is likely to be complicated, especially after his conversation with Socrates about Protagoras. He might reasonably see them as part intellectual, part schoolteacher, and part rhetorician or might even be confused as to whether Protagoras is a sophist or a philosopher. "Hunting" is unlikely to capture the full range of what Theaetetus thinks about the sophist's activity. Neither would the final definition of the sophist as an imitator who relies on false appearances necessarily help Theaetetus to make full sense of what he knows of Protagoras, for Socrates presents him more as a thinker with an inadequate theory than as a person who deliberately dissembles.

Moreover, the Stranger's divisions do not easily lend themselves to asking normative questions about the sophist's activity. Even if the sophist is a hunter, Theaetetus might still want to know what constitutes good or bad hunting, or what sorts of things are proper objects to hunt. While the Stranger revises his categories throughout the *Sophist*, his questions are centered on whether they have found the correct category and not the normative value of those categories. While the metaphysical sections of the dialogue delve deeply into the question of being, they do not address the moral or political problems attached to false appearances. The Stranger's concerns in the *Sophist* remain abstract and never link metaphysical questions to the personal or political. This absence of the person from the discussion of metaphysics stands in contrast to Socratic dialogues in which Socrates relates the forms to love of the good and the well-being of the city (as in the *Republic*); friendship, politics, and the creative arts (as in the *Symposium*); or the moral consequences of hedonism (as in the *Philebus*).

The *Theaetetus* also makes problematic the Stranger's view that knowledge is about finding a way to make a private notion public, through finding a common definition. The Stranger assumes that each person already has a notion of what the sophist is, and that his task is to find the right words to correspond to the right idea. The image of the aviary in the Theaetetus addresses problems with regarding knowledge in this way. Socrates uses the image shortly after Theaetetus has defined knowledge as "true judgment" (187b). One difficulty with this definition is that while false judgments seem to be possible, it seems impossible to say consistently that one can know things that one does not know, or that one can judge what is not (188a–189b). Instead, false judgment must be "a kind of 'other-judging,'" when a man, in place of one of the things that are, has substituted in his thought another of the things that are and asserts that it is" (189c). In other words, false judgment would seem to be placing the wrong object into the category under discussion – for example, calling an ugly thing beautiful or vice versa (189c). The Stranger's method of defining things according to categories relies on a similar assumption. He is explicit that good definition is a matter of matching up each private notion with a public, common name (218d). A false definition of the sophist would then be placing the sophist into the wrong category – for example, calling him a hunter of animals instead of men or categorizing him as one who makes likenesses rather than apparitions. Later, the Stranger attempts to find the right way of talking about non-Being, so that speech might be rescued (259a–260a). For the Stranger, philosophy is closely connected to the possibility of consistent speech (260a).

But Socrates goes on to test this model of knowledge with Theaetetus. While he makes a number of criticisms, one is particularly relevant here. Socrates distinguishes between the "possession" of knowledge and "having" it through comparing knowledge to an aviary. Whenever someone has taken possession of knowledge, he can be said to have put this knowledge into a "pen" along with other "pieces of knowledge," like birds kept in an aviary (197e–198a). Knowing a particular thing is a matter of possessing it in one's aviary (198b). False judgment, then, is a matter of grabbing the wrong piece of knowledge when one is seeking another. Again, this view of knowledge would be consistent with the Stranger's description and practice of trying to make the right internal idea match up to its proper external name. However, the aviary is eventually rejected as an inadequate account of false judgment, for it seems to make a person ignorant on account of his knowledge (199b). That is, if one grabs the wrong piece of knowledge (e.g., taking "five" as the solution to 2 + 2 instead of "four"), then one's knowledge of five is somehow responsible for the mistake. Socrates says we are left with the absurdity of claiming that one's knowledge of five has produced ignorance. But it seems then that the person did not know five after all; and yet, it is in his "aviary" precisely because he does know it. While Theaetetus suggests that there might be pieces of "ignorance" flying around in the aviary, this too leads to absurdity since the problem of identifying ignorant pieces and the knowledge pieces only pushes back the question of judgment one more level. We must still find a coherent way to talk about distinguishing between true and false judgment. In short, Socrates suggests that viewing knowledge as simply matching up the right words to the right internal idea is insufficient. The Stranger's understanding of good definition as putting the right name on the right idea falls prey to this same criticism. The Stranger cannot explain how to identify whether one has chosen the right or the wrong definition of the sophist from among a variety of possibilities. That is, he gives no rules or method for determining when the correct answer has been found; there is no guarantee that the right "internal idea" will be plucked from within his or Theaetetus' mind. Neither does a harmony between the Stranger's and Theaetetus' ideas guarantee the correct answer since they might both be ignorant of the sophist but believe themselves to know.

Interestingly, in developing his image of the aviary, Socrates uses the same language of hunting found in the *Sophist*. But here, the division is not into the different kinds of objects hunted (e.g., human or animal). Instead, the division is between two different phases of hunting: initially catching knowledge in order to possess it and then catching it from one's aviary in order to make it present (198d). The object is the same in each phase, but the way in which it is hunted is different; the initial experience of learning is distinct from recollecting knowledge already possessed. Moreover, Socrates is also said to always be on the lookout for promising young men with whom to speak (143d). The opening of the *Protagoras* has a friend asking Socrates whether he is on the hunt for Alcibiades (309a). Socrates seems to hunt for men with whom to converse, whom he hopes to benefit through conversation, and yet his hunting has a different purpose than hunting others for his own gain. Plato, then, presents the possibility of understanding hunting in more than two ways in these dialogues. The divisions that the Stranger makes are not the only kinds that could be made within the category of hunting. Part of what is reflected in the process of making cuts and separating ideas into different kinds are the sorts of things that are valued by the person making the cut. In the *Theaetetus*, Socrates uses the image of hunting to explain the difference between learning and remembering in order to illuminate something about false judgment. The Stranger treats hunting as if there were only two kinds (animal and human) and that he has correctly identified them. What is a useful metaphor for Socrates – one used to unfold some of Theaetetus' ideas about knowledge – takes a greater ontological importance in the Stranger's scheme. Socrates' divisions are valuable tools for discerning whether Theaetetus' ideas will stand up to testing, but Socrates claims no permanence for these categories. They disappear once they have been used for good purpose. Again, Socrates' use of division here exhibits his attention to the right moment (*kairos*). His division of hunting into two kinds is rhetorical and practical insofar as his aim is to act as a midwife who aids *Theaetetus*. The Stranger treats bifurcation much more literally, as the grasping of the nature of things themselves.

The gap between the Stranger's and Socrates' understanding of knowledge becomes even clearer in examining the criticisms of Theaetetus' last definition of knowledge as "true judgment with an account (*logos*)" (201d). A person who offers a definition of a concept – whether of a sophist or knowledge itself – seeks to capture the nature of the thing through words. But the aporetic ending of the *Theaetetus* suggests that definitions are not adequate to describe knowledge. Socrates' questions about the definition of knowledge as "true judgment with an account" focus on the impossibility of analyzing simple elements into smaller components. Larger complexes, such as words, can be reduced into smaller elements, such as letters in the alphabet (203a). However, the same cannot be said of simple elements, such as the letters themselves. An account cannot be given of these elements because if one could offer an account, this would mean breaking them down further into even simpler elements. At some point, the process of analysis would have to stop. Moreover, Theaetetus also thinks that the whole of something is not identical to the sum of its parts. For example, the concept of two times three is distinct from the concept of six, even though the two are mathematically equivalent (204a-d). But if this is so, then even apparently complex ideas (e.g., six) are elementary in their own way: these complexes have a nature that is distinct to them, as Socrates puts it, "an absolutely single form, indivisible into parts" (205c). Accounts that attempt to reduce six to two times three, or four plus two, miss something about the concept of six. Similarly, analyses of other concepts that reduce them to something simpler are likely to fail to capture something about the concept as a whole as well.

Socrates then elaborates on how this problem causes difficulties for those who say that knowledge is true judgment with an account. By an account (*logos*), we cannot simply mean the ability to say anything whatsoever about what one thinks; anyone can give a speech, and yet this does not show that he possesses knowledge (206d–e). Perhaps an account would mean breaking down the complex into its simpler elements and giving a description of its elements.[12] However, we know of people who only have partial or incomplete knowledge of the whole and yet can give some account of the parts. Socrates gives the example of a student who can write the first syllable of Theaetetus' name correctly but misspells "Theodorus" (207e–208a). This student does not have knowledge of writing letters as a whole and yet can write the elements correctly. He identifies each element correctly but does not put them together correctly in the case of Theodorus' name. He has commands of the elements but not the whole made from the elements (208a–b). So an "account" cannot be a command of the elements alone.

A third way of understanding "account" might be to see what distinguishes one thing from another. For example, one could claim that the sun is the brightest of all the heavenly bodies (208d). However, at least some things seem impossible to differentiate in this way; for example, we might have a hard time differentiating Theaetetus from other snubnosed people, such as Socrates (209c). If instead we say that the person who gives the account must "know" the difference between one thing and another, then we have come full circle and defined knowledge in terms of knowledge. The definition of knowledge will then be: correct judgment with knowledge. The definition of knowledge has become self-reflexive. Socrates' conclusion is to admit that they have ended up with a "wind egg" and yet that Theaetetus may conceive better "children" in the future as a result (210c). Here, Socrates emphasizes once again his partial state of knowledge. The result of the *Theaetetus* is not simple *aporia*: they

---

[12] As Burnyeat argues in his commentary on the *Theaetetus*, it is unclear whether in this section by an "account" Socrates means a statement or a completed analysis. See *The Theaetetus of Plato*, translation by M. J. Levitt, commentary by Myles Burnyeat (Indianapolis and Cambridge: Hackett Publishing Company, 1990), 145.

have learned much about the nature of knowledge through coming to understand what it is not. Theaetetus, for example, now understands that judgment is an important element of thought and that perception alone will not do. However, Socrates also asserts that neither he nor Theaetetus have complete knowledge of the whole of knowledge. They are like the writing students in Socrates' example who at times proceed well in their classes but sometimes misstep.

This last refutation of knowledge as "true judgment with an account" produces at least one positive result. Socrates effectively shows that the ability to speak clearly about a subject does not guarantee the state of knowledge in a speaker. Ignorant people can offer accounts, and those who know things only partially, like novice writing students, also can give accounts that are correct at least some of the time. Moreover, we can also "know" something – for example, that Theaetetus is not Socrates – and yet be unable to articulate the idea clearly. The overall claim seems to be that there is something about the state of possessing knowledge that is distinct from the ability to give an account per se, at the same time that an account is crucial for discerning whether one knows or is ignorant. Speaking clearly and dividing things into smaller categories is not itself a guarantee of knowledge; neither is the inability to speak adequately a guarantee of complete ignorance. Socrates' arguments here suggest that definition in general might be an inadequate means of understanding knowledge.

Given the problems raised in the *Theaetetus*, a reader of the *Sophist* ought to hesitate at whether the Stranger's method of division and collection necessarily reflects his knowledge of the sophist. We especially might wonder what makes his particular set of divisions the most accurate account of the sophist's nature. Why not use other categories to capture the sophist's nature – for example, focusing on the differences in the subject matter that the sophists teach, their love of money, or their character? Plato points to the possibility of other ways of making the cuts since the Stranger is forced to go back and reformulate the divisions several times in the dialogue. But – especially in light of Socrates' cautions to Theaetetus about the limitations of analysis – we as readers ought to be asking ourselves whether the initial categories used are the best ones for grasping and expressing the nature of the sophist. Plato does not decide the issue for us in offering these two different approaches to the dialogues. Instead, Plato encourages his readers to question the identity of the Stranger, to consider whether he is a philosopher or a sophist.

The *Theaetetus*, then, provides grounds for a series of potential criticisms of the *Sophist*'s method. The Stranger sees the method of good inquiry as finding what is common between a compliant interlocutor and himself. Socrates uses opposition in argument in order to test the ideas of his interlocutor. The Stranger expresses his ideas through diaresis that leads to definitions intended to capture the nature of the sophist. Socrates raises a number of difficulties as to whether the ability to offer a definition guarantees a speaker's knowledge. A careful reading of both the *Theaetetus* and the *Sophist* alongside one another ought to produce a kind of dissonance in the mind of the reader. Socrates and the Stranger offer two entirely different approaches to inquiry. Anyone who has read both dialogues will be forced to ask the question for himself as to which approach is better and why. Next, I explore the content of the Stranger's divisions and definitions of the sophist, comparing them to Socrates' descriptions of the philosopher as a midwife in the *Theaetetus*.

IV.

The first model the Stranger offers for making proper divisions is angling. Angling is divided along the following lines: someone who possesses expertise (not a layman); one who possesses a getting art (not an art of making); a manipulative getting (not exchanging); a hunting kind of manipulating (not competing); a hunting of the ensouled (not the soulless); hunting creatures that swim (not footed creatures); fishing (not fowling); fishing by striking (not by enclosure); hook-hunting (not fire hunting); finally arriving at angling (not tridentry) (219b–221c). In offering these categorizations, the Stranger is responsible for how the divisions take place. He does not ask Theaetetus to consider how the subject matter might be divided and never asks Theaetetus whether the divisions should proceed in any other way. Theaetetus' role seems to be only to assent to the divisions, or to choose between each pair, but not to determine how the cuts themselves ought to be made. In this sense, he is significantly more passive than in Socratic questioning. While Socrates insists that Theaetetus turn to himself in order to offer a definition (148d; 151d; 187b), with the Stranger, Theaetetus is less responsible for the content of the discussion.

The Stranger offers a similar set of divisions in defining the sophist as a hunter. It is interesting that Theaetetus is hesitant as to how to make the very first cut. The Stranger asks whether the sophist is a layman or "in every way a 'professor of wisdom'" (221d). Theaetetus responds: "In no way is he a layman. For I do understand what you mean: that he's far from being 'wise' and yet does have this name" (221d). Theaetetus sees a possible flaw in the adequacy of the division between expert and layman in labeling the sophist, and he assumes that the Stranger sees it too. The sophist calls himself wise, but everyone knows that he is not. He seems neither to be a layman nor an expert. The Stranger then places the sophist in the category of expert, but Theaetetus remarks, "Then what in the world is this expertise?" (221d). Theaetetus is already perplexed, and rightly so: the Sophist makes claims to wisdom that would set him apart from the layman who does not pretend to possess knowledge, and yet he does not seem to have a specific area of expertise. Theaetetus sees a gap between the sophist's claims to wisdom and his own understanding of genuine expertise – perhaps in part because of Protagoras' defeat at Socrates' hands the day before. He seems confused by the Stranger's desire to place the sophist in the category of expert with such ease.

The Stranger attempts to resolve Theaetetus' perplexity rather than to explore the question of the difference between real and pretended expertise further (although the Stranger will later decide on his own to take up the question of false appearance). Again, we see the difference between the Stranger and Socrates, who is delighted when Theaetetus sees a problem in the way in which the categories of the argumentation are laid out, as in the example of the dice (154d). Instead, the Stranger suggests that there is a similarity between the angler and the sophist (221a). When Theaetetus is surprised by the comparison, the Stranger goes back to the same cuts as before: the sophist is a hunter of animals (not water creatures); who hunts tame creatures (not wild ones); by producing credulity (not hunting by force); in private (not public); through pay-earning (not gift-bearing during the erotic hunt); through pretending to care for virtue while demanding payment (not flattering) (221e–223b). Again, in these cuts, the Stranger is responsible for most of the divisions. Only in the case of the division between tame and wild animals is Theaetetus asked to consider whether the categories are appropriate, and the Stranger's indifference to how Theaetetus makes the cut is telling: "If man is a tame animal. But put it any way you like, whether you set down no animal as tame, or some other animals as tame but man as wild, or again, whether you say that man is tame but you consider there to be no hunt for men – whichever of these ways of saying it you consider congenial, mark off that one for us" (222b). The Stranger is surprisingly uninterested to the philosophical question of whether human beings are wild or tame, or how persons are distinct from animals. His only concern is that

Theaetetus somehow make a cut that will efficiently separate humans from non-humans so that the next division can be made. He seems to take an almost nominalist approach to making divisions between kinds; in this way, his diaresis is very different from the division according to natural kinds described in the *Phaedrus* (*Phaedrus* 265d–266b).

Again, the contrast with Socrates is striking. Socrates describes the philosopher as one who is not bound by a concern for time but who is willing to wander wherever an argument may take him:

When he talks, he talks in peace and quiet, and his time is his own. It is so with us now: here we are beginning on our third new discussion; and he [the philosopher] can do the same, if he is like us, and prefers the new-comer to the question at hand. It does not matter to such men whether they talk for a day or a year, if only they may hit upon that which is (*Theaetetus* 172d).

Socrates is willing to wander wherever the argument takes him, even if this means that his method is less systematic or efficient.

However, the Stranger's first definition of the sophist does not stand. The Stranger goes back to revise the series of divisions that they had made. The sophist is defined through a new series of divisions in expertise in exchange instead of manipulation: as a marketing (not gift-giving) expert; trafficking the products of others (not self-selling); trading (not peddling) products; engaged in soul-nourishing (not body-nourishing) trading; and as selling "learnables" in virtue (not displaying) (223c–224d). Again, the Stranger fails to ask any questions about his own divisions. The very fact that the sophist belongs in both categories of hunting and exchanging would seem to subvert the adequacy of the divisions themselves. Moreover, the division between earning pay and gift-giving occurs at entirely different "levels" in the hierarchy of divisions in the two definitions of the sophist offered so far. In the first division, the sophist is distinguished from erotic lovers who "hunt" men by his willingness to accept payment instead of gifts. That is, he is implicated as being something like a prostitute: in the Athenian lover–beloved relationship, while gifts were perfectly acceptable expressions of affection, monetary payment was considered base and to be rejected by a virtuous beloved. In the second definition, the contrast between marketing and gift-giving is a fundamental division in exchange itself, but there are no moral overtones. One can easily imagine Socrates asking the following kinds of questions, however: Is the sophist more like a beloved who prostitutes himself or a legitimate businessman? Is his deficiency in money-making itself or in the nature of the product that he sells? When is earning money good or bad? Is the sophist's expertise in making money or in teaching virtue, or both or neither? What is virtue? Similarly, in the Stranger's third and fourth definitions of the sophist, he fails to ask evaluative questions about the sophist's "trafficking" in learning or in selling products. While the Stranger's effort is put into finding the right category, Socrates spends significant time in the dialogues inquiring into the adequacy of categories that we tend to use without sufficient reflection. In the first four definitions, the Stranger's method is impersonal and entirely concerned with finding the right categories rather than inquiring into the value of the sophist's activity or its place within a larger vision of the good.[13]

In seeking the fifth definition, the Stranger returns to the category of getting (in contrast to making) in order to find the sophist. He argues that part of the getting art is the competitive, which can be divided into battling and contending. The sophist is a fighter who uses words to battle. Instead of brute violence, he uses the disputing art but only the part of the disputing art that involves debating in private rather than pleading in public. He debates not about contracts but rather about notions such as justice and the like, and so practices "polemics"; he is the sort of polemicist who uses his debating skills in order to earn money (225a–226a). While the Stranger disparages these sophists who earn money from their practices, his description of those who debate without the aim of money-making is also negative. The latter become "careless of their own affairs" and take pleasure in passing the time in polemics while their audiences do not. The Stranger says that this practice is best described as nothing more than "yammering" (*adoleschikos*) (225d). This is another occasion in the dialogue when the Stranger offers a description of the sophist's activity that seems close to Socrates' own practice. Socrates is notable for his lack of concern with practical affairs because of his devotion to philosophical questioning, as we saw in the *Apology*. While in the *Gorgias* he claims that he takes pleasure in being questioned, the same cannot be said of most of Socrates' interlocutors. In these respects, he seems like the person one step away from sophistry. However, the dialogue is not clear as to where Socrates ought to be placed into this fifth set of divisions. One could argue that Socrates is exactly the sort of man who takes pleasure in polemics at the expense of his own affairs – but then

---

[13] As Catherine Zuckert states of the first definition, "He [the Stranger] never characterizes angling – or sophistry – in terms of its purpose, motive, or any other sort of good. He describes what the angler or sophist does, where, with what, and to what or whom, but not why." See Zuckert, "Who's a Philosopher?," 71.

argue that much more than mere yammering is going on, if his pleasure stems from teaching others of their own ignorance for their benefit. Or one might exclude Socrates from this category for the exact reason that his aim is not the pleasure of debate per se, in which case his version of polemics is not adequately captured by this set of divisions. The dialogue does not decide the issue for us but instead requires us to engage in a debate about the merits of Socrates' activity. The question as to whether Socrates' neglect of his own affairs and love of debate (at times, seemingly for its own sake) is good, bad, or morally neutral is forced back upon the reader. To answer such a question, the reader must have in mind some sort of vision of the purpose of good polemics, but such a *telos* is lacking in the Stranger's approach to division and collection.

The Stranger's sixth definition also implicitly raises the question of philosophy's place in the divisions that lead to a definition of sophistry. The Stranger finally addresses the results of the sophist's activity on the souls of his students or auditors. The first four sets of divisions into kinds focus on what the sophist does, but with no obvious purpose in mind other than earning money. This time, however, the Stranger includes normative concerns. In ordinary discourse, the Stranger notes, we often use the term *separation* (*diakrisis*) to describe the difference between the better and the worse (226d) – as in the phrase, "separating the wheat from the chaff." The Stranger says that the concept of "cleansing" in particular seems suited to describe the process of separating what is better from what is worse and getting rid of what is worse (226d). Gymnasts, doctors, bath attendants, and coroners all focus on separating the better from the worse in the body and disposing of what is worst. At this point, the Stranger remarks upon the limitations of methods that only sort and separate but do not also value different activities:

But as a matter of fact, the Way of Accounts happens to care neither more nor less for sponging than for drinking medicine, for whether the one type of cleansing benefits us a little or the other a lot. The reason is that, in trying to understand – for the sake of getting insight – what is akin and not akin in all the other arts, it honors them all equally and does not, in making its comparisons, consider some any more ridiculous than others; nor has it ever regarded the one who clarifies hunting through the general's art as any more awesome than one who does so through louse-catching but only, for the most part, as more vain (227a–b).

The Stranger goes on to say that his method will not attend to whether the name for cleansing of the soul is "most becoming," as long as all cleansings of the soul are accurately classified and separated from cleansings of the body. That is, the Stranger is explicit that his method does not – and, in fact, cannot – make normative judgments in how it classifies, for the method by its nature does not stop to reflect on the essence of the categories by which it separates and binds together. The Stranger never asks, "What is the soul?," but only asks what name we might give for those activities that claim to cleanse the soul. The questions of value that arise in the *Phaedo* or *Phaedrus* about the nature of the soul and its good are set aside here in the effort to classify with precision. The risk, of course, is that good and bad sorts of soul-cleansing will be lumped together if these sorts of questions are not addressed. The philosopher and sophist might both seem to be engaged in the same activity of attending to the soul, even if one's activity is better than the other's.

The Stranger describes all soul-cleansing as separating what is good from what is bad in the soul, and here he does briefly describe the virtue and vice of the human soul. He claims that there are two vices to the human soul – ugliness and sickness (227d–228a). The Stranger describes the sickness of the soul as a lack of measure; a soul that cannot achieve its goal cannot do so because of this lack. As an example of this lack of measure, the Stranger gives two examples: villainy and ignorance. According to the Stranger, ignorance is the soul's attempt to gain the truth while being deflected from the achievement of truth (228d). The worst form of ignorance is to believe that one knows when one does not know. This kind of ignorance can be cured through education or vocational training. Teaching can cure ignorance through either direct admonishment or refutation. This latter method refutes others through questioning others, showing them that their own ideas are inconsistent, and shaming them, until they no longer believe that they know when they do not know (230b–d). The Stranger fears that calling this practice sophistry would be to give the sophists too much honor (231a) but nonetheless settles on this cross-examining process as the fifth definition of sophistry.

Once again, the Stranger's definition raises more questions for the dialogue's audience than it answers. On the one hand, the Stranger seems to identify Socratic questioning and cross-examination with sophistry. On the other hand, he notes that this seems to be too high of an honor to grant to the sophists, and Theaetetus declares that recognizing one's own ignorance is "the best and most sound-minded" state in which to be (230d). We might wonder why the Stranger does not identify this practice with philosophy rather than sophistry since in the *Apology* it is marked out as central to Socrates' philosophical practice. One reason might be that the Stranger places a high value on the ability to classify things into kinds. Such classification requires knowledge of things in a positive sense – that

is, understanding what is essential to them and not only what is lacking in
them. For this reason, merely showing others of their lack of knowledge is
not yet philosophy for the Stranger since it does not indicate the positive
possession of knowledge.

Accordingly, the sort of Socratic midwifery described in the *Theaetetus*,
in which a speaker is himself barren of knowledge but leads others to
better understand their own ideas (especially the limitations of their own
ideas), is not yet wisdom in the Stranger's eyes. In contrast, for Socrates,
his own philosophical practice is first and foremost about the state of the
soul of his interlocutor: not his state of knowledge alone but also his ability to understand himself and what he still lacks. Socrates is concerned
with affecting the whole person and not only his intellectual grasp of
a particular topic. The Stranger has little concern for his interlocutor,
Theaetetus, in his unwavering attempts to get at the essence of sophistry
and to find an adequate definition. While Socrates might agree that villainy is a sickness of the soul, his understanding of ignorance is quite
different from that of the Stranger. Recognizing one's own ignorance is
not merely acknowledgement of a fact about one's intellectual state – for
example: "I do not know what x is." Recognizing one's own ignorance for
Socrates also involves some further understanding of one's own humanity – for example: "I am the sort of being who desires to know things but
lacks full knowledge of them. To be human is to be in this middling state."
For the Stranger, ignorance is a state to be cured through teaching, while
for Socrates it is always, to some extent or another, part of the essential
human condition, never something to which to completely capitulate or
to completely overcome.

In the next sections of the dialogue, the Stranger appears more similar
to Socrates. He questions whether any human being can know all things
(233a), recalling Socrates' idea that we ought not to confuse human and
divine knowledge (see, e.g., *Symposium* 207e–208b). The Stranger asks
whether a non-knower could debate well with a knower (233a), reminiscent of Socrates' comparison of doctors and other craftsmen with those
who lack knowledge, as in the contrast between crafts and knacks in
the *Gorgias* (*Gorgias* 464b–466a). The sophist must be a person who can
appear to be wise, someone who has "a certain opinion-producing knowledge about all things, but not true knowledge (*ouk alêtheian*)" (233c). The
Stranger compares the sophist to a painter who can imitate all things in
his speech instead of his painting. His language of contrasting appearances to "the things that are" and opinions to knowledge is reminiscent
of the *Republic*'s contrast between opinion and knowledge as well (*Sophist*

234b–d; *Republic* 479d–480a). While the Stranger and Socrates seemed to be quite different in their approaches to inquiry earlier, here they share some similar ideas about the nature of wisdom, expertise, and knowledge.

The Stranger goes a step further, however, in developing an account of appearances, an account we do not find Socrates offering in other dialogues in this sort of detail. The Stranger's inquiry into the question as to how a non-knower can appear to be a knower leads naturally into the question of how to understand false appearances. It arises in the context of the Stranger's definition of the sophist as one who is an imitator, not of likenesses but rather of apparitions (236b–c). The painter at least imitates what is real in his painting. However, the sophist presents a thing as beautiful that, if it were seen from the correct perspective, is not like what it claims to be like (236b). The problem of how to articulate the concept of a thing that is unlike what it pretends to be produces one of the richest sections of the dialogue. Because of the inherent interest of the metaphysical question of talking about non-being and the subtlety of the Stranger's position here, this section has often been taken to be Plato's own account of the nature of non-being.[14] Indeed, it may well be true that Plato uses the Stranger to develop a metaphysics. However, it does not necessarily follow that because the Stranger offers an articulate or persuasive account of metaphysics that he is an adequate philosopher in Socrates' or even Plato's eyes. Here, I set aside a discussion of the details or the adequacy of the metaphysical claims of the dialogue in order to focus on what those claims tell us about the Stranger and his broader approach to philosophy.

A brief summary of the problem is in order even for our limited purposes here. As the Stranger puts it, for him the problem is "how, in speaking, one is to say or to opine that falsehoods genuinely are, and not, in having uttered this, be hemmed in by contradiction" (236e–237a). Non-being cannot exist, be thought of, or be spoken about since "non-being" cannot be (237a–238c). It seems that even to state that it cannot be spoken about is itself contradictory since this is to assert something positive about what is not (238d–239b). The claim that sophists teach false opinions also seems to be impossible since it means that the sophist asserts that what is, is not, or that what is not, is (240e–241a). Those thinkers

---

[14] See, e.g., two excellent accounts of Plato's metaphysics in Allan Silverman, *The Dialectic of Essence: A Study of Plato's Metaphysics* (Princeton, NJ: Princeton University Press, 2002); and Mary Margaret McCabe, *Plato's Individuals* (Princeton, NJ: Princeton University Press, 1994).

who have tried to solve this problem by asserting that the beings are "two" (e.g., hot and cold or wet and dry) also fall into difficulty since they then are saying that Being, a unity, is also a multiplicity. But to say that the One is a multiplicity also seems to be contradictory, for we must then say that Being is a third thing that unifies the two contrary qualities; so we have still not solved the question of what that unity, Being, is. Even to claim that Being is affected by the One (in an effort to grant unity to being) seems to separate being from oneness; but to deny Being oneness seems to be to deny being to Being. Being, then, will seem to be not being (244e–245c).

To solve this problem, the Stranger gives an account of five genera of Being, Rest, Motion, Sameness, and Otherness and how they mix with one another. By allowing different forms to mix with one another, ordinary speech can be saved since we can now speak of one thing as possessing another quality and can talk not only about what is true but also what is false and deceptive (260a–d). Thought, too, as the soul's conversation with itself can now be true or false. It seems that the question of false appearance has been solved. The last definition of the sophist follows pretty quickly on the heels of the metaphysical solution: he is "the man, then, who has arisen from the contradiction-making art of the dissembling part of the opining art – the imitative man – who himself has sprung from the apparition-making kind descended from the image-making art and has marked off for himself the portion of making, not divine but human, that makes wonders in speeches" (268c–d). In addressing this problem, the Stranger claims that the man who struggles with these sorts of questions is the one who is "philosophical and most respects these things" (249c–d). The Stranger identifies the philosopher as one who gives the "highest honor" (*malista timônti*) to metaphysical questions (249c). Just as the musical man knows which notes harmonize and which do not, a person who is to understand Being must learn which things can mix with one another (253b). The Stranger exclaims, "Or by Zeus, have we stumbled without noticing it on the knowledge (*epistêmê*) that belongs to free men? And have we, while seeking the sophist, by some chance found the philosopher first?" (253c). The philosopher is the person who has dialectical knowledge or the power to divide according to kinds and to identify different forms in distinction from one another (253d). He possesses knowledge of the "look" of each thing and where each thing can commune with each other thing (253d–e). While the sophist is difficult to see since he hides in non-being, the philosopher is hard to see because he is among things that are so bright and divine (254a–b).

These passages might seem to imply that the Stranger is Plato's model of a philosopher as well. Since he is committed to an understanding of Being and seeks to apply rational arguments to understand Being (and not only appearances), the Stranger is a philosopher according to his own categories.[15] He seems to follow in the footsteps of philosophers such as Parmenides, who sought to understand difficulties in *logos,* such as the seeming impossibility of talking about non-being; he makes speech about such things more coherent. To this extent, the Stranger, like Socrates, is also concerned with the power and limitations of *logos.* Moreover, the intelligence and complexity of his metaphysical account seems to indicate that Plato himself is offering at least a partial answer to his predecessors on the question of Being and appearance. If the Stranger offers Plato's account of Being, then it would seem that the Stranger is a philosopher; perhaps he represents a shift in Plato's thinking about the practice of philosophy, away from Socratic refutation and toward a more metaphysical system.[16]

Certainly, we see that philosophers, sophists, and strangers alike are concerned with the power of *logos* and the difficulty of relating *logos* to what is. If, however, we keep in mind the dramatic connections between the *Sophist* and the *Theaetetus,* then we also have reason to question the adequacy of the Stranger's description of philosophy and his use of *logos* here. For, as I have argued in previous chapters, Socrates identifies philosophy closely with particular moral virtues and not only intellectual ones. The philosopher is presented primarily as someone who questions with care for his interlocutor, not only with a view to getting the correct answer. Socrates is personal, asking those with whom he is in conversation to bring themselves to the discussion, and he also brings himself to it. Socrates does not treat knowledge as though it were either simply present or simply absent. Socrates does not reject the possibility of metaphysics, although it is beyond his immediate set of concerns with Theaetetus. However, his understanding of human nature and especially the need for acknowledging the limits of human knowledge make the possibility of a complete metaphysics unlikely. When Socrates speaks of the forms, he

---

[15] Zuckert argues that the Stranger is not a philosopher but only a sophist since he falls short of the possession of full knowledge of the whole that characterizes the philosopher on her reading. However, I disagree, as the Stranger claims to have knowledge of sophistry and how it fits into a collection of these divisions, and in that sense these collections might constitute a whole of which he possesses knowledge.

[16] See, e.g., Kenneth Sayre, *Plato's Late Ontology* (Princeton, NJ: Princeton University Press, 1983).

uses imagery and metaphor – as in the *Republic*, which admits to describing only a "child" of the good and not the good itself – or he engages in criticism of metaphysical issues – as in the *Parmenides*, which does not resolve the problems it sets out.[17] Myth and criticism are both modes of speaking that take account of the limitedness of one's own knowledge. In this sense, Socrates is always rhetorical at the same time that he is philosophical; that is, he is ever attentive to his interlocutor's soul in how he speaks to him.[18] To this extent, the Stranger has not addressed the sorts of fears of *logos* which Aristophanes' *Clouds* and Gorgias' essays raise – namely, the moral dimensions of *logos* as a powerful tool that can persuade us of untruths and make us believe that we have grasped the truth when we are still at least partially ignorant. The Stranger has a stronger sense of his own mastery of knowledge, while Socrates emphasizes his ignorance and devotion to the care of souls and to the city even in his old age in his trial in the *Apology*. If we take Socrates' reflections on the philosopher and on questioning seriously, then the Stranger's shortcomings are personal rather than epistemological ones.

Plato emphasizes, then, in the presentation of these two figures, that sophistry itself is dependent upon a prior positive notion of philosophy. That is, to understand the question of the sophist's identity requires that we first develop a positive understanding of what it means to be wise. Plato's Socrates represents the moral and political dimensions of the question, while his Stranger is emblematic of a certain dispassionate speculative orientation toward the truth. We as readers are asked to ask ourselves about the relative value of their methods. Any reader who undertakes the project of understanding whether the Stranger or Socrates ought to be labeled as a sophist or a philosopher has already committed himself to an understanding of philosophy in the very act of attempting to evaluate the Stranger and Socrates. That is, the dialogues as a whole emphasize that part of philosophy includes evaluating what moral values are constitutive of philosophical practice as well as what kinds of characters are really philosophical. In this sense, the reader is put into a position that is more Socratic than Eleatic. That is, the reader is required to ask questions of character, value, and meaning, and to look into himself to determine what the most important elements of philosophy are. To do so, the reader must open himself up to moral and political questions about the value of

---

[17] As Gordon points out, even the term *form* itself is an image for something that we cannot literally grasp. See *Turning*, chapter 6, on the forms as a species of image.
[18] Rosen, *Plato's Sophist*, 20.

philosophy that go beyond epistemological and metaphysical problems (without excluding them either). Then the philosopher is not primarily identified by his state of knowledge but rather by his love of truth and his commitment to care of his interlocutor as a moral concern. Socrates the midwife admits to his own ignorance and questions others in an effort to promote their self-knowledge. The dialogues function in a similar fashion, as midwives to our own conceptions of philosophy, bringing to birth a philosophical rhetoric that links abstract ideas to the souls of people with whom one is in conversation.

7

Love and Rhetoric in Plato's *Phaedrus*

I.

Plato's *Phaedrus* contains Plato's most explicit and well-developed account of rhetoric. The dialogue provides an account of good rhetoric as philosophical *psychagôgia*, the leading of souls toward the forms. For the first time in the dialogues, we have a clearly articulated account of rhetoric in its positive sense. Socrates' account of good rhetoric describes good speech as an organic unity of collection and division. However, the dialogue's account of philosophical rhetoric in distinction from sophistical rhetoric is complicated when one considers the dialogue as a whole. Socrates' use of rhetoric in the Palinode shows that there is more to rhetoric than a technical method of organizing material according to kinds. In addition, Socrates' technical account of rhetoric is itself rhetorical in how it seeks to persuade Phaedrus to care about philosophy. Both Socrates' Palinode and his general description of rhetoric are rhetorical. Both are designed to lead Phaedrus' soul away from sophistical rhetoric and toward love of the forms.[1] While my focus in this chapter is primarily on the contrast between Socratic and sophistical rhetoric, I also briefly address the issue of the dialogue form and its rhetoric of leading souls. The *Phaedrus* helps to tie up many of the concerns in the previous chapters insofar as the unifying feature of good, philosophical rhetoric is love: love of the forms and love of those to whom the rhetorician speaks.

---

[1] Due to limitations of space, I do not treat the first of Socrates' speeches but instead note here that Socrates relies upon many of the same devices of antithesis, parallelism, and use of imagery as Lysias does in his speech.

II.

I argue that Socrates' Palinode reflects the principles that he will later describe to Phaedrus in terms of good rhetoric. Before turning to the Palinode, then, let us examine Socrates' speech about the nature of good rhetoric which follows the Palinode. For the Palinode is not a simple and straightforward exhibition of these principles of good rhetoric. While the Palinode displays some of the features of that description of good rhetoric, it also departs from that account of rhetoric in significant ways. This suggests that the prose description of good rhetoric is not a comprehensive articulation of good rhetoric's qualities. In fact, I argue that the prose description is itself rhetorical and designed to lead Phaedrus toward philosophy and away from his love of a style of speech inattentive to philosophical concerns.

Socrates' description of good rhetoric arises in the context of Phaedrus' wondering aloud about Lysias' rhetoric; in particular, whether Lysias' oratory is sophistic in a pejorative sense. Phaedrus has heard much talk about the claim that Lysias is a logographer, a writer of speeches, and fears that Lysias might be accused of being a sophist on account of his writing (257d). Socrates replies that writing speeches is not itself a shameful activity; what matters is whether speeches are written well or badly (258d).

Socrates' first criterion of a good speech is that the speaker must have "a discursive understanding (*dianoia*) of the truth (*to alêthes*) about the subject he means to discuss" (259e).[2] Phaedrus tells Socrates that he thought that what matters in persuading is not what is just, beautiful, or good but only what seems to be so (260a). But Socrates insists that a speaker must have knowledge, lest one who is unaware of good and evil persuade the city to do what is evil, at its own peril (260c). Socrates personifies Rhetoric and has Rhetoric offer a brief speech in defense of itself: "[W]ithout me, in no way will a man who knows the truth be able to persuade with art" (260d). Socrates at first seems to separate philosophy from rhetoric, presenting them as if the order of preparation for a good speech is: first, mastery of a philosophical truth and, second, presentation of it through a separable art of rhetoric. Socrates' presentation of philosophy and rhetoric appears to concern two separate skills, with philosophy as primary and rhetoric as secondary.

---

[2] Translations in this chapter are from Stephen Scully (translator), *Plato's Phaedrus* (Newburyport, MA: Focus Library, 2003).

However, in the very next sentence, Socrates qualifies Rhetoric's claim. He says that he would agree with Rhetoric's speech *if* rhetoric is an art. However, Socrates has heard some arguments testifying to the claim that Rhetoric is not an art (*technê*) but instead devoid of art (260e). By offering up this opposition, Socrates engages Phaedrus in philosophical inquiry about the nature of rhetoric. Rather than simply stating his own views on the technical or non-technical nature of rhetoric, Socrates here draws Phaedrus into philosophizing about rhetoric. What matters is Phaedrus' participation in the process of inquiry into its nature. Socrates begins with Phaedrus' love of speeches and draws Phaedrus into an inquiry into the nature of his "beloved" *logoi*. Socrates can see that Phaedrus wishes to understand that which he loves; a philosophical inquiry into the nature of rhetoric turns out to be the best way in which to draw Phaedrus into the practice of philosophy. Socrates' practice with Phaedrus is simultaneously philosophical and rhetorical: philosophical insofar as it asks questions about the nature of rhetoric but also rhetorical in persuading Phaedrus to ask philosophical questions, when before he had been interested only in the beauty and cleverness of speeches.

Socrates then describes rhetoric as a "leading of souls" (*psychagôgia*) through words, in both in public and private settings (261a). Phaedrus is a bit confused by Socrates' explanation, saying that he is only familiar with rhetoric in its public uses (261b). Because the term *rhetor* was commonly used to refer to speakers in the Assembly and has an overtly political connotation, Phaedrus' reaction should be no surprise to us. If the primary purpose of the rhetoric with which Phaedrus is familiar is to persuade an audience to act or to please and gratify a crowd, then the practice of rhetoric for a private speech makes little sense. Socrates, however, notes that the practice of offering two different arguments, one on each side of an issue, takes place not only in the courts but also in the Assembly and in the works of thinkers such as Parmenides. The leading of souls cannot be reducible to psychology but instead requires some understanding of one's topic as well as one's audience. Misleading one's audience also requires using terms whose meanings are controversial (e.g., justice or love) rather than easily agreed upon (e.g., silver or iron; 263a–c). Effective rhetoric requires a sense of how one's audience perceives the meaning of one's words.

Socrates next engages in a bit of literary criticism, arguing that Lysias' speech is not finely made; his criticisms focus around the speech's arrangement. Lysias' speech is simply a "heap" of words. A good speech ought to be like a living organism: "Every speech like a living creature should be put together with its own body so that it is not without a head or with a foot but has a middle and extremities, written in such a way that its parts fit together and form a whole" (264c). This image of a good speech as like a living thing is not limited to Plato's own work. Plato's contemporary Alcidamas also praises a good speech as akin to an "ensouled" thing in his work, *On the Sophists.* The larger context of Alcidamas' essay is an argument that good speech ought to be spoken and not written; those who write deserve the name of sophist, while those who speak can properly be called wise. The spoken word is better able to adapt to the shifting circumstances of the moment; those who focus on learning how to speak rather than how to write well are better able to influence the desires and actions of others and to win honor for their excellence as a speaker. Those who spend too much time writing become inflexible and helpless when faced with a new or unexpected circumstance. Alcidamas argues that written speeches are like statues, whereas

the speech spoken straight from the heart on the spur of the moment has a soul in it (*empsuchos*) and is alive and follows upon events and is like those real bodies, while the written speech whose nature corresponds to a representation of a real thing lacks any kind of living power (27–28).[3]

Alcidamas' claim that oral speech is "ensouled" (*empsuchos*) is of special interest since he applies this term to the speech and not only the speaker. Alcidamas' main point is to emphasize the ways in which the spoken word is more flexible, adaptive, and responsive to changing temporal circumstances. An oral speech also holds more intrinsic appeal for an audience than a written one, even if the product is somewhat less polished, as real human bodies have more appeal than polished and perfect statues.

Alcidamas and Socrates both use the image of a living thing rather than an inanimate object as the proper model for understanding speeches; for both thinkers, a speech must seem to be "alive" to its audience. But while Alcidamas emphasizes how a good speech possesses the dynamism of a living body, Socrates adds the need for an internal ordering of the parts to the whole, the underlying organization of how the parts interrelate. An effective speech must exhibit harmony in its parts, where each part contributes something to the overall structure of the entire animal. An author must consider how each part contributes to the overall structure of his argument, while also keeping the discussion lively and active. Here,

---

3 J. V. Muir, translator and editor. *Alcidamas: The Works and Fragments* (London: Bristol Classic Press, 2001).

Socrates implies that Lysias has not adequately ordered his thoughts and so his speech lacks an organic coherence.

Socrates claims that an artful speech must both collect and divide its subject matter systematically. First, if rhetoric is going to be an art (*technê*), then the subject matter which one discusses must first be understood as a whole. Socrates tells us that we will need a speaker "whose sight can bring into a single form things which have previously been scattered in all directions so that by defining each thing he makes clear any subject he ever wants to teach about" (265d). Such collection into a unity will give a speech "clarity" (*saphes*) and "consistency" (265d). Socrates offers as an example their earlier definition of Eros. Socrates had defined love as a force of passion apart from reasoning that rules over opinion and is driven toward the pleasure of beauty, especially the beauty of the body (283b–c). Presumably, Socrates thinks that if both speaker and audience have in mind a clear sense of the boundaries of the topic, then there is less likely to be confusion in the communication between speaker and audience. For example, if a speaker means by Eros love of the good but his audience equates Eros with lust, then miscommunication is likely.

However, Socrates' mention of "consistency" along with clarity also suggests an interest in more than agreement between speaker and audience. Socrates wants the speaker himself to be consistent about his subject matter and to be able to "see" the form that unifies it; if rhetoric is to be a *technê*, a speaker must understand what a thing is and what it is not. The boundaries of what the thing is must be clear to him. Socrates says that this takes place by some sort of ability to gather up diverse particulars (*sunoraô*): somehow, the speaker must understand the nature of the thing as a whole so that he may include what really belongs to it, while excluding what does not belong. Socrates says that it must be brought together into a single "idea" (265d). Given that Socrates in the *Palinode* describes the ideas as real entities outside of ourselves, which philosophical souls long to gaze upon, Socrates seems to require that the rhetorician with art have just this kind of insight into the nature of the whole of a topic; he must understand the form of justice, or beauty, or love in order to collect it into a unity before making his speech. Socrates sets a high standard for the rhetorician who will meet the requirements of a *technê* – particularly when one considers how elusive the sight of the forms is to even the most ardent seekers in the Palinode.

The second requirement for a technical rhetoric is for the rhetorician to divide up the whole into parts again. He must have "the power, conversely, to cut up a composition, form by form according to its natural

joints and not to try to hack through any part as a bad butcher might"
(265e). Just as an animal has two arms, two legs, and so on, a good speech
must present its material into organized parts that follow the nature of
the thing being described. Socrates gives as an example the division of
madness into its divine and human kinds (266a). While human madness
is bad, divine madness is praiseworthy. While Socrates is not insistent that
the division must always be into two parts, his examples in this section
are all of equal pairs. Here, Socrates takes up elements of the rhetorical
device of antithesis, where two ideas are opposed in a speech, into the
proper division of the content of a thing according to its nature. While
Lysias, Gorgias, and others treat antithesis as a pleasurable element of
style, Socrates says that dividing one's topic into two parts must proceed
according to nature. Socrates does not ignore style altogether: rather,
he offers a theory of composition that demands a harmony of style and
content with one another. The *idea* of a speech must mirror and reflect
the form *idea* of the thing that it is describing. Again, the standards for
rhetoric as an art are high: Socrates demands insight into the nature of
the whole, knowledge of how to divide the whole properly, and knowledge
of how each of the parts fits into the whole upon which it is dependent.
Socrates does not offer details on how this process is to be accomplished;
there is no reason, for example, to assume that the method named here is
identical to the Stranger's method in the *Sophist* and *Statesman*. In fact, as
I argue herein, Socrates' Palinode exhibits some of these characteristics
of collection and division into kinds, but in the form of a myth.

However, Socrates' description of rhetoric is not only driven by the
content of a speech's subject matter. Socrates is not only interested in the
proper philosophical categorization of each thing according to knowledge of its form; he also wants the relation of part to whole to be communicated to one's audience with clarity and understanding. The rhetorician
must identify how one's audience already understands the topic in question and then lead souls toward a better understanding. If one adds to this
task the need to make one's speech lively and active, as in the metaphor
of a living being, the rhetorician's art is clearly difficult to achieve.
Socrates describes those who in this way collect and divide "dialecticians"
(266c).

Phaedrus agrees that this process sounds like dialectic but thinks that
rhetoric has somehow been lost in the process of describing division
and collection. Socrates responds by listing a number of rhetorical techniques, from the structure of speeches (e.g., *prooimion, diêgêsis, marturiai*,
and the like) to the use of maxims, similes, and reduplication found in

rhetorical handbooks (266d–267d). Socrates does not discount the value of any of these techniques; instead, he emphasizes that they are incomplete without the art that he has just described. Although no fifth-century ancient handbooks survive, most were likely made up of examples of figures of speech and rhetorical topics, with limited discussions – if any – of how these techniques worked.[4] Socrates suggests that such lists are insufficient. Just as we would call "mad" a man who claimed to be a doctor after reading about how to bring down a fever, or a man who said he was musical because he could hit the highest and lowest notes, a person who has studied rhetorical techniques in books has only studied the "prerequisites" (*mathêmata*) for rhetoric but not rhetoric itself (268a–269c). Rhetoric requires knowledge that the handbooks lack. Part of the rhetorician's knowledge is knowledge of the soul (270c).

To begin, Socrates asks Phaedrus, "Do you think that it is possible to understand the nature of the soul at all intelligently without understanding the nature of the whole (*tês tou holou phuseôs*)?" (270c). Socrates does not explain what he has in mind, but Phaedrus' answer provides a clue: "If we are to follow Hippocrates at all, Ascelpius' heir, it is not possible to understand anything about the body either without this method" (270c). As Lloyd has argued, the meaning of the "whole" for Hippocrates here is unclear and could mean anything from (1) the whole universe, (2) the whole body, (3) the whole body–soul complex, or (4) the whole of the subject under discussion.[5] What we can say, however, is that just as a good doctor must know how the parts fit into a whole, good rhetoric brings a coherence of part and whole such that one's audience can make sense of the diverse phenomena at hand and find order and unity in multiplicity, without losing multiplicity altogether.

Socrates goes on to say that the rhetorician must understand the nature of the soul with precision. The true rhetorician must know: (1) whether the soul is simple or multiformed; and (2) what it has a capacity to do and what it has a capacity to suffer, whether as a simple whole or in its various parts (270d). The soul must be described with total "precision" (*akribeiai*, 271a). Then, having classified both souls and speeches, he will align each type of soul with each type of speech, "explaining the reason why one soul is necessarily persuaded by speeches of a certain sort and another is not" (271b).

4 See Kennedy, *A New History*, 34–35.
5 G. E. R. Lloyd, *Methods and Problems in Greek Science* (Cambridge: Cambridge University Press, 1991), 194–223.

Moreover, once a student has learned this art at school, "he must apply these particular words in that particular way to persuade him of these things. After the young rhetorician has mastered all this and understood the appropriate times (*kairous*) – both opportune and inopportune – for speaking and holding back, for concise speech, for speech which stirs pity, for exaggeration, and for each of the other forms of speech he has learnt, only then, and not before, has the art been beautifully and perfectly mastered" (272a–b). Socrates distinguishes between *knowing* about souls, speeches, and their correspondence and having the ability to *apply* this knowledge to a specific context and situation. Again, Socrates emphasizes that a sense of *kairos* is required in order to apply this knowledge: if the speaker does not use the right speech at the opportune moment, then all of his knowledge will have done no good. The rhetorician must know when to speak but also when not to say anything for the sake of his interlocutor's well-being. Socrates is not interested only, then, in intellectual knowledge of soul and subject matter but also in practical knowledge that consists of how to apply this knowledge in particular contexts.

The language of *kairos* apart from the Platonic philosophical context has a history in the crafts of archery and weaving, as Eric White has shown. *Kairos* in archery refers to the aperture through which the archer's arrow must pass, whereas in weaving, it is the momentary opening through which the weaver's shuttle must go.[6] The use of the term in each of these arts, then, implies that *kairos* is difficult to find because the right moment appears and disappears quickly, like the opening in the weave of a textile on the loom. Moreover, the opening is narrow: the archer cannot err much on either side and still hit his target. In the case of the weaver and the archer, the practitioner of the art acts intuitively in order to achieve his goal; the weaver slides the shuttle in and out of the loom after years of practice. So too, it seems, Socrates includes this intuitive sense of seizing the right moment, correctly identified in the *Gorgias* as a "knack," as a necessary part of the art of rhetoric. But the myriad of ways in which a speaker seizes the moment cannot – by the very nature of the practice – be taught through the use of general principles any more than we could give rules for how the archer should shoot his arrow. What we need is a good deal of practice shooting.

In summary, to possess the art of rhetoric one must (1) understand the truth about the subject at hand, both the whole and how its parts fit

---

[6] Eric Charles White, *Kaironomia: On the Will-to-Invent* (Ithaca, NY: Cornell University Press, 1987), 13.

together; (2) understand the nature of the human soul; (3) understand one's particular audience's beliefs; (4) know how to lead one's particular audience toward the truth; and (5) do so with a clear and lively speech that is in accordance with the nature of the material. Combining all of these different elements in the "here and now" requires a sense of good timing, or *kairos*. As Phaedrus puts it, "this seems to be no small undertaking" (272b).

III.

Socrates' Palinode in defense of love exhibits many of these qualities of good rhetoric. I suggest that Socrates does not think that the rhetorical art can be perfectly mastered: such perfection is divine and beyond human beings. Socrates emphasizes throughout the Palinode that human beings are always in an erotic state, that is, always in a state of moving toward or away from the ultimate objects of their love (the forms). Human knowledge of the forms and human self-knowledge are never complete.[7] At the same time, the rhetorician's art is nonetheless set up as the standard for which a good rhetorician strives. Even if this standard is not possible to achieve flawlessly, there is the possibility of exhibiting the virtues of the philosophical rhetoric in a better or a worse way. We have the possibility of being closer to or farther away from this standard and ought to emulate it as closely as possible. As the Palinode demonstrates, philosophy is neither prior to rhetoric nor entirely separable from rhetoric. Philosophy is not the art of discovering the truth, to be followed by a distinct art of rhetorical persuasion. For Socrates, the philosopher by his nature is always incomplete in knowledge and continues to learn about the truth through conversation. The philosopher's soul is drawn closer to the truth through speeches, particularly through speeches between friends. To phrase it another way, the Palinode describes philosophy in terms of love: love of the forms and love of other persons.

The Palinode is, first of all, a myth. Socrates attributes it to Stesichorus, a sixth-century lyric poet. Socrates closely follows Steisochorus' approach in his own speech, both in his lyrical style and in how he takes up an epic theme. Socrates alludes to a story told about Stesichorus, who was

---

7 As Griswold in *Self-Knowledge* argues, one way of unifying the disparate themes of the dialogue is the theme of self-knowledge. While I focus on love as its primary theme, the two are not unrelated: as the lovers in the Palinode more deeply understand themselves and their own love, they are also led closer to the forms.

said to have been struck with blindness after writing a slanderous story about Helen. He regained his eyesight only after telling a second version in which he claimed that only Helen's phantom had been carried off to Troy. Socrates, too, describes his own speech here as a recantation of his first speech in criticism of love. The Palinode praises love when formerly Socrates criticized it. At the same time, Socrates never recants his claims that lovers do sometimes focus only on their own well-being with no genuine concern for their "beloveds." Socrates' first speech correctly identifies the evils of selfish lovers who care only for their own satisfaction. The shortcoming of the first speech is that it was too simple-minded and slandered Eros, which is divine.

Given that Socrates describes the division of speeches into their natural joints in terms of pairs, one can also understand Socrates' two speeches as forming a natural pair. Socrates' first speech describes a non-lover who believes himself to be a lover, while his second speech describes the true lover. The two speeches together suggest that genuine love goes beyond the lover's desire for his own satisfaction and attends primarily to the well-being of the beloved. Both lover and beloved must pursue a higher, transcendent good if we are to call their love for one another genuine. Socrates' first speech criticizes the shortcomings of human love apart from its context in the larger "whole," while his second speech extols *eros* when it is properly related to the divine. In other words, the Palinode exhibits this attention to the relation between parts and the whole, as well as an understanding of the human soul in relation to that whole – two of the most important characteristics of good rhetoric in the passage of rhetoric just analyzed. The Palinode is an epic and lyrical description of the human person being led through love to the good; that is, the Palinode is a poetic treatment of rhetoric itself.

The Palinode gives the following account of love. Socrates first asserts that although love is a form of madness (*mania*), we can identify other accounts of madness that are divine and good: the madness of prophecy, of purification, and of the Muses (244a–245b). We need not fear the madness of love, seeing that there are other forms of *mania* that are good and beneficial. While it would take a god to describe the soul's form completely, Socrates says that we can still talk about what the soul is "like" (246a). He then offers the comparison of the soul to a winged team of horses and a charioteer, in which one horse is of noble stock and the other of poor stock, making guidance of the soul difficult. The soul's feathers are nourished by the beautiful, wise, and good, but if a soul loses its feathers through shame and vice, it is joined to a body that weighs it down. In heaven, souls can follow the paths of the gods until they climb the steepest paths in order to feast, at which time only the divine chariots are sufficiently obedient to make the trip. Vicious souls cannot follow, and even good but non-divine souls have difficulty. Souls able to look upon the "place beyond heaven" where they can see Being itself are nourished and filled with love (*agapê*) and enjoyment (247d). Later, they travel farther around the circuit and see the forms of Justice, Moderation, and the Knowledge so that they have knowledge of Being, not becoming. Only divine souls do this well; even the best human souls are barely able to get a glimpse of such things before being confused by the horses, while other, less virtuous souls see nothing at all in their efforts to control their own horses and avoid being trampled by other horses. In all cases, these non-divine souls leave the rim of heaven unfulfilled and feed only on opinion (*doxastêi*; 248b). Those in the entourage of the gods who were able to see the truth are free of pain until the next cycle, but those unable to see it are overcome by "forgetfulness and wrongdoing" and fall to earth. Depending on how much of Being each soul has seen, he will become one of nine different types of soul on earth.

The best type of soul is a lover of wisdom, beauty, the musical, or erotic, while the other eight types in descending order are a law-abiding ruler, a political man or money-maker, a gymnast or doctor, a prophet or seer, a poet, a craftsman or farmer, a sophist or demagogue, and a tyrant (248d–e). Each of these souls receives different rewards or punishments after their lives on earth, depending on how each has lived. Most souls will have to wait ten thousand years to regain their wings, and some will fall into animal rather than human bodies in future lives. Some souls will forget what they have seen and lose interest in regaining it. Only the philosopher, who is in love with wisdom, can grow new wings (249c); those who love wisdom "without deceit" or who love both boys and wisdom are capable of getting back their wings before the usual ten-thousand-year time period is up. Those who have forgotten true beauty seek only their own physical pleasure in others, while true lovers, who remember it, revere the beauty of the beloved and feel divine reverence for it (251a–b). This soul's wings are nourished whenever he sees this beauty, initially causing him to feel throbbing, itching, and aching, but later joy as his wings sprout again (251b–d). His longing for the beauty of his beloved is so great that he wants only to be with him and aches in his absence; this causes him to forget family, friends, and all else in his desire to see his beloved's beauty. Depending on which god they accompanied in heaven, lovers manifest their love in different ways: those who followed Ares are angry and violent when they feel betrayed, while those who followed Zeus are able to bear their burdens with dignity (252c–d). Each lover seeks after a beloved who has the qualities of the god that the lover's soul had previously followed in heaven. All lovers treat others in imitation of the god that they had previously followed and "sculpt" their beloveds in accordance with this ideal, making the beloved into a statue to revere. Both lover and beloved, then, develop the qualities of the type of god that the lover follows.

Eventually, as the boy matures and the lover is received into his company, the lover will be filled with a sense of love for the boy: "As a breeze or perhaps an echo bounces off a smooth hard service and is carried back to the source from which it sprang, just so the flow of beauty goes back into the beautiful one through his eyes, arriving where it naturally goes into the soul, causing movement of the wing. There the stream waters the pathways of the feathers, urges them to sprout, and fills the beloved's soul in turn with love" (255c–d). In contrast to ordinary Greek conventions, the boy, too, will find himself in love with his lover but cannot quite explain it. He does not understand "that in his lover he is seeing himself as in a mirror" (255d) but only knows that when his lover is present, his pain ceases, while when he is absent, he longs for him. But he experiences this love as friendship (*philia*), not *eros* (255e). While the beloved desires to grant his lover sexual favors, his better horse and charioteer attempt to restrain him with a sense of shame. Both lover and beloved must undergo the same process of learning to restrain the worse horse and find a harmony of the soul. If lover and beloved are both able to prevail in virtue and live out a life of wisdom, then "they have won the first round of the wrestling falls in these, the true Olympic games" (256b). Even those who live a life according to honor instead of wisdom and who occasionally give in to physical desire will still desire wings when they leave their bodies and in time grow them (256e). Socrates ends with a prayer to the god Eros, asking him to turn Phaedrus toward a love devoted to wisdom-loving speeches (257a–b).

Socrates' Palinode exhibits many of the traits discussed in Socrates' account of rhetoric as examined herein. First, Socrates uses this speech to lead Phaedrus' soul through love. Socrates does not shy away from using erotic language with Phaedrus. From the very earliest dramatic moments of the *Phaedrus*, Socrates playfully suggests that he may be trying to "seduce" Phaedrus. When he first asks Phaedrus to read Lysias' speech, Socrates teases, "Only if first, my love (*philotes*), you show me what you have in your left hand under your cloak" (228d); here, the sexual double entendres of Aristophanic comedy come to mind. Later, Socrates alludes to a line from Sappho's erotic poetry (230b).[8] Socrates also mentions that he "loves" Phaedrus (228e), using the term *philein*, which can be used either to connote friendship in either its more austere or romantic forms and uses the word "*pai* (my boy)," a term that can be used to refer to the beloved in a lover–beloved relationship (267c). Using the same term in his preface to the non-lover's speech, Socrates says, "There once was a darling boy, a young man really, a very beautiful young man, and he had a great number of lovers" (237b). A heartfelt delivery of such a line, with its series of embellishments on the beauty and youth of the "unnamed boy," might well be directed at Phaedrus.[9]

At the same time, Socrates' "seduction" of Phaedrus is designed to reorient Phaedrus' love away from speeches themselves and toward the forms and philosophy; his seduction is not carnal in nature, although it borrows from the language of carnal love. This idea of *psychagôgia* is also dramatically foreshadowed: when Socrates agrees to accompany Phaedrus on a walk and listen to him, Phaedrus says, "Lead on (*proage de*)" (227c). Socrates repeats the same line back to Phaedrus a bit later (229a), suggesting that Phaedrus' words might lead Socrates closer to the good too. Not only Phaedrus but also Socrates is a lover of speeches (228c). Like the philosophical lover in the Palinode, Socrates sees in his "beloved" Phaedrus a kindred soul.[10] Socrates' claim that he knows Phaedrus as well as he knows himself is reflected in the Palinode's idea that the beloved sees himself as in a mirror: both lover and beloved mutually recognize in one other something of themselves.[11] It is through this mutual recognition that the love between lover and beloved can help lead them both closer to the forms and so also closer to the truth of the meaning of their own love.

Socrates' speeches take account of Phaedrus' love of words in their use of style that surpasses Lysias' speech. Each speech in turn is intended to lead Phaedrus farther away from the love of speeches themselves and toward the love of the forms.[12] Socrates' first speech (of the non-lover) reveals Socrates to be as capable as Lysias of writing a speech against

---

[8] See Scully, *Plato's Phaedrus*, 6, n. 17.

[9] See Jill Gordon, "Eros and Philosophical Seduction in the *Alcibiades I*," *Ancient Philosophy* 23 (spring 2003): 11–30, who argues that Socrates "seduces" Alcibiades since only through greater self-knowledge can Alcibiades satisfy his true ambitions.

[10] As Griswold argues, rhetoric and *eros* are already connected in the very person of Phaedrus. See Griswold, *Self-Knowledge*, 21.

[11] See Griswold, *Self-Knowledge*, 126–129; and Sallis, *Being and Logos*, 112–113.

[12] See Harvey Yunis, "Eros in Plato's *Phaedrus* and the Shape of Greek Rhetoric," *Arion* 13 (2005): 101–125, who argues that Socrates' artfulness here is specifically his ability to "exploit the soul's natural capacities for desire and transcendence" (115).

love, a speech that is paradoxical in content and fluid in style. With some surprise, Phaedrus tells Socrates, "a most uncustomary fluency has seized you" (238c) after Socrates' speech. While Phaedrus may have viewed Socrates only as an audience for Lysias' speech, the speech of the non-lover opens up the possibility of becoming Socrates' audience. Socrates puts himself in the position of Lysias as both an orator and as a lover to Phaedrus, allowing Phaedrus to become receptive to listening to Socrates. While Phaedrus was excited by Lysias' speech at the beginning of the dialogue, he soon demands that Socrates speak more. By the time Socrates has completed the *Palinode*, Phaedrus says that Socrates' second speech is even more beautiful than his first, adding, "It's actually made me anxious lest Lysias seem second-rate by comparison – if, that is, he even wanted to match your speech with one of his own" (257c). Socrates draws Phaedrus into philosophical concerns in part through his superior use of style; he also draws Phaedrus away from a speech that advocates not loving to one that places love at the center of human meaning.

The content of the Palinode is also conducive to leading Phaedrus, the speech lover, away from love of speeches themselves and toward a love of the forms. Socrates' argument that some kinds of madness are divine and good entices Phaedrus into considering whether the intensity of his own desires is directed at the right objects. His identification of the desire to see the forms with the desires of the gods in heaven lifts philosophical love to nearly divine status.

In general, Socrates' use of erotic language (e.g., throbbing, aching, stinging, madness, and desire) to speak about philosophy exhorts Phaedrus to consider the familiar yearning of love for another person in connection to the forms. Socrates suggests that if Phaedrus thinks that he already knows the extent of erotic desire for another person, he still has not yet plunged into the full depths of love. His description of the profundity of philosophical love is also a challenge to Phaedrus to experience it for himself. Socrates' aim of converting Phaedrus to philosophy is clear in his prayer to Eros, in which he urges the god to make Phaedrus "devote his life solely to Love with wisdom-loving speeches" (257b). Socrates' Palinode is an instance of soul-leading rhetoric, specifically oriented to the soul of a person who is already erotic and in love with what is beautiful, musical, and erotic – that is, to a person just like Phaedrus.

Socrates' speech also exhibits a kind of collection and division akin to that described in the non-mythical description of rhetoric. To begin, his myth gives an account of the "whole" by literally situating each type of human being in a cosmological context in which gods and human beings alike desire the forms found at the rim of heaven. Socrates locates love within this divine scheme; the topic is no longer the relative value of the non-lover and lover in relation to a boy but instead the love of the beautiful, good, and true. It is hard to imagine a greater "whole" in which to begin than the movement of the gods and human beings in the heavens in relation to the forms. Socrates also divides his subject matter into parts. For example, the speech of the non-lover and the lover form a pair, in which selfish love is denigrated but love of the forms praised. Madness is divided into the human and the divine, and the divine itself is divided into four parts. Nine types of soul are classified, and each soul is further divided into its parts of charioteer and two horses. The image of the charioteer itself displays the kind of "organic unity" of the animal body that Socrates extols as ideal: the image gives us both an image of the soul as a whole, working in harmony, while allowing for the possibility of inner psychic conflict through the imagery of two horses that may not want to follow each other or their master. Throughout his speech, Socrates uses the division and collection of things into their parts, while often using images that keep these parts together in an organized unity that reveals the proper relationship of part to whole. The fact that the Palinode is a myth ought not to bar us from also seeing how its order follows some of the principles set out in the description of division and collection. Furthermore, the language of change, growth, and motion throughout the speech allows Socrates' speech to be active and "ensouled," like a living thing. Images such as horses are quite literally living things. Socrates' speech contains little stasis, with its constant emphasis on movement and being drawn upward away from what is base and toward what is higher.

However, as several commentators have noted, the Palinode and the non-mythical description of rhetoric are not harmonious in other ways.[13]

---

[13] Griswold first raises this problem, arguing that the *technê* of division and collection is unerotic and does not include the sort of recollection of the forms that is so central to knowledge in the Palinode. See Griswold, *Self-Knowledge*, chapter 5. However, I argue that both Socrates' presentation of the *technê* of division and collection and the Palinode are rhetorical descriptions of rhetoric, designed to draw Phaedrus into philosophy. In arguing this point, I do not wish to undermine the value of division and collection as a method; I only note that it cannot be a comprehensive picture of philosophical rhetoric. Others who see the rift include Charles H. Kahn, *Plato and the Socratic Dialogue: The Philosophical Use of a Literary Form* (Cambridge: Cambridge University Press, 1996), 373; James Kasteley, "Respecting the Rupture: Not Solving the Problem of Unity in Plato's *Phaedrus*," *Philosophy and Rhetoric* 35 (2002): 138–152; and Alexander Nehamas, *Virtues of Authenticity: Essays on Plato and Socrates* (Princeton, NJ: Princeton University Press, 1999), 352.

The Palinode's emphasis on *eros* is absent from the description of division and collection. In addition, Socrates claims that if rhetoric is to be an art, the rhetorician must possess mastery and knowledge of the topic about which he is presenting. But the Palinode claims that the ultimate objects of knowledge, the forms, are *not* perfectly mastered by *any* human being. The gods alone can gaze upon the forms with ease; most human beings see little of them. Even the best souls who accompany the gods and get a glimpse of the forms are always in a state of trying to recollect the forms once embodied on earth. No living and embodied human being possesses the complete truth about them. So, the Palinode would seem to claim that no human being is in a state of complete knowledge if the object of knowledge is the forms. While it might be possible to give a technically rigorous speech about some other subject matter (e.g., a topic in medicine or carpentry), the Palinode makes clear that no human being ever achieves comparable mastery and precision in his understanding of the forms. If this is true, then Socrates' Palinode cannot be seen as a perfect exhibition of the rhetorician's art as he defines it in the *Phaedrus*.[14]

Nonetheless, neither does the Palinode claim that human beings are completely ignorant of the nature of the forms. Socrates argues that the only way that human beings will strive to understand the forms is if they do possess some faint memory of having seen them (even if they are not always fully aware of such a memory); the stronger the memory, the more a soul will be inspired to love and seek the forms. Socrates describes knowledge in terms of a middle ground between complete mastery and complete ignorance. The soul that seeks to know the forms and is in a process of coming to know them is in motion. When Socrates describes the soul of a person in love, he connects that love of persons to the love of the forms. Lovers seek out the souls of those like themselves. So, *all* human love is described in terms of a common love of something outside of the two lovers. One soul is first drawn outside of itself by being drawn to another human being, but if the two lovers grow to understand the nature of their own love, then this love will also draw them to love the forms, which transcend them both as individuals and as a couple. This outward emphasis of Socrates on the forms has an effect on his rhetoric too. Because his aim is to draw Phaedrus nearer to the forms, Socrates' speeches are not oriented exclusively toward drawing Phaedrus to himself. Socrates speaks to Phaedrus and seeks his attention ultimately in order to lead the boy beyond Socrates. In a certain sense, philosophical

---

[14] See Griswold, *Self-Knowledge*, chapter 5, for a longer argument on this point.

rhetoric attracts its audience with the final aim of making the speaker superfluous.

Socrates' account of love in the *Phaedrus* harmonizes with Diotima's account of love in the *Symposium*, where even the love of bodies is implicitly a love of the forms. All love, including carnal love, is somewhere on a ladder toward the forms as our ultimate objects of desire, although some forms of love are closer to the forms than others. The human soul in love is neither completely happy nor desolate; the loving soul is always in a middle state between the perfect possession of the object of love and a longing for something that is entirely absent. When he is moving toward the forms (or his beloved, who reflects the forms), he experiences joy; when he is moving away, desolation. The soul in love is in a state of drawing closer to that for which it yearns and growing better to understand itself, the beloved person, and the forms in the process.

As a result, Socrates' rhetoric about love cannot be understood either as the presentation of precise, technical knowledge or as a persuasive presentation without regard for the truth. Instead, Socrates' rhetoric is in between the presentation of secure and complete knowledge and the presentation of ideas that do not even intend to reveal a truth outside of the speaker. On the one hand, Socrates insists that good rhetoric cannot simply persuade one's audience of what seems to be so. The philosophical speaker is guided by a truth that transcends both himself and his audience, but to which they are both drawn. On the other hand, the philosophical speaker does not impart perfectly mastered knowledge that he possesses to his audience. Instead, Socrates' sort of rhetoric, which is committed to both the idea of a transcendent and objective truth and to the recognition of the imperfection of human knowledge on the part of both audience and speaker, is "erotic rhetoric." It is erotic not only in how it leads the soul of the audience toward the forms but also erotic insofar as the rhetorician *himself* admits to being in motion, in love with – but not in total possession of – knowledge of the forms. Socrates tells Phaedrus that Socrates still does not adequately know himself and is still inquiring into his own nature (229e–230a). The *Palinode* makes clear that self-knowledge is a condition for understanding one's love of other people and the forms, and vice versa, but this is true for the speaker no less than the audience.

Perhaps this is what Socrates has in mind when he declares that he possesses the art of love (257a).[15] By this, Socrates cannot mean that

---

[15] See Roochnik, "Erotics," for a discussion of Socrates as an expert in *eros*.

he has reached a full understanding of love since he still does not fully understand his love's object (i.e., the forms). However, he understands something essential about the nature of human desire – namely, that the highest of our desires are oriented toward the forms. In other words, Socrates' technical mastery, if he has any at all, is a kind of deep insight into human psychology, particularly into the nature of human desire. But, because his fundamental insight *is* to claim that desire is never properly turned inward upon ourselves but rather always outward to the forms, Socrates' subject matter can never limit itself to that which he masters. Any discussion of love cannot rest satisfied with describing only the human soul but instead must go beyond the soul to the object of its desires. Socrates' rhetoric is designed to inspire a love of the forms so that his listeners might more actively seek them. For this reason, we cannot argue either that rhetoric and philosophy are two distinct arts, in which rhetoric persuades while dialectic teaches,[16] or that philosophy and rhetoric are identical.[17] The dialogues show that some rhetoric is philosophical, while some is not. Good philosophical rhetoric leads the soul closer toward the truth. But, because the lover's encouragement of his beloved also feeds into his own love of the forms, philosophy and rhetoric remain intertwined.

We can now return to the problem posed in the chapter on the *Protagoras*, namely, the link between the performative and constitutive aspects of rhetoric. There, we argued that in the *Protagoras*, the performative aspects of Socratic questioning could not be fully separated from their constitutive aspects. The *Phaedrus* continues this approach to the interconnection between the performative- and content-based aspects of speech. Here, however, this connection between performance and content can be seen in terms of the links between rhetoric as the leading of souls (as performance) and the content of speech. As I have argued herein, the form of the Palinode cannot easily be separated from its content.[18] The Palinode does not simply *describe* through mythical language what Phaedrus needs

---

[16] See, e.g., Yunis, *Taming Democracy.*
[17] As examples of this way of construing the *Phaedrus*, see M. M. McCabe, "Arguments in Context: Aristotle's Defense of Rhetoric," in *Aristotle's Rhetoric: Philosophical Essays*, D. J. Furley and A. Nehamas, eds. (Princeton, NJ: Princeton University Press, 1994), 129–165; and C. J. Rowe, "The Argument and Structure of Plato's *Phaedrus*," *Proceedings of the Cambridge Philological Society* 32 (1986): 106–125.
[18] Gordon, *Turning*, makes a similar point about the dialogues as literary and dramatic structures. She argues that devices such as irony, images, and the dialogue form are not merely questions of literary style but also convey philosophical content.

to know about the nature of love and the forms. That is, it does not contain a fully formed truth, already mastered by Socrates, about which he then wishes to instruct Phaedrus. The Palinode explicitly tells us that our knowledge of the truth, the forms, is always partial and limited. We are never in a state of mastery or possession of knowledge of the forms but, at most, only en route to a greater understanding of them. The Palinode is an account of what it means to discover the truth, a description of the experience of seeking the truth, and a performed speech, a piece of rhetoric that draws Phaedrus into wanting that experience for himself.[19] In this sense, the content of the speech is not separable from the form in which it is presented. Part of the "content" of the speech *is* its effect on Phaedrus – that is, its rhetorical value for him and how it affects who he will become as a human being. The mythical presentation of the Palinode using terms that lead Phaedrus to desire this truth for himself is not accidental to the material but rather is essential to it. While Socrates' speeches seem to be tailored to Phaedrus, to the extent that Socrates sees all human beings as erotic, his rhetoric is more universal. However, what most affects Phaedrus is not the accurate division and collection of the subject matter. Without the mythical elements and verbal flourishes, without Socrates' evocative descriptions of the experience of being in love, without the description of all of its attractions and perils, Phaedrus is not likely to be persuaded.[20]

Plato also presents the *Phaedrus* to his audience in order to inspire his readers to a greater understanding of the nature of our own desires and so also to the forms. However, to inspire his audience to philosophy also requires that the audience of the dialogue actively ask questions about the nature of the soul, desire, and forms rather than being passively instructed. The *Phaedrus* as a whole can be understood as a form of erotic discourse, leading the soul toward philosophical inquiry into the nature of love, the self, and the forms. In this sense, Socrates' first words of the dialogue – "My dear Phaedrus, where have you been and where are you going?" – are words for Plato's audience as well (227a).[21] In the

---

[19] See Matthew Linck, "Unmastering Speech: Irony in Plato's *Phaedrus*," *Philosophy and Rhetoric* 36 (2003): 264–276, who shows how irony in the *Phaedrus* functions to lead Phaedrus' soul. Linck also sees the use of such rhetoric as an example of how Socrates' speech is "ensouled" (275).

[20] To this extent, I agree with Ferrari's thesis that non-logical persuasion is a key part of the *Phaedrus*. See G. R. F. Ferrari, *Listening to the Cicadas: A Study of Plato's* Phaedrus (Cambridge: Cambridge University Press, 1987).

[21] Sallis notes that this line in the *Phaedrus* can be understood in three ways: in terms of Phaedrus' literal journey; where Phaedrus is headed as a human being; and in terms of

Palinode, Socrates tells us that all human souls, by nature, are in motion, either toward or away from the forms. Plato's dialogue asks each of its audience members to ask himself, "Where have I been, and where am I going?"

V.

We can now return to Socrates' abstract description of rhetoric in order to examine its rhetorical dimensions. Socrates' description of the art of good rhetoric is itself a rhetorical description, designed to persuade Phaedrus to pursue philosophy. Socrates uses humor, myth, personification, and even elements of forensic rhetoric to draw Phaedrus nearer to Socrates' own understanding of good rhetoric. I suggest that the shift from overtly erotic language to other techniques is intended to move Phaedrus beyond Phaedrus' interest in the philosophical lover and his beloved to the forms.[22]

Rather than giving a speech, Socrates explores rhetoric through opposing two different sets of ideas about it. Phaedrus seems to be unsure of whether or not writing is shameful. He implies that those who criticize logographers such as Lysias might be right. At the same time, Phaedrus is disappointed at the prospect of Lysias quitting writing; he is considerably anxious at the prospect (257c–258d). Socrates responds that writing can be good or bad, depending on how it is done. One must find out what it means to write well or poorly, through "cross-examining" (*exetasai*) Lysias. Phaedrus responds with great enthusiasm to the prospect of cross-examination, asking whether there is any other pleasure "worth living for" aside from this kind (258d). By first granting Phaedrus' wish that there might be a good form of writing but then asking Phaedrus to join him in cross-examining Lysias, Socrates makes Phaedrus into his ally. Rather than defending Lysias, Phaedrus now opposes Lysias in the discussion, enticed by the prospect of a forensic exercise. Socrates' approach gives Phaedrus license to criticize Lysias.

---

the origin and destiny of the human soul with which the Palinode will concern itself. See Sallis, *Being and Logos*, 107–108.

[22] Kasteley also sees this section as rhetorically oriented toward Phaedrus but argues that Socrates describes good rhetoric in a technical way because Phaedrus is too much of a technician and not sufficiently erotic to be persuaded by the Palinode. See Kasteley, "Respecting the Rupture," 138–152. I take the opposite point of view: it is precisely because the Palinode's myth is so successful with the erotic Phaedrus that Phaedrus can now take an interest in the nature of rhetoric in a more technical sense as well.

Socrates also uses a number of myths, images, and jokes to make Phaedrus' disposition gentle and receptive to the criticisms of Lysias. Phaedrus says that he would rather have the pleasure of discussing speeches than anything else, contrasting this love of speeches to the love of bodily goods, which he finds "slavish" (258e). Socrates in reply offers a myth about the origin of cicadas: the mythical origin of the cicadas is of human beings who sang, forgetting to eat and drink, and so died before they even knew what had happened. The Muses then gave the cicadas the honor of never needing to eat or drink but only to sing (259b–d). Through this myth, Socrates implies that he too finds pleasure and honor in speaking rather than in pursuing bodily pleasure. Again, Socrates emphasizes the harmony between Phaedrus and himself. Later, Socrates uses a humorous analogy of a horse and an ass. Socrates jokes that if one's audience did not know what a horse is and believed it to be an ass, perhaps one ought to create a speech in praise of the ass as the creature best suited for warfare. Phaedrus naturally calls this speech to be "ludicrous" (260c). But Socrates' more serious point is that a rhetorician must have a discursive understanding of his subject matter and not only teach what "seems" to be the case, as Phaedrus has heard.

Then, Socrates poses a much more philosophically serious question in relation to his joke: "[I]sn't it better to be ludicrous (*geloion*) and friendly (*philon*), rather than clever (*deinon*) and hostile (*echthron*)?" (260c). Socrates challenges Phaedrus to consider whether it is better to be friendly or hostile to an audience if the friendly idea is crazy but the wiser idea is one to which the audience will be hostile. If we look to Phaedrus' character earlier in the dialogue, we can see that Phaedrus values both cleverness and wisdom, which act as competing desires in his soul. Phaedrus is "sick with desire to hear speeches," Socrates tells us (228b), but the fundamental question is what aspect of a speech he most values. When Phaedrus asks Socrates whether any other Greek could make a better speech on the same subject, Socrates asks him whether he really thinks that a speech should only be praised for its being "clear, compact, and well-turned." Socrates implies that Phaedrus' only concerns are stylistic (234e).

However, at times, Phaedrus insists that his praise of Lysias is *not* limited to stylistic concerns. He responds to Socrates, "The material was handled extremely well. He didn't leave out any of the items that are naturally implied by the topic, and everything was given worthy treatment, so that no one could add to what he said or say more and say it better" (235b). Phaedrus displays interest in the content of a speech as much as its style. Moreover, at least two remarks earlier in the drama suggest that Phaedrus cares about the truth. When Socrates mentions that he has heard that there is an altar to Boreas farther downstream, Phaedrus asks whether Socrates thinks "this mythical story is true" (229c). Later, when Socrates says that his speech of the non-lover has been "simple-minded, even slightly irreverent; what could be more terrible than that?," Phaedrus responds, "Nothing, if you speak the truth" (242d). Plato indicates that Phaedrus does hope that the truth informs speeches. Still, only moments after his claim that the truth matters, he tells Socrates that he will insist that Lysias write on the same theme as Socrates. Phaedrus' concerns shift back and forth between a focus upon truth of a speech and its pleasing style. So, Socrates' question as to whether the point of a speech is to please one's audience or speak what is true at the risk of incurring an audience's hostility is exactly the question that Phaedrus needs to answer for himself. Socrates is careful not to admonish Phaedrus for his love of style. We know from Aristotle that Gorgias thought humor could be an important strategy in arguing matters of controversy (*Rhetoric* 1419b). Here, Socrates uses humor to defuse the question of the conflict between pleasing an audience and speaking what one knows to be true. The joke about the ass disarms Phaedrus and makes him more receptive to the introduction of the theme of knowledge as crucial to writing a good speech.

Socrates also personifies Rhetoric and argumentation in his presentation of the arguments for and against the question as to whether rhetoric is an art. His defense of rhetoric as an art is first presented by a personified female Rhetoric (260d), while the counterarguments are presented as going "on the war path," testifying that Rhetoric is "lying" (*pseudetai*) and is not an art (260e). This personification (*prosopopoeia*) of Rhetoric and her opponents functions in at least two ways. First, personification makes Socrates' argument more emotionally effective. Presenting the conflict as an attack on a woman gives Socrates' topic much more weight than if it were merely presented as an intellectually interesting question. Second, by making Rhetoric a woman under attack, Socrates indirectly implies sympathy for rhetoric, once again suggesting to Phaedrus that their concern for rhetoric is shared. Socrates' account of good rhetoric is initially set up as a defense of it from its assailants. Socrates makes himself Rhetoric's – and so also Phaedrus' – knight in shining armor at the same time that he offers serious criticisms of how Lysias actually practices rhetoric.

If indeed Socrates' strategy here is to give Phaedrus a way in which to criticize Lysias' rhetorical practice without also letting go of rhetoric, his great passion, altogether then we need not see the *Phaedrus* as Plato's "later" account of good rhetoric. While most commentators view the *Phaedrus* as a shift from Plato's "earlier" position against rhetoric in the *Gorgias*,[23] perhaps the difference between the two accounts rests primarily in the differences between Socrates' interlocutors. Gorgias and Polus present themselves as in love with their own practice of *epideixis* and with pleasing the audience; their commitments demand a showier, more hostile Socrates who takes them down publicly. Callicles, too, seems to be shameless in his willingness to use rhetoric for his own ends, and Socrates' extreme examples of the *kinaidos* and "leaky jars" address the need to attend to matters of shame and honor. All three characters are in need of admonishment, for none display concern with the problem of knowledge. They are also speaking in a public setting, before others who have come to admire Gorgias and to pay the sophists for their teachings. In the *Phaedrus*, Socrates is in a private conversation with Phaedrus, a young, excitable man with a sense of the noble and good, at least some concern for the truth, and a great love of the musical and the beautiful. Plato presents Phaedrus as a potential philosopher, one who is not in need of admonishment but rather encouragement to develop an understanding of rhetoric in harmony with his other ideals.

Socrates' strategy of personification is effective. Phaedrus asks to hear the arguments, telling Socrates: "Lead them out so we can review what they say and how they say it" (261a). Here, Phaedrus' concerns are both for the content – "what they say" – and the style – "how they say it" – of the attacks on Rhetoric. Socrates makes his purpose clear: "Approach my noble creatures; persuade Phaedrus, this beautiful boy, that unless he loves wisdom sufficiently, he will never become a competent speaker about anything" (261a). Socrates' Palinode had earlier linked the love of wisdom to the love of speeches, beauty, and the musical by giving the soul who loves these things the highest ranking. Here in the non-mythical account of rhetoric, Socrates links good rhetoric to the need to inquire into the "nature" (*phusis*) of subject matter at hand. Socrates' image of a living body functions to link the natural order to the order of speech. One cannot artificially separate the arrangement of an animal's parts without destroying the animal itself. Similarly, Socrates says that the arrangement of a speech cannot be wholly separated from the proper collection and division of its content according to nature. Dialectic, in other words, is central to good rhetoric.

---

[23] See, e.g., Yunis, *Taming Democracy*.

The temptation might be to reduce rhetoric to philosophy or at least to view the essence of good rhetoric as dialectic. However, if my analysis of the rhetoric of the Palinode is correct, then Socrates' own understanding of philosophical rhetoric is not reductive. That is, Socrates is not developing an account of rhetoric where rhetoric must be equated with the correct use of a particular philosophical method, such as division and collection. The Palinode persuades through the use of images that are designed specifically to draw Phaedrus' soul to care for philosophical goods. The Palinode is not primarily a speech about the collection and division of things according to nature, although it does classify some things (i.e., madness and different types of soul) in a way that is similar to division and collection. The Palinode attempts to lead souls through a beautiful style and erotic imagery and also through encouraging Phaedrus to identify with the "best" souls – that is, those of the philosophers. To this extent, Socratic rhetoric shares something in common with the claim in Gorgias' *Encomium to Helen* that rhetoric is like a lord that seduces the soul, or a powerful drug (8; 14).

Another alternative would be to treat collection and division as philosophy, while understanding speeches such as the Palinode to be rhetorical, perhaps preparatory for genuine philosophy (e.g., the sort of philosophical dialectic alluded to in the *Republic's* middle books). However, if we take Socrates' idea in the Palinode that the distinctive essence of the philosophical soul is that it seeks the forms, then division and collection cannot be the only way in which good philosophy is practiced.[24] Instead, any way of speaking that leads the soul to seek the forms and increases its desire to pursue them rather than other, lower goods counts as philosophical rhetoric. When Socrates gives the first speech of the non-lover, he moves Phaedrus a bit further away from his devotion to Lysias. Thus, when Socrates insists to Phaedrus that good rhetoric must divide and collect its subject matter properly, this need not be to the exclusion of other elements of philosophical rhetoric. I suspect that Socrates places so much weight on the elements of knowledge and the nature of the subject matter here because Phaedrus himself already values matters of style, phrasing, and the like. But we as readers of the dialogue ought not take Socrates' description of good rhetoric in terms of collection and

---

[24] I leave aside the relation of division and collection to the forms because the scope of it is beyond this work. For one account, see David White, *Rhetoric and Reality in Plato's Phaedrus* (Albany, NY: SUNY Press, 1992). However, division and collection is limited to the extent that the forms cannot be captured by it. See also Ferrari, *Listening*.

division to be *the* definitive account of good rhetoric. It is the dialogue's use of rhetoric as a whole that really illuminates Socrates' use of rhetoric. Philosophical rhetoric is characterized by love. Good rhetoric is guided by a love of the forms and of one's audience. But in the Palinode, love of another person is closely connected to love of the forms: love leads the lover to care for the beloved and the beloved to return favors, and this mutual love leads both lovers toward the forms. Human love is integrally connected to the love of the forms.

In fact, if we take Socrates' Palinode seriously, then the ultimate force of philosophical rhetoric is not to be found in a speaker, for the Palinode shows that the forms have an almost gravitational pull on human souls. While some souls are better than others at rising to the heights of the forms, and different souls seek them alongside different gods, the Palinode makes all souls subject to them in some way or another. We could then say that in some sense, the forms are the real "rhetoricians": they alone have the power to move the soul. The lover or rhetorician who leads the soul of his beloved toward the forms is only identifying in another person the same sense of attraction to the truth that he already feels. For Socrates, the beauty of the truth is naturally attractive. It is this naturally attractive quality of the forms that draws souls nearer to it; the forms are the genuinely beautiful objects, and beautiful speeches and the love between lover and beloved are always reflections of a prior (if sometimes hidden) love of the forms.

Here, Socrates departs substantially from Lysias and the sophists in giving a priority to the forms as the real leaders of the soul. Rhetoricians merely imitate, to a greater or lesser extent, the truth and the beauty that belong more fully to them. With his acceptance of rhetoric, Socrates does not wish to eliminate from discourse all questions regarding truth, being, or the real. On the contrary, Socrates' affirmation of the concept of forms reveals a genuine commitment on his part to truth apart from our individual or cultural expressions of those truths. That is, good rhetoric and good philosophy are not merely poetry or invention; they seek a real existence apart from themselves. We see again that the love of the forms is prior to knowledge of them. Desire is the driving force that spurs souls to seek the forms; Socrates locates that desire as part of the fundamental nature of the human being.

Moreover, no speech is identical to a form, for the forms are unified and transcend our full comprehension, while speeches are by nature composed of parts and reflect the impartial state of human knowledge (at best). Every speech, to some degree or another, is constructed; all speech is partly poetic, whether mythical (as with the Palinode) or not (as with Socrates' analogies, jokes, and prose descriptions of good rhetoric). That Plato thought we ought to seek it or move closer to it, however, is not to say that he thinks that human beings are capable of reaching some pure and unmediated conception of the forms. Rather, Plato locates us, the human beings, in a middle ground between the real or universal and the merely constructive. Our speeches are a mixture of the poetic and the real. Socrates presents this orientation toward the universal as a moral or regulative ideal rather than as a completed project. Still, a good speech points beyond itself, to a truth that is not itself verbal but objective; a good speech subjects itself to the truth of the forms insofar as they can be known.[25] What sets Socrates' rhetoric apart from that of the sophists is the commitment to seek the forms and to lead others to them, not mastery of language or a particular method of doing philosophy. Socratic rhetoric is defined by its service to love. While Lysias argues in favor of the non-lover, Socrates affirms love above all other human activities.

While the final sections of the dialogue are well known for their criticisms of writing, Socrates allows for the possibility of writing that might address different souls differently. If a writer knew each of the forms of soul, he might offer complex speeches to a complex soul and simple speeches to a simple soul (278c). Commentators have found the Platonic dialogues to be exemplars of such a form of writing.[26] Socrates acknowledges that writing is problematic because it can fail to address its particular audience's needs and because it can give the illusion of knowledge on the speaker's part when none is present (276a; 275b). But, the Platonic dialogues are capable of addressing different souls differently. As we have seen in previous chapters, even the problem of the relationship between philosophy and rhetoric is not addressed in one single way. Instead, Plato raises the issue of the relationship between philosophy and rhetoric in ways that address different kinds of audiences and take account of different concerns: politics, the love of speech as a display, the question of the relative value of power and knowledge, and so on. There is no single Platonic treatise on the nature of sophistry or rhetoric because the needs of one interlocutor may not be identical to the needs of another.[27]

[25] See Sallis, *Being and Logos*, 174.
[26] See Ronna Burger, *Plato's Phaedrus* (Birmingham: University of Alabama Press, 1980); Cole, *The Origins of Rhetoric*; Ferrari, *Listening*; and Griswold, *Self-Knowledge*, chapter 6.
[27] See Drew Hyland, "Why Plato Wrote Dialogues," *Philosophy and Rhetoric* 1 (January 1968): 38–50, on the issues of how the dialogues address different souls in different ways.

For example, for one reader, the *Gorgias* may better address the question of whether philosophy is as powerful as certain forms of sophistic rhetoric. The *Gorgias* does not address this issue through solving the problem in a transparent and obvious manner, however; rather, it engages the reader and draws him into examining the problem of knowledge and power and their relative value. But any reader who examines these two competing values and begins to weigh and to discuss them is already engaged in practicing philosophy. In this way, the *Gorgias* as a dialogue functions rhetorically, too, since it draws the reader into the active practice of philosophy, even when or perhaps especially when it does not offer final answers to questions. The *Phaedrus*, too, asks the reader to engage in an analysis of rhetoric and its relationship to philosophy. However, its emphasis is apolitical; virtually nothing is said about the relationship between philosophy and politics. Perhaps the *Phaedrus* best addresses a reader who is enamored with epideictic speeches, as Phaedrus is. Once again, the dialogue functions both philosophically and rhetorically: it both offers an account of rhetoric and tells a myth about philosophical lovers; throughout, the reader must engage with the text in order to make sense of the relationship between philosophy and rhetoric. In neither dialogue does Plato simply transmit knowledge: the dialogue is not an epideictic display designed to please, or a deliberative speech that persuades an audience to take a concrete political action, or a forensic defense of one person or point of view. The dialogue form takes up and refashions a number of rhetorical devices and commonplaces. At the same time, the dialogue transcends all of these devices in its aim of leading the soul toward the forms.

In summary, Socrates' philosophical rhetoric in the *Phaedrus* is characterized by his love of the forms and of Phaedrus. Philosophical rhetoric, while it includes methods such as division and collection, is not reducible to a single method. Socrates uses myths, similes, erotic language, humor, personification, antithesis, and other devices as part of his *psychagôgia* with Phaedrus. These devices themselves are neutral and must be evaluated in terms of how well they serve the speaker's purpose of drawing the soul through love toward the forms. The philosopher is distinguished from the sophist not by a method but rather by how well he loves.

VI.

I have argued that Plato's approach to philosophical rhetoric is far more complex than is often supposed. Even in dialogues such as the *Gorgias* that take sophistic rhetoric to task, Plato does not reject rhetoric in favor of a rhetoric-free philosophy. Neither does he propose a new method of philosophical rhetoric that can be limited to one type of argumentation or method of speaking. Instead, we see that Plato presents philosophy as being intertwined with rhetoric. Socrates prefers to ask questions when possible, for questioning is a way for both speakers and audiences to express many of the virtues of being a philosopher, including knowledge of one's own ignorance, a sense of wonder about the world, responsibility for one's speech (*parrêsia*), goodwill, and love of those with whom one speaks. However, Socrates' practice of questioning is not limited to a specific method. His questions are guided by a sense of *kairos*, knowing when and how to speak to his interlocutors in particular circumstances. Socrates makes choices as to how to question those with whom he is speaking, but those choices cannot be exhausted by a limited set of universal principles. Perhaps it is for this reason that Plato presents Socrates in dramatic dialogues, where we can see how his questioning is guided by attention to *kairos* and his ubiquitous individualized care for the souls of those to whom he speaks.

Socrates' rhetoric in the dialogues is not limited to a questioning stance, however. Socrates uses a number of other modes of speaking, such as longer speeches, myths, or defense speeches in order to lead his audience closer to the good. Many of these ways of speaking share a great deal in common with the ways in which his sophistic opponents speak. Perhaps we can say that part of the brilliance of Socrates' rhetoric with his sophistic opponents is to take up their styles of speaking but in ways that support philosophical goods.

I have also argued that, for Plato, the primary difference between philosophers and sophists is their theoretical stance, a stance that is grounded upon attention to human desire. The sophist is not defined by a difference in his method, for Socrates often uses some of the same ways of speaking that his sophistic opponents do. Rather, in keeping with Isocrates and Alcidamas, Plato uses the vocabulary of philosophy and sophistry in a normative way. *Philosophia* is a way of identifying a way of living according to a certain vision of the world, based on the understanding of oneself and one's deepest desires. It is not defined by a method or even by a particular intellectual doctrine so much as it is by the practice of living well. Part of this practice of living well includes seeking the forms. Accordingly, for Plato the difference between philosophical rhetoric and sophistic rhetoric is also normative: sophistic rhetoric is deficient because it does not seek to lead its audience toward the forms. Socrates' rhetoric is always informed by care of his interlocutors, a care that is ultimately exhibited in his attempts to lead them closer to the forms so that they might find the object of their deepest love.

We also see in the Platonic dialogues a close relationship between form and content in Socrates' arguments. Socrates does not separate the discovery of the truth through philosophy from its presentation in speeches, for conversation is part of how we come to better know the truth for ourselves as well as lead others toward it. Moreover, Socrates' questioning stance itself exhibits the virtue of knowing one's own relative ignorance and limitation. That is, an important part of the content of philosophy is this acknowledgment of limit in how one speaks. The acknowledgment of the incompleteness of knowledge is conveyed as much through Socrates' style of speaking as through the content of what he says. Socrates repeatedly speaks of the limited nature of what he knows in the dialogues. We see this, for example, in the *Apology*'s statement that Socrates' "knows only that he does not know"; Socrates' claim in the *Protagoras* that the discovery of the truth is best undertaken by two people in conversation; or his caution in the *Republic* that images of the sun, divided line, and cave are merely images that do not reflect a stance of complete knowledge. Questions, images, and aporetic conversations are all forms of speech that can reflect the ways in which the content of our knowledge remains partial. We see in Plato's presentation of Socrates the recognition that good philosophical rhetoric is not only about articulating what we do understand but also about admitting that our words do not yet capture the fullness of the truth. For this reason, Socrates continues to question others as a midwife of ideas who is "barren" rather than as a dogmatic philosopher who authoritatively collects and divides the world as the Stranger does.

Socrates' attention to *kairos*, to the right moment, and in how he speaks shows sensitivity to the situated nature of human knowledge. If *kairos* includes a sense of improvisation in how responds to one's audience, then Socrates is a master improviser. At the same time, Socrates is always oriented to that world of forms, immutable truths to which he is drawn and to which he hopes to draw others. Accordingly, his stance as a speaker is always a middle one, in between either of the extremes of the total invention of meaning and the discovery of an unchanging and objective truth. Socrates speaks with his interlocutors as if *both* the discovery of eternal truths outside of ourselves *and* the attention to the individual person standing in front of him, here and now, are of the utmost importance. In other words, Socrates' attention to *kairos* reflects his love and care for his interlocutor. His use of rhetoric, however, is not oriented toward persuading his interlocutor to believe in him, Socrates, but rather to love and to seek the forms. That is, genuine love of one's audience requires loving them enough to lead them beyond one's self as a speaker or a writer, toward the forms. Philosophical rhetoric can be viewed, then, as the bridge between the unchanging and eternal forms and the partial, created, limited understanding of the truth that characterizes the human condition.

In this way, Plato is neither a proponent of a philosophy that claims it has grasped the forms or the nature of being in its totality nor of a rhetoric that sees all meaning as created by us. Truth, for a human being, is always partly poetical and partly situated in our conversations, arguments, and questions about the world. Yet, the eternal forms are the ultimate objects of inquiry, and good speeches at least attempt to bring us to seek the forms, even as our grasp of the truth remains limited. Plato rejects sophistry for its refusal to acknowledge an objective truth that ought to inform how we seek and how we live because this higher good is what we really most desire. In a sense, Plato's rhetoric is guided by a strong sense of humility, the humility of a philosopher willing to subject himself to a transcendent truth outside of himself and simultaneously to acknowledge that his grasp of that truth is always incomplete. His love of the forms is so great that he wishes to lead others to them. Plato's dialogues present the philosopher as a person who embodies both humility and love.

Bibliography

Primary Sources

Alcidamas: The Works and Fragments. Edited with Introduction, Translation, and Commentary by J. V. Muir. London: Bristol Classic Press, 2001.

Aristotle, *The Rhetoric and Poetics of Aristotle*. Introduction by Edward P. J. Corbett. New York: McGraw Hill, 1984.

Burnet, John, ed. *Platonis Opera, Volumes I–IV*. Oxford: Oxford University Press, 1989.

Diels, Hermann, and Walter Kranz. *Die Fragmente der Vorsokratiker*, 3 vols., 6th ed. Berlin: Weidmann, 1951–1952.

Edwards, M., and S. Usher, eds. *Classical Texts Series: Greek Orators, Vol. 1*. Warminster, PA: 1985.

Euripides. "Fragmenta Euripides: *Antiope*," in *Thesaurus Lingua Graece* cd-rom, Regents of the University of California, 1999.

Isocrates. *Isocrates I*. With an English translation by George Norlin. Cambridge, MA: Loeb, 2000.

_____. *Isocrates I*. Translated by David Mirhardy and Yun Lee Too. Austin: University of Texas Press, 2000.

Plato. "Apology," *Five Dialogues*. Translated by G. M. A. Grube. Indianapolis: Hackett Publishing Company, 1981, 23–44.

_____. *Plato: Gorgias*, with introduction and commentary by E. R. Dodds. Oxford: Clarendon Press, 1959.

_____. *Plato: Gorgias*. Translated with notes by Terence Irwin. Oxford: Clarendon Press, 1979.

_____. *Plato: Gorgias*. Translated by Donald Zeyl. Indianapolis: Hackett Press Hackett Publishing Company, 1987.

_____. *Plato's Phaedrus*. Translated with notes, glossary, appendices, interpretive essay, and introduction by Stephen Scully. Newburyport, MA: Focus Library, 2003.

_____. *Plato's Phaedrus*. Translated with commentary by C. J. Rowe. Wiltshire, England: Aris and Phillips, 1986.

————. *Protagoras.* Translated with notes by S. Lombardo and K. Bell. Introduction by M. Frede. Indianapolis: Hackett Publishing Company, 1992.

————. *Protagoras,* revised edition. Translated with notes by C. C. W. Taylor. Oxford: Clarendon Press, 1991.

————. *Protagoras.* With an introduction, notes, and appendices by J. Adam and A. M. Adam. Cambridge: Cambridge University Press, 1971.

————. *Protagoras,* Edited with an introduction by G. Vlastos. New York: Liberal Arts Press, 1956.

————. *The Republic of Plato,* 2nd edition. Translated with notes by Allan Bloom. New York: HarperCollins Publishers, 1991.

————. *Sophist.* Translated and with a commentary by Seth Benardete. Chicago and London: University of Chicago Press, 1984.

————. *Plato's Sophist: The Professor of Wisdom.* Translation, introduction, and glossary by Eva Brann, Peter Kalvakage, and Eric Salem. Newburyport, MA: Focus Library, 1996.

————. *The Theaetetus of Plato.* Translation by M. J. Levitt and commentary by Myles Burnyeat. Indianapolis and Cambridge: Hackett Publishing Company, 1990.

Sprague, Rosamond Kent, ed. *The Older Sophists.* Indianapolis: Hackett Publishing Company, 1972. *Thesaurus Lingua Graecae* CD-ROM. Irvine, CA: Regents of the University of California, 1999.

Xenophon. *The Shorter Socratic Writings: Apology of Socrates to the Jury, Oeconomicus, and Symposium.* Translations with interpretive essays and notes. Edited by Robert C. Bartlett. Ithaca, NY: Cornell University Press, 1996.

Secondary Sources

Adkins, Arthur. "Arete, Techne, Democracy, and Sophists: *Protagoras* 316b–328d." *Journal of Hellenic Studies* 93 (1973): 3–12.

————. *Merit and Responsibility: A Study in Greek Values.* Oxford: Clarendon Press, 1960.

Allen, R. F. *Socrates and Legal Obligation.* Minneapolis: University of Minnesota Press, 1980.

Annas, Julia. *An Introduction to Plato's Republic.* Oxford: Clarendon Press, 1981.

Anton, John. "Dialectic and Health in Plato's *Gorgias:* Presuppositions and Implications." *Ancient Philosophy* 1 (1980): 49–60.

Arendt, Hannah. "Philosophy and Politics." *Social Research* 57 (1) (1990): 73–103.

Arieti, James. "Plato's Philosophical *Antiope:* The *Gorgias* in Plato's Dialogues." In Press, Gerald (ed.), *Plato's Dialogues: New Studies and Interpretations.* Lanham, MD: Rowman and Littlefield, 1993, 197–214.

Arp, Robert. "The Double Life of Justice and Injustice." *Polis* 16 (1999): 17–29.

Ausland, Hayden. "Socrates' Argumentative Burden in the *Republic.*" In Michelini, Ann (ed.), *Plato as Author: The Rhetoric of Philosophy* (Leiden: Brill, 2003), 123–144.

Austin, J. L. *How to Do Things with Words.* Oxford: Oxford University Press, 1962.

Avnon, Dan. "'Know Thyself': Socratic Companionship and Platonic Community." *Political Theory* 23 (1995): 304–329.

Bailly, Jacques. "What You Say, What You Believe, and What You Mean." *Ancient Philosophy* 19 (1999): 65–76.

Bateman, J. J. "Lysias and the Law." *Transactions and Proceedings of the American Philological Association*, Vol. 89 (1958): 276–285.

Bauman, Richard. "Performance." *International Encyclopedia of Communications*, vol. 3. Oxford: Oxford University Press, 1989, 262–266.

Bauman, Richard, and Charles Briggs. "Poetics and Performance as Critical Perspectives on Language and Social Life." *Annual Review of Anthropology* 19 (1990): 59–88.

Benitez, Eugenio. "Argument, Rhetoric, and Philosophic Method: Plato's *Protagoras*." *Philosophy and Rhetoric* 25 (1992): 222–252.

Benson, Hugh. "Problems with Socratic Method." In Scott, Gary, ed., *Does Socrates Have a Method?* University Park, PA: Pennsylvania State University Press, 2002.

————. "The Problem of the Elenchus Reconsidered." *Ancient Philosophy* 7 (1987): 67–85.

Bett, Richard. "Is There a Sophistic Ethics?" *Ancient Philosophy* 22 (2002): 235–262.

Beverslius, John. *Cross-Examining Socrates*. Cambridge: Cambridge University Press, 2000.

Black, Edwin. "Plato's View of Rhetoric." *Quarterly Journal of Speech* 44 (1953): 361–374.

Blondell, Ruby. *The Play of Character in Plato's Dialogues*. Cambridge: Cambridge University Press, 2002.

Bonner, Robert J. "The Legal Setting of Plato's *Apology*." *Classical Philology* 3 (1908): 151.

Bowra, C. M. *Greek Lyric Poetry*, 2d edition. Oxford: Clarendon Press, 1961.

————. "Simonides and Scopas." *Classical Philology* 29 (1934): 230–239.

Brickhouse, Thomas, and Nicholas Smith. "Socrates and the Unity of the Virtues." *Journal of Ethics* 1 (1997): 311–324.

————. *Plato's Socrates*. Oxford: Oxford University Press, 1994.

————. *Socrates on Trial*. Princeton, NJ: Princeton University Press, 1989.

————. "The Paradox of Socratic Ignorance in Plato's *Apology*." *History of Philosophy Quarterly* 1 (1984): 125–131.

————. "The Origin of Socrates' Mission." *Journal of the History of Ideas* 44 (1983): 657–666.

Brogan, Walter. "Plato's Dialectical Soul: Heidegger on Plato's Ambiguous Relationship to Rhetoric." *Research in Phenomenology* 27 (1997): 3–15.

Brown, Malcolm. 1969. "Theaetetus: Knowledge as Continued Learning." *Journal of the History of Philosophy* 7: 359–379.

Burger, Ronna. *Plato's Phaedrus*. Birmingham: University of Alabama Press, 1980.

Burnet, John. *Euthyphro, Apology of Socrates, and Crito*. Oxford: Oxford University Press, 1977.

————. *Greek Philosophy*. London: MacMillan, 1968.

Burnyeat, M. F. "The Impiety of Socrates." *Ancient Philosophy* 17 (1997): 1–12.

Cairns, Douglas. *Aidos: The Psychology and Ethics of Honor and Shame in Ancient Greek Literature.* Oxford: Clarendon Press, 1993.

Chroust, Anton-Hermann. *Socrates, Man and Myth.* London: Routledge, 1957.

Coby, Patrick. *Socrates and the Sophistic Enlightenment: A Commentary on Plato's Protagoras.* Lewisburg, PA: Bucknell University Press, 1987.

Cole, Thomas. *The Origins of Rhetoric in Ancient Greece.* Baltimore and London: Johns Hopkins University Press, 1991.

Consigny, Scott. 1992. "Gorgias' Use of the Epideictic." *Philosophy and Rhetoric* 25.3: 281–297.

Coulter, James. "The Relation of the Apology of Socrates to Gorgias' Defense of Palamades and Plato's Critique of Gorgianic Rhetoric." *Harvard Studies in Classical Philology* 68 (1964): 269–303.

Crombie, I. M. *An Examination of Plato's Doctrines,* volume I. London: Routledge and Kegan Paul, 1962.

Cronquist, John. "The Point of Hedonism in Plato's *Protagoras.*" *Prudentia* 12 (1975): 63–81.

Cross, Robert, and Anthony Woozley. *Plato's Republic: A Philosophical Commentary.* New York: St. Martin's Press, 1964.

Cross, Robert, and Anthony Woozley. "Knowledge, Belief, and the Forms." In Vlastos, G., ed., *Plato: A Collection of Critical Essays* (Notre Dame: University of Notre Dame Press, 1978), 70–96.

Crowley, Sharon. "A Plea for the Revival of Sophistry." *Rhetoric Review* 7 (1989): 318–344.

de Strycker, SJ, Emile, and S. R. Slings. *Plato's Apology of Socrates.* Leiden: Brill, 1994.

Desjardins, Rosemarie. "Why Dialogues? Plato's Serious Play." In Griswold, Charles (ed.), *Platonic Writings, Platonic Readings.* London: Routledge, 1988, 110–125.

Dickie, Matthew. "The Argument and Form of Simonides 542 PMG." *Harvard Studies in Classical Philology* 82 (1978): 21–33.

Donlon, Walter. "Simonides Fr. 4D and P. OXY. 2432." *Transactions of the American Philological Association* 100 (1969): 71–95.

Dorion, Louis André. "La Subversion de l'elechos juridique dans l'Apologie de Socrate." *Revue Philosophique de Louvain* (1990): 311–344.

Dorter, Kenneth. "Philosopher-Rulers: How Contemplation Becomes Action." *Ancient Philosophy* 21 (2001): 335–356.

Dyson, M. "Knowledge and Hedonism in Plato's *Protagoras.*" *Journal of Hellenic Studies* 96 (1976): 32–45.

Evans, David. "Dialogue and Dialectic: Philosophical Truth in Plato." *Diotima* 31 (2003): 21–26.

Fattal, Michael. "L'alethes Logos' en Phedre 270c10." In *Understanding the Phaedrus,* Livio Rossetti, ed., Sankt Augustin: Academia, 1992.

Feaver, D. D., and J. E. Hare. "The *Apology* as an Inverted Parody of Rhetoric." *Arethusa* 14 (1981): 205–216.

Ferrari, G. R. F. *Listening to the Cicadas: A Study of Plato's Phaedrus.* Cambridge: Cambridge University Press, 1987.

Fish, Stanley. *Doing What Comes Naturally*. Durham, NC: Duke University Press, 1989.

Fontenrose, Joseph. *The Delphic Oracle: Its Responses and Operations, with a Catalogue of Responses*. Berkeley, CA: University of California Press, 1981.

Frede, Dorothea. "The Impossibility of Perfection: Socrates' Criticism of Simonides' Poem in the *Protagoras*." *Review of Metaphysics* 39 (1986): 713–753.

Freydberg, Bernard. *The Play of the Platonic Dialogues*. New York: Peter Lang, 1997.

Friedlander, Paul. *The Dialogues of Plato*, volume 2. Translated by Hans Meyerhoff. Princeton, NJ: Princeton University Press, 1977.

Furley, D. J., and A. Nehamas (eds.). *Aristotle's Rhetoric: Philosophical Essays*. Princeton, NJ: Princeton University Press, 1994.

Fussi, Alessandra. "Socrates' Reputation of Gorgias." *Proceedings of the Boston Area Colloquium in Ancient Philosophy* 17 (2001): 123–145.

Gagarin, Michael. *Antiphon the Sophist*. Austin: University of Texas Press, 2002.

———. *Early Greek Law*. Berkeley: University of California Press, 1989.

Gallagher, Robert. "Protreptic Aims of Plato's *Republic*." *Ancient Philosophy* 24 (2004): 293–319.

Gill, Christopher. "Plato and the Education of Character." *Archive für Geschichte der Philosophie* 67 (1985): 1–26.

Goldberg, Larry. *A Commentary on Plato's Protagoras*. New York: Peter Lang, 1983.

Goldman, Harvey. "Reexamining the 'Examined Life' in Plato's *Apology of Socrates*." *The Philosophical Forum* 35 (2004): 1–33.

Gonzalez, Francisco. "The Socratic Elenchus as Constructive Protreptic" In Gary Scott (ed.), *Does Socrates Have a Method? Rethinking the Elenchus in Plato's Dialogues and Beyond*. University Park, PA: University of Pennsylvania Press, 2002, 161–182.

———. *Dialectic and Dialogue: Plato's Practice of Philosophical Inquiry*. Evanston, IL: Northwestern University Press, 1998.

Gordon, Jill, "Eros and Philosophical Seduction in the *Alcibiades I*." *Ancient Philosophy* 23 (spring 2003): 11–30.

———. *Turning Towards Philosophy*. University Park, PA: Pennsylvania State University Press, 1999.

Griswold, Charles L. "Irony in the Platonic Dialogues," *Philosophy and Literature* 26 (2002): 84–106.

———. "Relying on Your Own Voice: An Unsettled Rivalry of Moral Ideals in Plato's *Protagoras*." *Review of Metaphysics* 53 (1999): 533–557.

———. (ed.). *Platonic Writings, Platonic Readings*. New York: Routledge, 1988.

———. "Philosophy, Education, and Courage in Plato's *Laches*." *Interpretation* 14 (1986): 177–193.

———. *Self-Knowledge in Plato's Phaedrus*. New Haven, CT: Yale University Press, 1986.

Grote, George. *History of Greece, Selections*. Eds. J. M. Mitchell and M. O. B. Caspari. New York: Routledge, 2001.

Grote, George. *Plato and the Other Companions of Sokrates*, Volume II. Bristol, England: Thoemmes Press, 1992.

Guthrie, W. K. C. *A History of Greek Philosophy*. Volume III. Cambridge: Cambridge University Press, 1969.

———. *A History of Greek Philosophy. Volume IV: Plato the Man and His Dialogues, Earlier Period*. Cambridge: Cambridge University Press, 1986.

Hackforth, R. "The Hedonism in Plato's *Protagoras*." *Classical Quarterly* 22 (1928): 38–42.

Haden, J. C. "Two Types of Power in Plato's 'Gorgias'." *Classical Journal* 87 (1992): 313–326.

Harrison, E. L. "Was Gorgias a Sophist?" *Phoenix* 18 (1964): 183–192.

Haskins, Ekaterina. *Logos and Power in Isocrates and Aristotle*. Columbia: University of South Carolina Press, 2004.

Hathway, Ronald. "Law and the Moral Paradox in Plato's *Apology*." *Journal of the History of Philosophy* 8 (1970): 127–142.

Hays, Steve. "On the Skeptical Influence of *Gorgias's* On Non-Being." *Journal of the History of Philosophy* 28 (1990): 327–337.

Hemmenway, Scott R. "Sophistry Exposed: Socrates on the Unity of Virtue in the *Protagoras*." *Ancient Philosophy* 16 (1996): 1–23.

———. "Philosophical Apology in the *Theaetetus*." *Interpretation* 17 (1990): 323–346.

Henderson, T. J. "In Defense of Thrasymachus." *American Philosophical Quarterly*, 7 (1970): 218–228.

Hitchcock, David. "The Origin of Professional Eristic." In T. Robinson and L. Brisson (eds.), *Plato Euthydemus, Lysis, Charmides: Proceedings of the V Symposium Platonicum*, Sankt Augustin: Academia Verlag, 2000.

Howland, Jacob. *The Republic: The Odyssey of Philosophy*. New York: Twayne Publishers, 1993.

Hyland, Drew. *The Virtue of Philosophy*. Athens, OH: Ohio University Press, 1981.

———. "Why Plato Wrote Dialogues." *Philosophy and Rhetoric* 1 (January 1968): 38–50.

Irwin, Terrence. *Plato's Moral Theory: The Early and Middle Dialogues*. Oxford: Clarendon Press, 1977.

Jarratt, Susan. *Rereading the Sophists*. Carbondale: South Illinois University Press, 1991.

Johnson, Curtis N. "Socrates' Encounter with Polus in Plato's *Gorgias*." *Phoenix* 43.3 (1989): 196–216.

Kahn, Charles H. *Plato and the Socratic Dialogue: The Philosophical Use of a Literary Form*. Cambridge: Cambridge University Press, 1996.

———. "Drama and Dialectic in Plato's *Gorgias*." In J. Annas (ed.), *Oxford Studies in Ancient Philosophy, Volume I*, Oxford: Clarendon Press, 1983.

Kasteley, James. "Respecting the Rupture: Not Solving the Problem of Unity in Plato's *Phaedrus*." *Philosophy and Rhetoric* 35 (2002): 138–152.

Kaufmann, Charles. "Enactment as Argument in the *Gorgias*." *Philosophy and Rhetoric* 12 (1979): 114–129.

Kennedy, George. *A New History of Classical Rhetoric.* Princeton, NJ: Princeton University Press, 1994.

Kerferd, G. B. *The Sophistic Movement.* Cambridge: Cambridge University Press, 1981.

———. "Protagoras' Doctrine of Justice and Virtue in the *Protagoras* of Plato." *Journal of Hellenic Studies* 73 (1953): 42–45.

———. "The Doctrine of Thrasymachus in Plato's *Republic.*" *Durham University Journal* 9 (1947): 19–27.

Kidd, I. G. "Socrates." In *Encylopedia of Philosophy,* Paul Edwards (ed.), Volume VII, London and New York: MacMillan, 1967.

Klosko, G. "The Refutation of Callicles in Plato's *Gorgias.*" *Greece and Rome* 31 (1984): 126–139.

———. "The Insufficiency of Reason in Plato's *Gorgias.*" *Western Political Quarterly* 36 (1983): 579–595.

Klosnoski, Richard J. "The Preservation of Homeric Tradition: Heroic Reperformance in the *Republic* and the *Odyssey.*" *Clio* 22 (1999): 251–277.

Krentz. "Dramatic Form and Philosophical Content in Plato's Dialogues." *Philosophy and Literature* 7 (1983): 32–47.

Lanham, Richard. *Analyzing Prose.* New York: Continuum, 2003.

Ledger, G. R. *Re-Counting Plato.* Oxford: Clarendon Press, 1989.

Leff, Michael C. "In Search of Ariadne's Thread: A Review of the Recent Literature on Rhetorical Theory." *Central States Speech Journal* 29 (1978): 73–91.

Levi, A. "The Ethical and Social Thought of Protagoras." *Mind* 49 (1940): 284–302.

Lewis, T. J. "Refutative Rhetoric as True Rhetoric in the *Gorgias.*" *Interpretation* 14 (1986): 195–210.

Linck, Matthew. "Unmastering Speech: Irony in Plato's Phaedrus." *Philosophy and Rhetoric* 36 (2003): 264–276.

Lloyd, G. E. R. *Methods and Problems in Greek Science.* Cambridge: Cambridge University Press, 1991.

MacDowell, Douglas. *The Law in Classical Athens.* Ithaca, NY: Cornell University Press, 1986.

Marback, Richard. *Plato's Dream of Sophistry.* Columbia: University of South Carolina Press, 1999.

McCabe, Mary Margaret. *Plato's Individuals.* Princeton, NJ: Princeton University Press, 1994.

———. "Arguments in Context: Aristotle's Defense of Rhetoric." In *Aristotle's Rhetoric: Philosophical Essays,* D. J. Furley and A. Nehamas, eds., Princeton, NJ: Princeton University Press, 1994, 129–165.

McComiskey, Bruce. *Gorgias and the New Sophistic Rhetoric.* Carbondale, IL: Southern Illinois University Press, 2002.

McCoy, Marina Berzins. "Reason and Dialectic in the Argument against Protagoras in the *Theaetetus.*" *International Philosophical Quarterly* 45 (2005): 21–39.

———. "Sophistry and Philosophy in Plato's *Republic.*" *Polis* 22 (2) (2005): 265–286.

———. "Socrates on Simonides: The Use of Poetry in Socratic and Platonic Rhetoric." *Philosophy and Rhetoric* 32 (1999): 349–367.

———. "Protagoras on Human Nature, Wisdom, and the Good: The Great Speech and the Hedonism of Plato's *Protagoras.*" *Ancient Philosophy* 18 (1998): 21–39.

McPherran, Mark. *The Religion of Socrates.* University Park, PA: Pennsylvania State University Press, 1996.

———. "Recognizing the Gods of Socrates." *Apeiron* 30 (1997): 125–139.

Michelini, Ann. *Plato as Author: The Rhetoric of Philosophy.* Boston: Brill, 2003.

Miller, Mitchell. *Plato's Parmenides: The Conversion of the Soul* (University Park, PA: Pennsylvania State University Press, [1986] 1991).

Monoson, S. Sara. "Frank Speech, Democracy, and Philosophy: Plato's Debt to a Democratic Strategy of Civic Discourse." In *Athenian Political Thought and the Reconstruction of American Democracy,* Ithaca, NY: Cornell University Press, 1994.

Moser, S., and G. L. Kustas. "A Comment on the Relativism of the *Protagoras.*" *Phoenix* 20 (1966): 111–115.

Murray, James S. "Disputation, Deception, and Dialectic: Plato on the True Rhetoric (*Phaedrus* 261–266)." *Philosophy and Rhetoric* 21 (1988): 279–289.

Nagy, Gregory. *The Best of the Achaeans.* Baltimore: Johns Hopkins University Press, 1979.

Nails, Debra. *The People of Plato.* Indianapolis/Cambridge: Hackett Publishing Company, 2002.

———. "Plato's Middle Cluster." *Phoenix* 48 (1994): 62–67.

Nehamas, Alexander. *Virtues of Authenticity: Essays on Plato and Socrates.* Princeton, NJ: Princeton University Press, 1999.

———. "What Did Socrates Teach and to Whom Did He Teach It?" *Review of Metaphysics* 46 (1992): 279–306.

———. "Eristic, Antilogic, Sophistic, Dialectic: Plato's Demarcation of Philosophy from Sophistry." *History of Philosophy Quarterly* 7 (1990): 3–16.

Nightingale, Andrea. *Genres in Dialogue: Plato and the Construct of Philosophy.* Cambridge: Cambridge University Press, 1996.

Nussbaum, Martha. *The Fragility of Goodness.* Cambridge: Cambridge University Press, 1986.

Oehler, Klaus. "Protagoras from the Perspective of Modern Pragmatism." *Transactions of the Charles S. Peirce Society* 38 (1–2) (2002): 207–214.

O'Neil, Basil. "The Struggle for the Soul of Thrasymachus." *Ancient Philosophy* 8 (1988): 167–185.

Panagiotou, Spiro. "Lysias and the Date of Plato's *Phaedrus.*" *Mnemosyne* 28 (1975): 388–398.

Pangle, Thomas. *The Roots of Political Philosophy: Ten Forgotten Socratic Dialogues.* Ithaca, NY: Cornell University Press, 1987.

Parke, H. W. *A History of the Delphic Oracle.* Oxford: Oxford University Press, 1939.

Parry, Hugh. "An Interpretation of Simonides 4 (Diehl)." *Transactions and Proceedings of the American Philological Association* 96 (1965): 297–320.

Parry, Richard D. *Plato's Craft of Justice* (Albany, NY: SUNY Press, 1996), chapter 1.

Patterson, Richard. "Plato on Philosophic Character." *Journal of the History of Philosophy* 25 (1987): 325–350.

Penner, Terrence. "Desire and Power in Socrates: The Argument of *Gorgias 466A-468E* that Orators and Tyrants Have No Power in the City." *Apeiron* (1991): 147–202.

Peters, J. R. "Reason and Passion in Plato's *Republic*." *Ancient Philosophy* 9 (1989): 173–187.

Polansky, Ronald M. *Philosophy and Knowledge: A Commentary on Plato's Theaetetus.* Lewisburg, PA: Bucknell University Press, 1992.

Poster, Carol. "Being and Becoming: Rhetorical Ontology in Early Greek Thought." *Philosophy and Rhetoric* 29 (1996): 1–14.

Poulakos, John. "The Letter and the Spirit of the Text: Two Translations of Gorgias's 'On Non-Being or On Nature'." *Philosophy and Rhetoric* 30 (1997): 41–44.

———. "Toward a Sophistic Definition of Rhetoric." *Philosophy and Rhetoric* 16 (1983): 35–48.

Poulakos, Takis. *Speaking for the Polis.* Columbia: University of South Carolina Press, 1997.

Press, Gerald, ed. *Plato's Dialogues: New Studies and Interpretations.* Lanham, MD: Rowman and Littlefield, 1993.

Prior, William. "The Historicity of Plato's *Apology*." *Polis* 18 (2001): 41–57.

Putterman, Theodore. "Socrates/Thrasymachus: The Extent of their Agreement." *Polis* 17 (2000): 79–90.

Reeve, C. D. C. *Socrates in the Apology.* Indianapolis: Hackett Publishing Company, 1990.

———. *Philosopher-Kings: The Argument of Plato's Republic.* Princeton, NJ: Princeton University Press, 1988.

Robinson, Thomas, and Luc Brisson, eds. *Plato: Euthydemus, Lysis, Charmides.* Sankt Augustin: Academia Verlag, 2000.

Robinson, Richard. *Plato's Earlier Dialectic.* Oxford: Clarendon Press, 1953.

Roochnik, David. *Beautiful City: The Dialectical Character of Plato's Republic.* Ithaca and London: Cornell University Press, 2003.

———. "Self-Recognition in Plato's *Theaetetus*." *Ancient Philosophy* 22 (2002): 37–52.

———. *Of Art and Wisdom: Plato's Understanding of Techne.* University Park, PA: Pennsylvania State University Press, 1999.

———. "Socrates' Rhetorical Attack on Rhetoric." In *The Third Way: New Directions in Platonic Studies.* Francisco J. Gonzalez (ed.), Lanham, MD: Rowman and Littlefield, 1995, 81–94.

———. *The Tragedy of Reason: Toward a Platonic Conception of Logos.* New York: Routledge, 1990.

———. "The Erotics of Philosophical Discourse." *History of Philosophy Quarterly* 4 (1987): 117–129.

———. "Socrates' Use of the *Techne* Analogy." *Journal of the History of Philosophy* 24 (1986): 295–310.

Rosen, Stanley. *Plato's Sophist: The Drama of Original and Image.* New Haven and London: Yale University Press, 1983.

Rossetti, Livio, ed. *Understanding the Phaedrus.* Sankt Augustin: Academia, 1992.

Rowe, C. J. "The Argument and Structure of Plato's *Phaedrus.*" *Proceedings of the Cambridge Philological Society* 32 (1986): 106–125.

Russell, Daniel C. "Protagoras and Socrates on Courage and Pleasure: 'Protagoras' 349d." *Ancient Philosophy* 20 (2000): 311–338.

Sallis, John. *Being and Logos: Reading the Platonic Dialogues.* Bloomington: Indiana University Press, 1996.

Saxonhouse, A. W. "An Unspoken Theme in Plato's *Gorgias,* War." *Interpretation* 11 (1983): 139–169.

Sayre, Kenneth. *Plato's Late Ontology.* Princeton, NJ: Princeton University Press, 1983.

Schiappa, Edward. *Protagoras and Logos: A Study in Greek Philosophy and Rhetoric.* 2d ed. Columbia: University of South Carolina Press, 2003.

———. "Interpreting Gorgias' "Being" in "On Not-Being or On Nature." *Philosophy and Rhetoric* 30 (1997): 13–30.

———. "Did Plato Coin *Rhetorike?*" *The American Journal of Philology* 111 (4) (1990): 457–470.

Schleiermacher, Friedrich. *Introduction to the Dialogues of Plato.* Trans William Dobson. New York: Arno Press, 1973.

Scott, Gary. *Does Socrates Have a Method?* University Park, PA: Pennsylvania State University Press, 2002.

———. *Plato's Socrates as an Educator.* Albany, NY: SUNY Press, 2000.

Scott, Robert L. "On Viewing Rhetoric as Epistemic." *Central States Speech Journal* 18 (1967): 9–16.

Seeskin, Kenneth. "Is the *Apology* of Socrates a Parody?" *Philosophy and Literature* 6 (1982): 94–105.

Sharples, R. W. "Plato on Democracy and Expertise." *Greece & Rome* 41 (1994): 49–56.

Shorey, Paul. *What Plato Said.* Chicago: University of Chicago Press, 1933.

Silverman, Allan. *The Dialectic of Essence: A Study of Plato's Metaphysics.* Princeton, NJ: Princeton University Press, 2002.

Sloane, Thomas O., ed. *Encyclopedia of Rhetoric.* Oxford: Oxford University Press, 2001.

Tarrant, Harold. "Naming Socratic Interrogation in the *Charmides.*" In Thomas Robinson and Luc Brisson, eds., *Plato: Euthydemus, Lysis, Charmides.* Sankt Augustin: Academia Verlag, 2000.

Taylor, A. E. *Plato: The Man and His Work.* New York: Meridian Books, 1960.

Timmerman, David. "Isocrates' Competing Conceptualization of Philosophy." *Philosophy and Rhetoric* 31 (1998): 145–159.

Timmerman, David M., Edward Schiappa, and Wilfred E. Major. "Inferring Theory from Practice in Early Greek Oratory." Paper presented to the Biannual Meeting of the International Society for the History of Rhetoric, Los Angeles, CA, July 2005.

Turner, Jeffrey S. "'Atopia' and Plato's *Gorgias.*" *International Studies in Philosophy* 25 (1993): 69–77.

Vlastos, Gregory. *Socratic Studies.* Cambridge: Cambridge University Press, 1994.

Vlastos, Gregory. "Socratic Piety." *Proceedings of the Boston Area Colloquium in Ancient Philosophy* 5 (1989): 213–238.

Walters, Frank D. "Gorgias as a Philosopher of Being: Epistemic Foundationalism in Sophistic Thought." *Philosophy and Rhetoric* 27 (1994): 143–155.

Wardy, Robert. *The Birth of Rhetoric: Gorgias, Plato and Their Successors.* London: Routledge, 1996.

Weiss, Roslyn. "When Winning Is Everything: Socratic Elenchus and Euthydemian Eristic." In Thomas Robinson and Luc Brisson, eds. *Plato: Euthydemus, Lysis, Charmides.* Sankt Augustin: Academia Verlag, 2000, 68–75.

_____. "Hedonism in the *Protagoras* and the Sophist's Guarantee." *Ancient Philosophy* 10 (1990): 17–39.

White, David. *Rhetoric and Reality in Plato's Phaedrus.* Albany, NY: SUNY Press, 1992.

White, Eric Charles. *Kaironomia: On the Will-to-Invent.* Ithaca, NY: Cornell University Press, 1987.

White, Nicholas. 1985. "The Argument of Plato's *Gorgias*." In Dominic J. O'Meara, ed., *Platonic Investigations.* Vol. 13, Washington, DC: Catholic University of America Press, 139–162.

Woodbury, Leonard. "Simonides on *Arete*." *Transactions of the American Philological Association* 84 (1953): 135–163.

Yunis, Harvey. *Taming Democracy: Models of Political Rhetoric in Classical Athens.* Ithaca, NY: Cornell University Press, 1996.

_____. "Eros in Plato's *Phaedrus* and the Shape of Greek Rhetoric." *Arion* 13 (2005): 101–125.

Zaidman, L., and P. S. Pantel. *Religion in the Ancient Greek City.* Translated by Cartledge. Cambridge: Cambridge University Press, 1992.

Zuckert, Catherine H. "Who's a Philosopher? Who's a Sophist? The Stranger vs. Socrates." *The Review of Metaphysics* 54 (2000): 65–97.

Index